RETHINKING PASTORAL CARE

The issue of pastoral care in schools and how a teacher can provide it effectively is currently a topic of great debate in the media. With teachers increasingly bearing the brunt of their pupils' problematic personal lives, they feel under pressure to respond in an informed and professional manner.

This book looks at how teachers can attempt to give good quality pastoral care, whether as a form tutor in the first instance or in a managerial role further along in their career.

The volume uses practical case studies as examples of what can be achieved, and also explores the educational theory of this area. Its strength is its contributions from many reflective teachers who face the challenges of schooling today.

Úna M. Collins works with the National University of Ireland, Maynooth, and other education bodies.

Jean McNiff is an independent researcher who works across the island of Ireland and in other international contexts.

RETHINKING PASTORAL CARE

Edited by
Úna M. Collins and Jean McNiff

London and New York

First published 1999
by Routledge
11 New Fetter Lane, London EC4P 4EE

Simultaneously published in the USA and Canada
by Routledge
29 West 35th Street, New York, NY 10001

Typeset in Garamond by
M Rules
Printed and bound in Great Britain by
T. J. International Ltd, Padstow, Cornwall

British Library Cataloguing in Publication Data
A catalogue record for this book is available from the British Library

Library of Congress Cataloging in Publication Data
Rethinking pastoral care / [edited by] Úna M. Collins and Jean McNiff
p. cm.
Includes bibliographical references (p.) and index.
1. Counseling in secondary education–Ireland–Case studies. 2.
Teacher–student relationships–Ireland–Case studies. 3. Tutors and
tutoring–Ireland–Case studies. 4. Action research in
education–Ireland–Case studies.
I. Úna M. Collins. II. Jean McNiff.
LB1620.53.I73R48 1999
373. 14′046′09417–dc21   98–35448
                                            CIP
ISBN 0–415–19441–5 (hbk)
ISBN 0–415–19442–3 (pbk)

CONTENTS

CONTENTS

CONTRIBUTORS

Ron Best is Dean and Professor of Education at Roehampton Institute London. He is a founder member of the National Association for Pastoral Care in Education (NAPCE) and Executive Editor of its journal *Pastoral Care in Education*. He convenes the annual Roehampton Conference on 'Education, Spirituality and the Whole Child' and has written and edited widely in the areas of pastoral care and personal–social education.

Jean Clandinin is a former classroom teacher and school counsellor. She currently works at the University of Alberta where she is Professor and Director of the Centre for Teacher Education and Development. Jean is particularly concerned with issues of collaboration as it is lived out in relationships between those positioned at the university and those positioned in schools.

Úna M. Collins is joint coordinator of the Higher Diploma in School Guidance and Counselling at the National University of Ireland, Maynooth. She has developed and managed a number of school and teacher inservice courses in pastoral care and related areas. She has also been directly involved in the development and management of two full-time courses, the Higher Diploma in Pastoral Care, and the Higher Diploma in School Guidance and Counselling. Her most recent work has been in developing a process for whole-school planning and evaluation. She has published in the fields of pastoral care and school planning.

John Coolahan is Professor of Education at the National University of Ireland, Maynooth. He is author of many books and papers in Irish and international journals. He holds key positions of responsibility in Irish education, including advisory roles at National level. At a European level, he has been Leader and Chief Rapporteur of the three OECD teams on the country reviews of Education in Poland, Education in the Russian Federation and of Higher Education and Research in the Russian Federation, as well as being a member of the Steering Committee of the Council of Europe project 'Secondary Education for Europe'. He is currently Vice-President of the Study Group to advise the European Commission on education and training policy for the future.

Pauline Grenham is a teacher in Eureka School, Kells. She co-ordinates the Health Education Programme which includes pastoral and lifeskills aspects. She has professional qualifications in pastoral care and is particularly interested in issues of social justice for children and the welfare of young people with physical disabilities. Her personal interests include poetry, drama, music and theatre.

Ann Marie Kiernan is a teacher in Columba College, Killucan, Co. Westmeath, a school which caters for students from varying social backgrounds. She holds professional qualifications in home economics and pastoral care. Her interests include craft and design, and community development. Ann Marie is a director of the local Credit Union. She is married to Andrew Bracken and has two children, Aisling and Ciarán.

Joe Lynch is a secondary school teacher in St Joseph's C.B.S. Drogheda where he teaches science subjects. Over the years, he has done further studies in such areas as counselling, pastoral care and educational management. He is also Transition Year Coordinator in his school with responsibility for designing and running this optional senior cycle programme. He has had considerable success in establishing a European dimension to his school through student exchange and project work with many European schools.

Bríghid McGuinness is a teacher in a school in the Irish midlands. She has responsibility for student counselling and welfare in her school. She is particularly interested in issues of social justice and democracy in education, and how these aspects can be developed in schools curricula and management practices. Other interests include travel and theatre.

Jean McNiff is an independent researcher and writer. She currently works and lives in Dorset and Dublin, supporting educators and managers in undertaking their action enquiries into how they can improve their workplace practices, leading to Higher Awards and Degrees. She acts as a consultant to educational bodies in Ireland, Britain and North America.

Luke Monahan is a lecturer in the Marino Institute of Education Dublin, a consultant to schools, and Pastoral Care Coordinator in a Dublin post-primary school, Chanel College. He is author of a number of books, most recently *The Year Head – A Key Link in the School Community*. He has professional qualifications in Pastoral Leadership and is National Coordinator of the Irish Association of Pastoral Care in Education. He is a frequent contributor to conferences and workshops on educational issues in Ireland and abroad.

Frances Murphy, a Presentation Sister, began her teaching career in Presentation Secondary School, Cashel, in 1978. She became principal of the school in 1986 for seven years. When the school formed part of the new

Community School in 1994 Frances returned to full-time teaching in the Community School. Part of her work was to coordinate pastoral care in the school. She has been involved in co-presenting a number of courses around the role of the tutor to second-level teachers in recent years. From autumn 1998 Frances once again takes up the position of principal, this time in Presentation Secondary School, Warrenmount, Dublin.

Aidan O'Reilly is an English and music teacher as well as coordinator of pastoral care in an all-boys' school in the Irish midlands. He is a member of the executive of the Irish Association of Pastoral Care in Education and edits their journal. He is also a visiting lecturer on pastoral issues in education at Trinity College Dublin and University College Dublin. His interests include music, travel, sport, theatre and the history of education.

Jim Ryan is a teacher in a school in North Dublin where he has worked for twenty years. He is the learning support teacher in the school and has a special interest in the situation of disadvantaged students within the school system. He is actively involved in the Credit Union movement in Ireland. Other interests include gardening, environmental issues, Irish heritage and reading.

EDITORIAL PREFACE

This book is rooted in the experience of learning: the learning of students in school, of teachers with students, and of our work as editors with teachers and other educators. The context is an innovative programme for teachers in Ireland which began in 1993 when the Marino Institute of Education and the National University of Ireland, Maynooth, developed a Postgraduate Diploma in Pastoral Care. In 1996, the Diploma was developed into a professional study and training for guidance counsellors in a pastoral care context. The postgraduate diplomas were the first such programmes to provide formal, full-time study of pastoral care at this level. The study is rooted in teachers' school experience and their reflective learning during their classroom-based work.

The book contains teachers' stories of their professional learning in pastoral care contexts, and shows the development of their learning through their stories. Teachers are able to make justified claims that they have improved the quality of education for themselves and for the people in their care by producing empirical evidence to show what they did, and their influence on their own situations; and to make their implicit awareness of those processes explicit. It is also an account of how we, as editors, encouraged teachers to make their learning explicit, and in this way to contribute to an emergent body of education literature within an Irish context (Sugrue 1998).

We feel that the combination of teachers' accounts of living practice, together with their critical reflections on that practice, will go some way to developing the professional knowledge base of education. Personal practical theories of education offer new, effective ways of understanding teaching and learning processes. While we accept the validity and use value of dominant abstract conceptual forms of education theory that emphasise the theoretical bases of teaching and learning, we suggest that these be placed within the wider humanistic framework of person-centred enquiry. This, we feel, would provide a balanced approach to educational enquiry, showing how people use knowledge about the world in their personal attempts to understand how they might effectively use that knowledge. In this way abstract theory may be embedded within living theory; knowledge about the world is incorporated into wisdom of the self.

We believe that the accounts presented here do this. They show the living reality of people making sense of their work through self-reflection and collaborative working; they show how teachers generated new knowledge together, and then tested that knowledge against existing theories in the literature; and they show how teachers are able to approach their work in a thoughtful, critical way. Teachers have responded to a situation, yet are always aware that they still have room for growth. No answers are final. We still have much to learn.

The book contains extracts from a small number of dissertations of teachers, produced between 1993 and 1996. It needs to be emphasised that these are extracts only; the full accounts may be accessed through the library of the National University of Ireland, Maynooth. Aspects of research such as consideration of different research approaches, justification for choice of methodology, and ethical issues and their associated problematics are not reproduced; while these aspects featured in the original dissertations, they are not included here because of limitations of space and potential repetition.

Methodology

The methodology adopted for the research projects in the Higher Diploma in Pastoral Care was action research. This approach has grown in popularity in recent times, and, as happens in all evolutionary 'movements', it is interpreted in a variety of ways by different groups of action researchers. Such developmental processes are healthy for educational systems and lead to the kind of lively debate that keeps minds open and systems self-critical.

The methodology we adopted was the 'living theory' approach developed primarily by Jack Whitehead and associates at the University of Bath, UK, and which has wide credibility in international contexts. Descriptions of this approach appear in Chapter 1. One of its features is to challenge traditional theory-driven ways of doing research, requiring practitioners to engage actively in theorising their work as they do it. Practitioners offer descriptions and explanations for what they are doing, showing how they try to understand the reasons and potential consequences of their actions. In this way, practice becomes the ground for personal practical theorising; theory is drawn from experience, and reflection on that experience. Personal theories of education constitute the knowledge base of professional learning.

Further, this knowledge base demonstrates ethical practice: for 'action research is morally committed action which may be called praxis' (McNiff, Lomax and Whitehead 1996). Teachers carefully consider the values base of their work, and whether or not those values are being realised in practice. If there is some slippage, they work consistently and honestly so that they can arrive at a position where they may say that their values are being lived more fully in their practice. This is not a solitary exercise, for the justification for what we are doing as educators needs to be related to how we are influencing the quality of life for those with whom we work – our students and colleagues. Are we making a difference for good in their lives? Action research is always collaborative, requiring practitioners to check with others to see whether or not they are acting in the best interest of others, and not engaging in self-serving practices.

Presentation of the accounts

While the methodology for the accounts in the book actively embody the principles and practices of action research, their form of expression is often innovative. Contributors were invited to use whatever form of expression they wished in presenting their accounts; our guidelines asked them only to ensure that the process of systematic enquiry was evident throughout, as well as the process of their own learning and reflection. Some accounts use forms of expression that fit well with the methodologies of narrative enquiry and autobiographical research. All show the systematic nature of how participants identified a problematic area of practice and worked systematically to address it. In working through their identified issues, some participants raised more dilemmas than originally perceived; others reached a point at which they could say that the dilemma had been resolved; for others, resolution is still far away, yet understandings have been deepened. What is clear is that the situation always changed, whether at the personal level of improved insights, or at the systemic level of improved organisational practices. This is a basic principle of action research, and a common-sense observation on life processes: the fact that we exist in relation to each other means that the systems in which we work are always changing. No person is external to the system of which they are a part; they are an integral part of it, and, because they are themselves constantly changing, so is the system. Nothing is static; all is in flux. It is the responsibility of educators to ensure that such change is change for the good; and this requires educators to educate themselves, as well as others, so that their individual and collective processes of becoming may be judged as good. The purpose of action research is not only to change a situation, as the critical theorists would have us believe (for example, Zuber-Skerritt 1996), but to improve it by improving ourselves. The legacy we leave as educators should be a world better than we found it.

Ethical issues

In works such as this there is always the problematic of self-identification. While some people are happy to have their real names given, and rightly hope that their good practice will be celebrated and shared, there are others who would prefer to remain anonymous. The authors are named. All other real names have been included with the written permission of their owners. In accordance with good ethical practice, authors gained permission from students and other participants to name them in the stories. In some cases, where authors and participants felt it was appropriate, people are identified by symbols. As editors, we worked carefully with the authors to ensure that all participants' privacy had been safeguarded where appropriate, and that those who wished to share their practice had the opportunity to do so.

Context of the work

The teachers' accounts presented in the book are located within an Irish context. We believe that Ireland is one of the significant leaders in the field of pastoral care and its implementation in schools. However, that does not limit the potential influence or applicability of the accounts to other contexts, possibly at an international level. Michael Bassey (1990) says that good action research should be relatable: people need to see how they can learn from the descriptions and explanations offered by practitioners of their real-life experiences. We hope that the stories told by teachers here will be read and appreciated by teachers working in a variety of contexts. We hope that, by reading the stories of 'ordinary' teachers working in 'ordinary' classrooms, other teachers elsewhere will learn, will adapt and adopt, as suits their own situations, and in turn will feel inspired to share their stories of professional learning. Jean Clandinin notes in Chapter 13 that there is no such thing as an 'ordinary' teacher, or indeed an 'ordinary' moment. The moments of our lives are all special, and as such constitute quite extraordinary lives. Each one of us is special; the case is often, however, that we do not recognise this, nor recognise it in the lives of other people. Pauline Grenham shows in her account how this realisation jolted her into action, to ensure that the students she worked with were all recognised as special people, each with a story to tell.

The stories are located in Ireland, and many of them reflect a strong spiritual awareness. As educators, we hold that pastoral care is not only a personal–social process but it is also rooted in the human search for meaning. For us, 'religion' is a term associated with the organisation of belief, and is not always related to spirituality; this view is evident also in a growing critical literature (e.g., Noddings 1993; O'Murchu 1997b). Of course, pastoral care goes on in schools and organisational cultures that are more secular than the cultures of Ireland; yet it is inescapable that pastoral care emphasises the relatedness of people, and relatedness is a key feature of spirituality.

Our Irish context also colours our forms of expression. You will read the special Irish expressions of craic (fun), post-primary (secondary) education, and others; you will read of Irish games such as camogie and hurling; when you read of the Department of Education, be aware that it is the Irish National Department of Education (now the Department of Education and Science). It is often said that the importance of Irish affairs and influence is out of all proportion to the size of the country; the island as a whole carries about five million people, of whom about three and a half million live in the South. We believe that the importance of Irish commitments to pastoral care also out-weighs the physical size of our schools and communities.

A special time

This is a special time for us. On Good Friday, 10 April 1998, a momentous agreement was reached in Belfast. On 22 May 1998 there was a further occa-sion of unique significance: the people of Ireland, North and South, were asked to vote together and concurrently on the outcome of the negotiations and the agreement reached. This gave us another momentous outcome. The future is still uncertain, but at least we have the hope of a lasting peace.

The peace has been a long time coming. It has finally arrived because of the efforts of many people who refused to accept anything less than peace. Such is the commitment to care. The commitment to care begins in homes and schools, working together. The potential for care in schools is enormous, in terms of influencing what kind of society we will have and the kind of people who will constitute that society.

Knowledge of the future is impossible. All we have is knowledge of today. It is our responsibility, as thoughtful, caring educators, to make today the best it can be, in the interests of the children of tomorrow. To do this, we ourselves need to care, actively, honestly, and with less thought to self than to others.

Úna M. Collins and Jean McNiff
Dublin, May 1998

ACKNOWLEDGEMENTS

We wish to thank the teachers with whom we are privileged to work for their commitment in the preparation of this book.

We offer a special thanks to Simon Richey, UK Branch, Calouste Gulbenkian Foundation (Lisbon), for a grant towards production of the book.

INTRODUCTION

John Coolahan

There is currently striking evidence internationally of a vigorous concern about the nature of education systems and their suitability to serve the needs of individuals and society in a period of profound and accelerating social change. In recent times, most developed countries have brought forward new educational legislation, greatly expanded provision of secondary education, promoted many curricular reform initiatives, expanded inservice education opportunities for teachers, fostered close links between schools and parents and between schools and local communities, and so on. Yet there are uncertainties as to whether or not schools have adapted sufficiently to meet the needs of their expanded clienteles, and there is concern about the 'place' of the school within the concept of lifelong learning, which is likely to be the animating principle of educational policy for the twenty-first century.

A concern for quality in education has always been a feature of educational policy and debate, but recent years have witnessed much greater concentration on this issue and a tighter focusing on what quality means in terms of educational provision, processes and outcomes. Following several decades of great quantitative expansion in educational provision, public interest has shifted significantly towards establishing what is qualitative about the educational engagement. Governments and societies want to know more precisely if their very large investments in their education systems are in fact achieving the qualitative goals that are sought. Issues of accountability and evaluation pervade many aspects of public expenditure in contemporary society and, because of the strategic importance of their education systems, it is not unexpected that such accountability concerns are being applied to education, but the concerns go deeper than just a narrow value-for-money paradigm.

A range of OECD reports through the 1990s has focused on quality issues in school education, reflective of the interest of the twenty-nine OECD countries in this theme. It is also significant that the EU has focused more centrally on educational issues in the mid-1990s than heretofore. Notable in this regard were the following:

- European Commission, *White Paper: Teaching and Learning – Towards the Learning Society*, 1995
- European Commission Study Group, *Report: Accomplishing Europe Through Education and Training*, 1997.

These documents reflect the more centre-stage role being played by education within the Union in the post-Maastricht Treaty era. Underpinning many of their concerns and recommendations is the underlying one of improving quality in education in relation to human resource development within the European Union. The Council of Europe, too, through its major project 'A Secondary Education for Europe', has been endeavouring to promote best practice in school improvement.

It was noteworthy that 1996 was declared the international Year of Lifelong Learning to help promote new, vitalising concepts regarding the importance of learning and training throughout life. In January 1996, the Ministers of Education of the OECD issued a significant communiqué committing themselves to lifelong learning policies and the promotion of quality learning for all, with particular priority for those underachieving in the education system. The OECD published a major report on the theme, *Lifelong Learning for All*, in 1996. That year also saw the publication of the report by the UNESCO Commission chaired by Jacques Delors, on education for the twenty-first century, entitled *Learning: The Treasure Within*. It, too, stressed the centrality of educational policy within a rapidly changing world and made many proposals for qualitative reform and improving the character of pupil engagement within the school systems.

This concern for quality in education evidenced in so many recent international reports raises the question as to why such intense and concentrated attention is being given to the issue at this time. The following attempts to summarise many of the key concerns. The globalisation of the economy is having deep and wide-ranging ramifications on society. A key one is the greater competitiveness between large trading blocs. It is realised, with renewed emphasis, that a nation's wealth lies in its people. In the talents and skills of its human resources lies a society's greatest asset. The optimisation of the human resource potential becomes a significant goal for development in societies where the knowledge base is the foundation for further development. Accordingly, new emphasis is placed on quality education and training to foster the talents of all pupils.

The extent of change in the knowledge base with the acceleration of knowledge generation, particularly in the scientific and technological areas, also places urgent demands on educational systems to keep abreast of such changes and to adopt more dynamic approaches in styles of pedagogy. The ongoing revolution in information and communications technology impinges on education systems and requires many changes in the approach to teaching and learning. It is increasingly necessary that technological literacy be added to the repertoire of skills required by all pupils. New research has also highlighted the need to broaden traditional emphases, which tended to favour cognitive and abstract learning, towards a more embracive approach towards multiple intelligences.

One of the common themes in much of the current international literature in the field is the concern for the large minority of underachievers within the education systems. The proportion of underachievers tends to be put at 15–20 per cent of school cohorts generally. Many of these pupils tend to be from multi-deprived socio-economic backgrounds and failure at school and alienation from school tend to be their lot. This is a great human and social loss at present, but with the pace of technological and social change, such young people are in grave danger of being more socially marginalised in the years ahead. There is a wastage of human talent involved, but there are also grave threats to social and democratic cohesiveness in the future if these defects are not remedied. The role of schools as major social institutions working with the young is being focused on as one of the vital agencies wherein reformative action could be taken. Feeding these concerns is the research over recent years on school effectiveness. A great deal of school-based research has been examining the inner dynamics of school life, seeking to identify the characteristics that accompany successful achievement. These traits are being promoted as quality indices and efforts are being made to disseminate good practice. Particular efforts are being made in many countries to tackle the difficulties facing good quality school performance in areas of complex, socio-economic disadvantage.

In line with the greatly expanded role of the secondary school within contemporary society, closer attention is being paid to the inner quality of the life of the school. The area of interpersonal relationships, links with parents and community, staff teamwork and collegiality, school planning processes, the 'hidden curriculum' are all coming under fresh scrutiny. The impact of such factors on the quality of the living and learning environment of the school community is receiving new attention. The fact that the vast majority of teenagers remain at school until their late teens, forming a very heterogeneous clientele, imposes great demands on many schools. Many adjustments need to be made to traditional practices – curricular, pedagogic, assessment – and relationships within schools to ensure that the experience of these young people in the schools is qualitatively worthwhile.

Outside the schools, the changing nature of work provides another cause of concern for the promotion of quality in schooling. The type of personal qualities, competencies and skills now required differ significantly from those of an older and more stable era. This links to the needs to equip young people with the personal, cognitive and social skills and the motivation to engage in learning as a lifelong process. 'Learning to learn' becomes a key mantra for contemporary schools. In the era ahead, schooling will be a preliminary and preparatory part of the educational and training processes people will engage in, but the qualitative character of their school experience will be crucial for success in life.

Within this broad scenario the place of pastoral care, counselling and pupil guidance assume a new importance. I believe that any serious contextual analysis of the contemporary education situation indicates that such elements of school life need to move centre-stage in schooling. Changed conceptions of the role of the school, changed pupil clientele with varied needs, whole-school planning, curricular reform, new relationships with parents and school-to-work emphases all imply that pastoral care and guidance counselling services will be crucial factors in school success for the future.

The EU White Paper, *Towards the Learning Society*, focuses on various obstacles to guidance and counselling, and states:

> Information and guidance constitute the first condition for promoting access to education and training.
>
> (European Commission 1995: 34–5)

Concern for guidance and counselling was also evident in the communiqué issued by the OECD Ministers for Education in 1996, when they stated:

> Suitable academic and vocational pathways for learners at all levels and ages should be created, along with more sophisticated and transparent approaches for assessing and recognising competence. The development of career guidance and counselling, especially for adults, should be a priority.
>
> (OECD 1996a: 23)

The Council of Europe in its many efforts to promote civic education and human rights education implies a strong commitment to the practice of good interpersonal relationships and a regard for the effective and emotional dimensions of personal development that are underpinned by pastoral care and counselling provision within a school's repertoire of supports.

Many of the articles and reports in this book are rooted in the experience of Irish school circumstances. As such, they can be illustrative and illuminative of situations that are generalisable to other educational systems at this time. While certain local features indicate a specific context, the core issues being faced are encountered in many educational systems.

The Irish education system has been undergoing profound change in the 1990s. The system has been subject to wide-ranging analysis and appraisal. This is reflected in a range of policy documents, including an OECD review of the system in 1991 and a Green Paper, *Education for a Changing World*, in 1992. This was followed by unprecedented national debate on education which culminated in a National Education Convention in 1993. The report on the convention formed the basis for the Government's White Paper, *Charting Our*

Educational Future, in 1995. This has given rise to legislative measures such as the Universities Act of 1997 and the Education Bill of 1997. Within this changing framework, the school system has been undergoing the type of curricular, participation and planning changes common to most Western systems, and outlined above.

This book on pastoral care comes, then, at a most timely period. It represents part of the 'cutting edge' of change and reculturation of Irish school life. The perspectives and initiatives are carrying forward towards the implementation of the conception of school life set forth in the White Paper of 1995, namely:

> Schools actively influence all aspects of the growth and development of their students. This influence includes the school's environment and climate, its curriculum and its interaction with the community. The promotion of the social, personal and health education of students is a major concern of each school. Schools provide opportunities for students to learn basic personal and social skills, which will foster integrity, self-confidence and self-esteem, while nurturing sensitivity to the feelings and rights of others. The attainment of these objectives for all students is influenced by the climate of the school and the classroom, by the organisation and teaching methods, by the school's approach to students' personal difficulties and by the wider educational and spiritual values transmitted by the schools.
>
> (Government of Ireland, 1995: 161)

Many of the action research initiatives reported on here are reflective of an exciting new dimension of the expanded inservice teacher education policy of recent years. The teachers in question embody the role of reflective practitioners. They select specific issues within their own schools that require attention, particularly from a pastoral care perspective. Applying action research methodologies, they engage productively and cooperatively with pupils and colleagues towards devising solutions to, or amelioration of, the problems involved. The experience and competencies built up by such action research involvements greatly enhance the continued professional contributions of the teachers to their schools. There are incremental advantages for the future when teachers become focused in this way on the life and learning of their schools. The development of teachers as researchers is highly significant and it is this which gives such immediacy and credibility to the reports, while conveying a real 'feel' and atmosphere for the school settings. This trend in the teaching profession coincides with the Government's policy of establishing a Teaching Council as a self-governing body for the teaching profession in Ireland. The Ministerial Committee is to report shortly on how such a Teaching Council should be established. It will be a landmark in the history of the teaching profession in Ireland and is likely to promote a supportive framework for the type of professional activity engaged in by contributors to this volume.

The reports on specific action research projects are accompanied by key articles on aspects of pastoral care in education by eminent experts in the field. Pastoral care touches on all central areas of school life and, accordingly, is very close to concerns for quality in education. As a recent draft OECD document stated:

> The quality of teaching, the classroom culture and the relationship between teachers and pupils are the core of quality in education and, therefore, the main determinants of success or failure.
>
> (OECD 1996b: 51)

This volume illuminates how pastoral care dimensions are integral to promoting improved quality in the living and learning environment of the school for both pupils and teachers.

1

CONTEXTUALISING THE WORK

Úna M. Collins and Jean McNiff

This book is about pastoral care and action research. Although there is an intuitive link between the two concepts, they have not until now been made explicit. We believe that making the link visible will contribute to thinking in both fields: how the value of care can be made central to the methodology of action research, and how a critically reflective stance will raise our awareness about the need for care.

In this chapter we reflect on our own ideas regarding pastoral care in the secondary school, and action research as a form of disciplined learning for practising teachers.

Úna's reflections on pastoral care

In a paper presented to a European conference on pastoral care at the University of Warwick I developed the theme of 'Fiche Bliain ag Fás' (Twenty Years A-growing) (Collins 1998), using the title of a well known Irish/Gaelic novel. My thesis in that paper was that pastoral care as we now define it was always the experience of the 'good' school in Ireland, but it was not named or formalised. I argued that from 1974 to 1994 there was a gradual, sometimes difficult journey to the current position of recognising, owning, training and experiencing pastoral care in almost all secondary schools in Ireland. In 1994 came the first public statements acknowledging the need for pastoral care in official Department of Education literature (National Education Convention Secretariat, 1994).

The following is a personal reflection on my experience in that journey.

The recognition of current needs

In 1972 I began my work as a school guidance counsellor in a large state community school. Community and comprehensive schools were new in Ireland in the late 1960s and early 1970s, and their introduction marked a significant development in the articulation of needs, both academic and social, in secondary schooling. The introduction of guidance counsellors in schools was expected to be the response. Through reflection on my experience in this new situation, I realised that one person could not, and perhaps should not, respond to all the needs. A systemic or whole-school approach would be needed for the school to respond effectively to emergent trends such as larger numbers, co-education, comprehensive intake, comprehensive curriculum, and socio-economic difficulties.

Acquiring new learning

I went to Swansea University and studied with Douglas Hamblin and later with Leslie Button. The British system of pastoral care, which had developed in response to the needs experienced during the initiation and expansion of comprehensive schools in the 1950s, provided very useful guidelines for our experience in Ireland in the 1970s. My first visit to a pastoral care summer school in Swansea in 1974 was followed each summer into the 1980s, and on each visit there was an increase in the number of Irish teachers and counsellors who attended. This was a critical time of learning.

Sharing the learning

Each school year I became more involved in the provision of inservice education for school staffs. The expressed needs became more clearly articulated by principals and teachers, by parents, and by the students themselves. Inservice for staffs was random; there was no formal provision. Indeed, we had to deal with many difficulties about the meaning of the term 'pastoral care', and one of the teachers' unions had difficulties about how it was being introduced into Irish schools. Dealing with these difficulties enabled us to learn more about teachers' needs, and the structures that would support teachers.

Clarifying the learning

The most significant piece of this journey for me has been recognising the multitude of perceptions about the term 'pastoral care'. For some it means a programme in personal and social education. For others it means having a class tutor responsible for each class. I have heard it described as a 'back door for religious education', and, conversely, a 'front door for mere humanism'! Through my journey with students, with teachers, with parents and with university educators, I have learnt that all of these and much more contributes to an understanding of pastoral care. Pastoral care is that which the student experiences in their school life. It is the spirit, the culture, the heart of the school. It is the recognition, respect and support which each can claim as a right and as a responsibility within the learning community. The words provide a label through which we can wonder, question, share experiences and work together.

Institutionalising the learning

The 1990s saw the present piece of this journey. I had an opportunity to work full time in the provision of inservice education for school staffs, and, with the full cooperation of the National University, Maynooth, to offer full-time post-graduate study for teachers in pastoral care. This has been a significant milestone for Irish schools. We are currently providing a Higher Diploma in Guidance Counselling in a pastoral care context. Graduates of the studies have now formed the Irish Association of Pastoral Care in Education (IAPCE), and this body provides short inservice courses in all parts of the country. Parallel with these developments, the National Department of Education and Science has recognised in its literature, and in its provision of resources, the need for formal pastoral care (see National Education Convention Secretariat 1994: 51–2; Government of Ireland 1995: 156–9). Excellent work has also been happening in the development of programmes and of methodologies in personal, social and health education in the work of regional Health Boards, the National Council for Curriculum and Assessment (NCCA), and with the founding in 1996 of the Irish Association of Pastoral Care in Education (IAPCE). The threads are beginning to show a pattern.

Resourcing the learning

In Ireland, we have lacked resources for a whole-school approach to pastoral care. In 1980 my *Pastoral Care: A Teachers' Handbook* was a small beginning. This was reworked and a second edition was published (Collins 1993). IAPCE has begun to publish a series of books which will be of assistance to teachers, and that work will continue.

This book in the journey of learning

The teachers who studied in the Pastoral Care Diploma were required to be reflective in their study and in their practice. Action research methodologies became the discipline for the dissertations. This book reflects how that suc-ceeded . . . and the journey continues.

Jean's reflections on action research

I came to action research via pastoral care. A consistent aim in my research is to write up my learning episodes, and I have told the story elsewhere of my first encounters with pastoral care (McNiff 1986) and with action research (McNiff 1993). I also studied with Leslie Button during the 1980s, and only retrospectively do I now appreciate that he was ahead of his time in linking the ideas of pastoral care and action research. He said that teachers and students should be actively conducting research into what they were doing, both in terms of the content of what they were learning, and the processes through which they learned (Button 1974). Button's ideas were congruent with those of Lawrence Stenhouse, who imagined curriculum as a creative process in which teachers and students engaged thoughtfully about the nature of their work and relationships (Stenhouse 1975). Stenhouse popularised the idea of teacher as researcher; and it is in the ideas of theorists such as Button and Stenhouse that initiatives such as the Higher Diploma for Pastoral Care have their genesis.

I would like to give a brief summary of what I understand action research to mean. In our Editorial Preface we noted that there are several different interpretations of action research, and the one we have adopted is the living educational theory approach developed by Jack Whitehead and other researchers who have worked with him. I think it would be true to say that all interpretations of action research commit to the same core values and principles, and these act as significant features that identify action research as moving beyond empirical or interpretive research in terms of its methodology, epistemology and social purpose. These key features include the following:

- The individual practitioner is in charge of their own work; when they investigate their work it can become research.
- Research can be viewed, as Stenhouse (1983) said, as systematic enquiry made public; action research also embeds an explicit social intent of improving a situation.
- The individual does not work alone. While the research is undertaken by the individual who concentrates on what they are doing, the researcher always recognises that they are in relation with other people. Whatever the researcher does influences other people in some way, and whatever other people do influences the researcher in some way. It is a reciprocal relationship. People can never be out of relation with other people, even though their relationships might be conducted at a distance in space and time.
- The research must be subjected to the critical scrutiny and validation of other people. The individual cannot justify claims about having improved something unless other people approve that claim. This becomes very delicate when the researcher makes claims about her own subjective understanding. If a person says that her understanding has improved there is no way anyone else can validate that. The authenticity of subjective claims to knowledge is always open to question. The tentative nature of subjective claims to understanding leads, one hopes, to scepticism about one's own knowledge; opinions are always held loosely, and are open to challenge. Action researchers do not lay claim to absolute knowledge; everything is tinged with caution.

Work using the living educational theory approach can be seen in a variety of contexts. One in which its use value can be clearly seen is the work undertaken by the Ontario Public School Teachers Federation and the Teachers College (see Halsall and Hossack 1996; Delong and Wideman 1998; see also Hamilton 1998, for accounts of work in the USA; Atweh *et al.* 1998, for accounts of work in Australia).

Doing action research in this way requires researchers to engage in a dialectical form of question and answer that aims to address questions of the kind 'How do I improve my practice?' (Whitehead 1989). The questions and answers follow this kind of sequence:

What is my concern, or my research interest?
The researcher identifies a particular issue that they want to investigate.

Why am I concerned, or interested enough to think about this?
The researcher reflects on their educational values, and checks whether these values are being lived out in practice. If not, they might decide to do something about the situation, so that their practice can come more in line with their vision of what they would like to happen.

What do I think I can do about it?
The researcher thinks creatively about possible courses of action that could be taken to improve matters.

What kind of evidence can I gather to show the situation as it is?
The researcher gathers data to show the reality of the situation. There is a variety of data-gathering techniques, and the researcher decides, often in consultation with others, what kind of techniques might be most appropriate to their particular situation. They identify working criteria, in relation to their aims and objectives, about how they are going to show their situation, and, later, how it might develop. They highlight important pieces of the action, as it is captured by the data, and those episodes are pulled out as evidence to show what is happening in a focused way.

What will I do about it?
The researcher decides on a focused action plan, and begins to monitor their work, to see how it might be impacting on other people such as the students they are teaching.

What kind of evidence can I gather to show that I have made a difference for good?
The researcher gathers data at periodic intervals to show how the situation might have changed. There is always the hope in education that the difference will be for good, but sometimes things do not turn out as one might expect. Action research is seldom tidy. However, the way we deal with the situation is important. If we deal with it in an educational way, we assume that we will be working in ways that are beneficial and life-giving for others. The researcher aims to show the new situation by production of evidence to reveal specific pieces of action and how they relate to the criteria that have been identified.

Researchers always need to be aware that things are on the move: the research questions, how the data is organised, their own thought processes – everything might change. It can be very destabilising.

How can I explain that difference?
The researcher has earlier identified criteria by which to gauge whether or not their work has improved. These criteria might be obvious: are the students smiling more, for example, or is she as teacher talking less? In all research there must be some kinds of criteria by which to judge progress. Different research traditions require different kinds of criteria; and those different kinds of criteria require differentiated standards of judgement and assessment techniques to show that movement has taken place. In empirical research, criteria to show the effectiveness of the research project would be mainly related to behaviours, and a good research design would aim to render the research replicable and generalisable. In action research, the criteria would relate to the process of growth and educational understanding, as well as demonstrate overt actions and behaviours. Good action research would demonstrate its authenticity and use value in the life of the researcher(s), and its relevance to the lives of other people would be clear. There are strong debates about these issues throughout the education research literature.

How can I be reasonably sure that any conclusions I draw are justified?
Action researchers always need to check that what they say has happened really has happened. They might like to think that people have benefited from their interventions, but is this a reasonable assumption? A researcher always needs to check with their research participants. How can the negative feedback be built in with the positive? How can a balanced interpretation be given? This is a laborious and painstaking task, and, at the end of the day, one can never be absolutely sure that what someone is saying is completely true. However, we have to proceed on reasonable guesses, otherwise we should never make any progress, so we go on good faith, aware that we could be wrong, and that we need to season our work with scepticism. Doing action research is a salutary exercise.

What will I do then?
If the situation has improved, and the researcher can support that assumption with validated evidence, they may choose to proceed with this good practice. However, they will always need to subject that practice to constant evaluation. Becoming satisfied with a situation carries its own danger of complacency and potential stultification. Work, and people's situations, change all the time, so we need always to keep an eye open and modify practice where necessary.

I believe that doing research in this way is an ethical practice. It takes commitment, and commitment means that we care enough about other people to expend the energy to monitor and change our practice when necessary.

Summary

Here, then, is our link between pastoral care and action research. Pastoral care is a commitment to be aware of the needs of others, a commitment to respond to those needs in a way that will be life-enhancing for all. Action research is a methodology that requires educators to exercise discretion and tact in finding such responses. Together they constitute a formidable partnership that we may draw on in our search for ways to improve the quality of our educative relationships and, we trust, the educational experience of ourselves and our students.

2

PASTORAL CARE AND THE MILLENNIUM

Ron Best

Introduction

I am told by my historian friends that there is nothing of natural significance about the turn of a century or the end of a millennium. These occasions (it seems) are significant only because our society has chosen to make them so, and our culture to work (for some things, but not all) 'in base ten'. The psychological effects of these time periods are, however, remarkably strong. In art and literary criticism, for example, one reads of '*fin de siècle* works' explained or interpreted in terms of their coincidence with the end of a century. There is here some implication of social and cultural decadence and hope for the dawn of a new era. For some religious sects, the end of the millennium is hailed as the 'beginning of the end', the age of the apocalypse, the creation of Heaven on Earth or as the moment when all prophecies shall be fulfilled and all manner of things shall be revealed. For us all, the year 2000 stands as some sort of milestone in a history of a people which has so often used the century as a convenient division and for whose (nominally Christian) members the birth of Christ is the necessary starting point.

Despite my efforts to do so, I find it impossible to write about education at this time without pondering the scale and rate of change which our systems of schooling have experienced over the last hundred years, and to sense some hope for a better future. Yet it is easy to exaggerate the degree to which schooling is different now from what it was then. True, class sizes are much smaller, teachers are more highly trained, uniforms are less pervasive, pupils less often sit in rows of fixed desks and are allowed to talk and move more freely, discipline is less harsh and less physical, and a great many classrooms have computers in them. By the same token, teachers still stand or sit at the front of the room, write on the board (of a different colour perhaps, but a board nonetheless), fire questions at pupils, set tasks to be done out of books, set, administer and mark tests, punish misbehaviour and try to impose silence when they feel it right so to do. Arguably, a time-traveller from 1900 would quickly recognise a secondary school classroom for what it was, although the transformation of the regimented and repressive setting of the 'board school' to the colourful open-plan and 'free-range' environment of many a modern primary classroom might well take a good deal longer to assimilate.

One aspect of schooling which such a time-traveller might find striking is the degree to which (some) teachers do, and are expected to, engage in activities which are not immediately identifiable as part of the conventional curriculum. Teachers' roles in guidance and counselling, in tutorial activities and in 'delivering' aspects of the curriculum in personal, social and moral education would, in some schools, be a real 'eye-opener'. In others, change might be a great deal less apparent. Nor (I think) would these pastoral activities be quite as apparent now as they were ten or fifteen years ago.

The changing fortunes of pastoral care seem to me to be symptomatic of those of education generally this century. They also seem to relate particularly closely to the changes in wider political perspectives which have come to dominate social thought at different times since 1900. I suggest that the core value of pastoral care – that in our commitment to the well-being of the child, we should accept the rights, duties and responsibilities entailed in the concept of the teacher *in loco parentis* – has not significantly shifted, but that the emphasis given to teachers' caring, controlling and instructional roles has varied considerably over that period.

In what follows I shall attempt to establish the parameters of pastoral care as currently conceived. I shall argue that the term 'pastoral care' now encompasses a broader range of concerns and activities than hitherto. I shall suggest that these are better understood in their complexity, their potential and their problematics than would have been true even twenty years ago, but that for the last decade or so the political tide has been running against their further development.

But first, it is necessary to locate attitudes to pastoral care within a broad framework of assumptions about the nature of humankind and of the desirability of social engineering.

The nature of humankind

It is possible to see humankind in a more or less optimistic or positive light. We may look at small children in a nursery school and wonder at their innocence, seeing only their blameless characters as yet unstained by the worldliness of growing up. We may be moved by this experience to see in humanity the natural capacity for good, for altruism, for love and for fun. Or we may look at gangs of youngsters, already late, dragging their feet towards the gates of the secondary school, faces soured at the prospect and visibly antagonistic to school and what it stands for. As teachers we may feel a certain fear at the prospect of trying to teach them anything, seeing only their apparent malevolence and the threat of antisocial behaviour. Instead of natural goodness we see natural evil: humankind as Hobbes saw it, hedonistic and asocial to the point of mutual destruction unless controlled by some strong moral authority.

Daubner (1982) argued that these extreme models of man [*sic*] underpin competing approaches in the theory and practice of counselling. He juxtaposed 'man deified' (the romantic, Rousseauian image of natural goodness) with 'man depraved' (the Calvinist and Freudian images of humankind as, since 'the Fall' at least, fundamentally evil) (ibid. 184–7). Between these extremes, Daubner poses two further models, those of 'neutrality' and 'deprivation'. According to the former, we are neither naturally good nor naturally evil, but have the potential for both. Which we tend to become is a matter of our experience and, specifically, what we learn from it. The deprivation model emphasises our capacity for good, but stresses that our tendency to choose good rather than evil is undermined by our social and psychological heritage of 'fallen' values (ibid. 191–3).

These competing perspectives on the nature of humankind underpin different attitudes to our capacity to improve the human condition through social engineering, and on the way in which education should be organised. Writing in 1985, Best and Decker argue that political philosophies and political programmes may be seen as embracing more or less optimistic concepts of humanity. Following George and Wilding (1976), we suggest that the positions adopted towards collectivist approaches to social welfare are to be understood in terms of the assumptions they make about the capacity of individuals to live the good life and to support one another without working collectively to establish systems of care and support.

The 'anti-collectivists' are clear that we are fundamentally self-serving and individualistic – 'man depraved' – and that the greatest good of the greatest number is to be realised through maximising individual liberty and minimising the interference of the state. The 'welfare state' is seen as well-intentioned but counterproductive in the otherwise efficient system of capitalism.

The 'reluctant collectivists' share the anti-collectivists' basic belief in the *laissez-faire* economy, but recognise that capitalism is imperfect and needs to be regulated to some degree. In regard to social welfare, the state needs to intervene on economic grounds – the unemployed, the poor and the sick are a drain on the nation's wealth – and on humanitarian grounds, since there will always be some people who, through no fault of their own, simply cannot look after themselves.

The 'Fabian Socialists' assume a model of 'man deprived': given appropriate social engineering, the conditions can be achieved whereby the potential of humankind for good can be maximised. Collectivism is warmly embraced, centring on notions of equality of opportunity, cooperation and fellowship. Such a perspective is essentially optimistic. It sees in humankind the potential not only for altruism, but for creating the very conditions for promoting the good through the 'pragmatic, piecemeal social engineering' which became a central feature of British and other Western European countries (notably Sweden) as the century progressed (George and Wilding 1976: 75).

The fourth position identified by George and Wilding – that of the Marxists – is even more optimistic. It believes that through the subordination of the individual to the collective, human perfection is achievable to the point where the well-being of all members is guaranteed and the state can 'wither away'. Provisions made for the less fortunate under capitalism only postpone the dawn of the epoch of communism by ameliorating the worst of conditions and thus blunting the motivation for revolution. The possibility of utopia is predicated upon the natural goodness of 'man deified'.

The twentieth century may be seen as a field of battle between these different political philosophies – and of the competing models of humanity they entail. In Britain, the creation of a National Health Service, the Beveridge Report with its attack on the 'five giants' of disease, idleness, squalor, poverty and ignorance, and the post-World War II reforms to which it led – including the introduction of a National Insurance scheme and the provision of state secondary education for all – may be seen as the moments when collectivism reached its peak. The decades since have witnessed a 'swing to the Right' not just in Britain but in much of the world, in which collectivism has given way to a radical and market-oriented individualism. The prolonged period of Conservative rule in the UK was as much a symptom of this as was the dissolution of the USSR and the destruction of the Berlin Wall.

I want to suggest that the way in which education is viewed, and in particular, the place which pastoral care and personal and social education have filled within it, has to be understood within this broad context of social movements and political doctrines.

Pastoral care

There have been several attempts to map the historical development of the concept and practice of pastoral care in education. In a number of papers Peter Lang has evolved a historical account of pastoral care which traces it to its origins in nineteenth-century public schools where teachers' responsibilities for pupils' moral well-being and general welfare came to be recognised (Lang 1983: 61). He goes on to propose two stages of development this century: the application of the public school model to state secondary schools following World War II, and the development of the complex pastoral systems in comprehensive and other secondary schools during the 1970s. A similar chronology is provided by Blackburn (1983a; 1983b), where pastoral care is represented as evolving through phases in which a general concern for 'knowing' and 'tracking' children in new and large comprehensive schools gave way to the development of more focused forms of guidance and counselling of an academic, personal, social and vocational nature, culminating in the 1970s in more fully developed programmes of personal, social and vocational education. In yet another attempt to chart the development of this complex concept, Ribbins and Best (1985) also focus attention on the growth of pastoral care systems as a manifestation of comprehensive reorganisation in England and Wales, rationalised in a 'conventional wisdom' which found explanation in the works of such prestigious practitioners as Michael Marland (Marland 1974). The late 1970s and 1980s are described as a period during which both the techniques of pastoral care and the critique of its conventional wisdom were developed through professional application and academic scholarship. This period also saw the general acceptance of the idea of a pastoral curriculum (Pring 1984; Hargreaves *et al.* 1988) and the publication of a number of research projects (e.g., Best *et al.* 1983; Johnson *et al.* 1980), which examined the practice of pastoral care in schools and the welfare networks with which they meshed.

Whatever the relative accuracy of these histories, they are agreed on two points: first, that our understanding of the concept of pastoral care has become more elaborate and sophisticated with the passage of time; and second, that the range of activities which are encompassed by this term in schools has expanded. This is perhaps best demonstrated by considering the definition given by Her Majesty's Inspectorate in 1989:

> pastoral care is concerned with promoting pupils' personal and social development and fostering positive attitudes: through the quality of teaching and learning; through the nature of relationships amongst pupils, teachers and adults other than teachers; through arrangements for monitoring pupils' overall progress, academic, personal and social; through specific pastoral structures and support systems; and through extra-curricular activities and the school ethos. Pastoral care, accordingly, should help a school to achieve success. In such a context it offers support for the learning, behaviour and welfare of all pupils, and addresses the particular difficulties some individual pupils may be experiencing. It seems to help ensure that all pupils, and particularly girls and members of ethnic minorities, are enabled to benefit from the full range of educational opportunities which a school has available.
>
> (DES 1989: 3)

While hardly the crisp, dictionary definition we might like, this statement does seem to reflect the diversity and pervasiveness of what pastoral care means in most schools, pointing as it does to structures, systems, relationships, extra-curricular activities, arrangements for 'tracking' individual children's development and adjustment, and the overall ethos of the school.

Three types of care

Attempts to make our understanding of pastoral care more precise have led to a growing consensus about three distinct but related objectives. These are usually referred to as *reactive*, *proactive* and *developmental* care.

By *reactive pastoral care* is meant the attempt by the teacher or the school to respond to children who present problems of a personal, social, emotional or behavioural kind. The role of the form tutor is often seen as primarily concerned with getting to know the children in their form, and the children to know the tutor, sufficiently well for them to feel comfortable in bringing such problems to the tutor in the first instance. Motivated by a desire to help and comfort such children, the good form tutor is expected to provide some form of counselling, guidance or more generalised emotional support in response to perceived need. Because of the similarity with the work of doctors, social workers, educational welfare officers and other carers, this one-to-one help is often referred to as 'casework'. Good casework requires the teacher to be accepting and approachable and to have skills in active listening, negotiation, guidance and counselling. Where a problem is felt to be too complex, too severe, or in other ways beyond the capacity of the form tutor to resolve, the tutor is expected to refer the child to higher levels in the pastoral structure, from where they may subsequently be referred to outside, specialist help.

Proactive pastoral care is based on the old adage that prevention is better than cure. As long ago as 1978, Douglas Hamblin argued that limiting the help we give to children to the reactive, reduces teachers' caring to no more than 'emotional first aid'. He argued that the identification of 'critical incidents' in children's careers through school provided foci for the preparation and delivery of programmes of learning experiences which would equip children to cope when potential crises occur. This general principle was subsequently adopted by those writing materials for tutorial programmes, where attention came to be focused on the development of practical knowledge and coping skills which would allow children to make wise choices and respond positively to social, emotional and educational challenges.

However, there are educational grounds for developing such skills in youngsters which go far beyond equipping them to cope with predictable critical incidents, and this leads to the idea of *developmental pastoral care*.

In a seminal chapter, Michael Marland argued that the education of the child requires the mastery of much more than an academic curriculum (Marland 1980). He argued that there is a body of curriculum content which we want children to have acquired by the end of their schooling and which has as its subject matter the personal and social development of the child. He proposed that there is thus a pastoral curriculum consisting of concepts, facts, skills and attitudes which could, and ought, to be planned and provided by schools if they are seriously committed to education in its fullest sense. By emphasising in various degrees the personal and social dimensions of development, other writers (e.g., Watkins 1985; Pring 1988) have provided comparable justifications for the whole area of personal, social and moral education. What these writers have in common is their commitment to the idea that neither reacting to problems on a one-to-one basis nor providing specific skills in anticipation of critical incidents does justice to the *educational* dimension of pastoral work which is holistic, developmental and forward look-ing. Taken together, proactive and preventative measures along with developmental pastoral care comprise what is generally known in schools as 'the pastoral curriculum'.

Two other dimensions of schools' pastoral activities may be identified. The first of these is the whole area of order and control. It is arguable that much of the casework done by teachers 'wearing their pastoral hats' has been reactive to problems of behaviour identified as indiscipline. It was part of the critique of the 1970s and early 1980s that what was justified by the conventional wisdom as a response to the needs of individual children was too often a response to the needs of teachers who found certain children difficult to control (Best *et al.* 1977; Williamson 1980). While this has sometimes been thought of as a cyn-ical view, my own experience of secondary schools since then suggests that it remains true for many teachers in many schools today. Whether the child *has* a problem or is a problem *for the teacher* is something which might be debated *ad infinitum*. What is incontestable is that social and emotional problems most often manifest themselves in behaviour which is held to be unacceptable or inappropriate.

Schools may respond to such challenging behaviour in more or less positive ways. A purely reactive stance would seem to have little to commend it. Punishing children when they misbehave rather than taking preventative measures (as, for example, by identifying the circumstances which trigger such behaviour and challenging those circumstances) is short-sighted. Watkins and Wagner (1987) make a strong case for adopting a pastoral perspective in order to develop a systematic approach to school discipline at the levels of the school, the class and the individual. Their thesis is that misbehaviour must be understood as a social construct which involves one individual engaging in behaviour which is categorised as unacceptable by another within a social context in which other actors are present and significant. A rational approach is therefore to analyse not just the behaviour itself, but the effects of others pre-sent on the pattern of behaviour and the processes by which the teacher categorises, labels and responds to it. They argue that the teams of form tutors and their pastoral middle managers are ideally placed, by virtue of their holis-tic concept of the child, to lead such analysis and to coordinate the team response to which it should give rise. This response may appropriately be thought of as proactive and preventive.

However, as I have argued elsewhere (Best 1994a), to limit our attention to the needs of those who are defined as deviants is to overlook the needs and rights of all members of the school community. It is to undervalue the power-ful forces for good behaviour which are provided by the creation and strengthening of a sense of community in the first place. It is not only the deviants who need a framework of rules and a system of sanctions: these are the entitlement of all citizens in any community if their personal liberty is not to be infringed by the excessive behaviour of others. It is also the right of every citizen to have opportunities to share in the corporate life of the group, to feel a sense of belonging, to feel a shared destiny with other members, and to benefit from the acceptance of a mutual responsibility for one another. These are aspects of the ethos of the school to which Her Majesty's Inspectorate drew attention in their own definition of pastoral care.

Pastoral care and human nature

It is possible to associate these different aspects of pastoral care with the models of humankind and the political philosophies outlined earlier.

Those for whom pastoral care has only ever meant controlling individuals whose behaviour is unacceptable and contravenes the rules of the school, and who would argue that teachers should not be distracted by an expectation that they should act as 'agony aunts', are adopting an anti-collectivist perspective. They are arguing that individuals should be free to get on with the teaching and learning of the curriculum to their own advantage, and those who are not able or prepared to do likewise require correction.

Those for whom pastoral care is limited to preventive work with children who are perceived to have problems of a personal, social or emotional nature, originating outside the school and, most typically, attributed to 'the situation at home', may be compared with the reluctant collectivists. They perceive the needs which some children have for individualised support as resulting from the inadequacies of their parents, their neighbourhood and (in some cases) hereditary deficiencies in genetic endowment. Unable to look after themselves, they present a distraction and drain on the resources of the teacher, a hindrance to the achievements of their more adequate peers, and are on humanitarian grounds in need of special provision. The development of special schools and, within mainstream schools, of special classes or sanctuaries, may be seen as a natural response to this kind of thinking.

A more positive image of the child is adopted by those who see pastoral care as contributing in a more constructive way to the child's social adjustment and capacity to benefit from schooling. Here, the school and its teachers seek to compensate for some degree of social, material, emotional or cultural deprivation which is an obstacle as much to the child's psychological well-being as to their capacity to take advantage of what the curriculum has to offer.

This was the view of educational need most prominent in the late 1960s and 1970s, and was directly connected with Fabian socialism. Children from vulnerable groups – most notably at that time, those from the lower working class – were perceived as suffering from multiple deprivation to which some form of compensatory programme of education would be the most practical response. Compensatory schemes were a feature of the educational policies of many countries at that time, exemplified in England by the Schools Council/Nuffield Foundation experiment in 'educational priority areas' (Halsey 1972). The model of humankind underpinning this approach is clearly that of 'man deprived', with the designation of such areas as requiring remedial funding and positive discrimination intended to make good the deficiencies.

The capacity for social engineering through pastoral work of this kind is limited. Since its attention is restricted to the minority who are held to be deprived, the needs of the other children are not being addressed. It is possible to argue that this is tacitly conservative in that it deflects attention from the quality of education which is being provided for *all* children. Such was the thinking behind Williamson's (1980) thesis of 'pastoralisation' which posed the question: What if it is not the children who are inadequate but the curriculum?

Those who stress the developmental concept of pastoral care as making a positive contribution, through the curriculum, to the development of the child 'as a whole person' are making a similar point. Pastoral care is not limited to compensating for the imperfections of society, nor to humanitarian 'do-gooding' for those who, through accident of birth or hard times, are incapable of looking after themselves. Rather, it is seen as completing an education which is stunted by a conventional curriculum limited to the academic subjects. Underlying this is a humanistic view of the person which has much in common with the Romantics. Like Rousseau, and in a later generation Holt (1969; 1971), such a view implicitly or explicitly challenges the very concept of education which pervades schooling. Utopia is possible, but we must first release the child from the worst that schooling has to offer. Though rarely acknowledged, those who advocate the permeation of the entire curriculum with the values, attitudes, concepts, facts and skills necessary for the attainment of true personhood are not a million miles from Marx.

Pastoral casework in the 1990s

My own research and the content of contributions to the journal *Pastoral Care in Education* suggest that there has been relatively little change in the problems which teachers find themselves reacting to in the casework that they do. In a case study of a comprehensive school undertaken in 1992 (Best 1994b), teachers reported the following as the sorts of problems which were handled by form tutors and/or referred to heads of year:

- Problems with school work. Teachers found themselves providing emotional and practical support when youngsters became distressed or anxious because they could not cope with school work (particularly with homework). Teachers sometimes had to ask colleagues to be more sensitive to individual difficulties when they set work, and on occasions found parents' unrealistic expectations to be an added pressure.
- Physical disabilities. Although these might at first glance appear a learning need, teachers were clear that children with, for example, visual

impairment faced problems for which pastoral rather than academic support was required.

- Problems with relationships. Teachers talked at great length about personality clashes between teachers and pupils and the problems of friendships and peer relations amongst the children. Although sometimes appearing trivial to adults, such problems can assume enormous proportions for adolescents.
- Physical and sexual abuse of children.
- Anxiety and financial difficulties brought on by the recession in the late 1980s. Children were often seriously affected by significant changes in life style and the depression and anxiety of parents when made redundant.
- The use of cannabis and other drugs and their trade along the perimeter of the school site.
- Promiscuity, pregnancy and virtual prostitution (i.e., providing sexual favours in return for some benefit short of actual payment in money).
- Smoking.
- Truancy. Little was said in interview about this as a problem in its own right, but it was often mentioned in association with other problems such as children not coping with the break-up of their parents' marriage, problems of relationships at school, and so on.
- Bullying.
- Bereavement.
- Transition problems. Teachers talked at length about the difficulty some children have in making the transition from primary school to secondary school and from the earlier to later years in the secondary school where expectations can change radically.

Except for the emphasis given to child abuse and drugs, this list struck me as remarkably similar to the kinds of problems teachers talked about in a comparable study undertaken over a decade earlier (Best *et al.* 1983). I suspect that the new items reflect our raised awareness of both problems in the intervening years rather than any increase in either the use of drugs or the incidence of abuse. By and large, teachers continue to respond *in loco parentis* to a remarkable range of problems but with the added pressure of these particularly sensitive and problematic issues. Recent discussion with a colleague in Australia highlighted a growing problem there which schools are having to face: that of the rising rate of teenage suicides. Given a small number of highly publicised recent cases linked to bullying, one can only conjecture that this saddest of all events may soon also be added to the list in British schools.

In regard to discipline, teachers continue to deal with problems of behaviour, many of them related to the problems listed above. However, it is arguable that the challenges are greater because of a general decline in deference in society and youngsters' loss of a sense of purpose and direction in the face of high youth unemployment and cultural pluralism. As we shall see below, this has become a major issue in national politics and one to which a curricular response is now being sought.

A very significant year

The year 1988 may be seen as a watershed in educational policy in England and Wales. Comparable watersheds may be identified in other countries, but that is for someone else to determine. What is clear, is that the 1988 Education Reform Act both confirmed a range of changes that had been taking place in the administration of education and its policy determination throughout the 1980s, and heralded unprecedented changes in the curriculum and the management of schools. These changes have dramatic implications for pastoral care, and may be seen in a more or less positive light.

Paragraph 2 of the Act requires schools to offer:

a balanced and broadly based curriculum which
(a) promotes the spiritual, moral, cultural, mental and physical development of pupils at the school and of society; and
(b) prepares such pupils for the opportunities, responsibilities and experiences of adult life.

As Michael Marland has noted:

This over-arching pair of requirements, which are legally prior to the National Curriculum requirements, could have been drafted by a pastoral care enthusiast. Indeed (b) is virtually a succinct statement of the central aims of pastoral care.

(Marland 1995: 112)

Marland's optimism is understandable, for if schools were to take these clauses seriously, they might be expected to devote a great deal more time, energy and resources to the whole range of activities that come under the pastoral umbrella. Unfortunately, there have been powerful forces, legitimated by the very same Act, which run counter to such a development.

The conception of the National Curriculum as developed by the (then) National Curriculum Council (NCC) was remarkably conservative in its preoccupation with traditional academic subjects. Except for changes in technology (including a new emphasis on IT) the list of National Curriculum subjects looks surprisingly similar to the core curriculum in most schools before the Act and, indeed, at any time since the turn of the century. What was omitted was a range of subjects which had appeared on the curriculum of many schools and which might be described as having 'a pastoral flavour': subjects like careers education, health education, social studies and PSE.

In time, and in response to criticisms from the teaching profession and from bodies which saw such omissions as having serious implications for social order, the NCC belatedly generated what they called 'cross-curricular elements'. These were divided into cross-curricular *dimensions*, *skills* and *themes*. These included a concern for equal opportunities and preparation for life in a multi-cultural society, skills in communication, problem solving and personal and social skills, and such themes as health education, careers education and guidance and education for citizenship (NCC 1990).

The NCC was clear that these elements were the responsibility of all teachers and were to be delivered in all the National Curriculum programmes of study, and indeed elsewhere in the 'whole curriculum'. However, as a 'bolt-on afterthought' it was unreasonable to expect schools to give the cross-curriculum elements a high priority in a context in which they were under enormous pressure to accommodate the demands of the programmes of study themselves.

The fact that the National Curriculum was assessment driven, and that the Department for Education gave such prominence to the publication of 'league tables' of schools according to pupil performance in the National Curriculum, only added to the pressure against giving pastoral care anything like equal consideration. My own research (Best 1994b; 1995) confirms the anecdotal evidence that teachers have found pastoral care roles to be devalued in terms both of their priorities in the classroom and their career prospects. Teachers interviewed in case studies in a junior school and a comprehensive school in 1992 talked of the massive demands of the National Curriculum and its associated assessments, referring particularly to the bureaucracy and paperwork which this has added to their already busy lives. Some made it very clear that they had less time, resources and energy to care than they had ever had in the past.

However, schools have come under pressure to provide a pastoral curriculum from another quarter. The Office for Standards in Education (OFSTED) has been obliged to inspect schools not only in terms of the National Curriculum and Religious Education, but also in terms of the broad statements of paragraph 2 of the 1988 Act (see above). Thus, schools' provision for spiritual, moral, social and cultural development ('SMSC') is now prominent in the guidelines for school inspections, and both OFSTED and the Schools Curriculum and Assessment Authority (SCAA, the successor to the NCC), have produced discussion papers and consultation documents on this aspect of schools' work.

The developments which culminated in, and followed from, the 1988 Act have had important consequences also for the *management* of pastoral care. In particular, the emphasis given to the academic curriculum has led to a re-conceptualising of such roles as that of head of year. The division of the National Curriculum into key stages and the need for cross-curricular planning to be undertaken at each key stage and in each year within each key stage, has made the head of year a central position in curriculum planning and coordi-nation. In some schools this is reflected in changing nomenclature, with 'head of year' giving way to such titles as 'year curriculum coordinator'. We may con-jecture that similar changes may be happening at senior management level, but empirical research is needed to establish precisely what other structural and procedural changes are happening to schools' pastoral and academic sys-tems in response to legislation.

For the form tutor, so often identified as the 'foundation stone' of schools' pastoral systems, change is imminent. At the time of writing, people are start-ing to talk about the importance of *academic tutoring*. This may signal some realignment of the tutor's role to take account of the overwhelming emphasis being given to children's achievement within the academic curriculum. If this is so, the implications for the casework and tutorial work which are the tradi-tional tasks of the form tutor are considerable.

The market mentality

As already indicated, it is important to see these developments in the broader context of the changing fortunes of competing political ideologies.

The 1988 Education Act was a component in a broad move towards a more market-oriented education system. The devolution of budgets to individual schools (LMS), the promotion of parent power through a putative increase in choice of schools, the disempowerment of local education authorities, the cre-ation of a grant maintained sector, the development of an assisted-places scheme for independent schools, the creation of city technology colleges and the designation of other schools as specialist colleges in art, technology, and so on, and the introduction of league tables based on schools' performance in National Curriculum and other indicators of competitive success have together drastically changed the way the education service is seen. What schools may teach has in large measure been centrally ordained, but in all other respects schools are free to struggle for survival in a market-place where cut-throat competition for pupils (and thus for resources) has become the order of the day.

In the market-place everything has its price and price is the measure of value. In terms of the measurement of schools' effectiveness, those things which cannot be measured – and thus whose price cannot be determined and whose value must therefore be in doubt – are likely to go to the wall. It is arguable that this is what is now happening with much of the pastoral care which schools once accepted as an important part of teachers' work.

The recent concern shown by all political parties, and in particular the Government and its quangos (OFSTED and SCAA), in the promotion of moral education is striking, and may be grasped by some as an indication of a com-mitment to the pastoral curriculum. Such an interpretation would be simplistic. What seems to be the case is that an increasingly right-wing administration is seeking to impose greater social control through the socialisation function of schooling. Thus, SCAA established a National Forum for Values in Education and the Community whose aim was explicitly to identify a core of values upon which there is a consensus and which would be actively promoted through 'SMSC' in the curriculum. This is a million miles away from the concept of values clarification and the comparable approaches to personal, social and moral education advocated by bodies like the Schools Council in the 1960s and by such bodies as the National Association for Pastoral Care (NAPCE) at the present time.

It is ironic, to say the least, that the curriculum 'reforms' surrounding 1988 should have actively discouraged the further development of a pastoral curriculum which aimed to promote the knowledge and skills that would properly lead to personal autonomy in the context of social responsibility. It is ominous that central authorities should now be seeking to fill the gap with a programme for social *conformity*. The two are so widely different ultimately because they are premised upon those opposed models of humankind which were identified earlier: the reforms of the 1960s and the stance adopted by NAPCE have an optimistic concept of 'man deified' whereas current trends in SCAA are about the salvation of society through the socialisation of 'man depraved'.

Hope for the future?

Whether the turn of the century or the end of the millennium will signal a swing back towards a more humanistic concept of education, and thus of a renaissance in pastoral care, remains to be seen. Certainly, little real change has yet resulted from the return of a Labour Government in the UK in May 1997. In any event there is much which can be achieved by those in schools and colleges who have such a concept. One way in which pastoral care may be developed is through *action research*.

I suggest that action research and pastoral care go very well together precisely because both are based in those more optimistic models of humanity associated with progressive political philosophies. Those who believe in action research believe in our capacity to create structures and procedures which can improve the human condition. They also believe that it is 'ordinary' people and not some powerful or prestigious elite who have the experience and insight required to make change happen where it matters: in the classrooms, staff rooms and playgrounds of our schools. They are also at pains to emphasise the importance of collective and collaborative endeavour (Winter 1989: 55–9). In short, theirs is the perspective of the Fabian socialists, if not of even more radical reformers, and is diametrically opposed to the imposition on teachers of change from outside and above.

In principle there is no aspect of pastoral care which might not be improved through action research. However, it may be helpful to identify broad areas which might be addressed, and within those areas to begin to identify priorities.

The broad areas which suggest themselves are those which we have already discussed: pastoral casework, pastoral curriculum, discipline and social order, and pastoral management. Within each of these one might identify reactive, proactive/preventive and developmental practices. Taken together, these provide a matrix of possible foci for evaluation and improvement:

Table 2.1 A framework for identifying action research foci in pastoral care

	Casework	*Curriculum*	*Order/ discipline*	*Management*
Reactive	1	2	3	4
Proactive/ preventive	5	6	7	8
Developmental	9	10	11	12

Thus, for example Box 1 might represent an action research project which sought to improve teachers' active listening skills when providing guidance and counselling to individual pupils who have presented with a problem of a personal or emotional nature. Box 7 might represent an action research project which sought to analyse and evaluate current approaches to reward and punishment with a view to increasing the emphasis teachers give to the positive encouragement and reinforcement of pro-social behaviour. Box 8 might represent an action research approach to the review and improvement of systems of communication between teachers playing pastoral and academic roles within established structures of posts of responsibility.

I wish to encourage teacher-initiated action research in all areas. However, given the need to challenge the unhealthy dominance of schooling by the academic curriculum and its assessment, and the need to subvert the dehumanising trend of the market mentality, I suggest that top priority should be given to developmental approaches in Boxes 10, 11 and 12; that is to say, that action research should focus especially on:

- The development of whole-school approaches to the planning, implementation and evaluation of curricula in personal, social, moral, spiritual and health education. Within such projects, the developmental needs of the child as a whole person, and not the requirements of an imposed and impersonal National Curriculum, should provide the starting point.
- The promotion of the qualities of a community within the school. Within such projects, the entitlement of all members of the school community – pupils, teachers, ancillary staff – to experience a sense of belonging, of identity, of collective responsibility, of a shared destiny and of personal worth and dignity should be the starting point, and not the subordination

of the school to the imposition of a set of values from outside and above.

- Action research projects which develop the management of pastoral care in all its rich diversity. Within such projects, the training of staff for managerial roles would of course be significant, but it is important to remember that teachers also need personal and moral support, to feel appreciated and to be valued in their own right. The question which, more than any other, should give direction to such projects is this: what kind of development do pastoral managers need in order to be able to meet the needs of the staff they manage in order that they, in turn, can more effectively meet the needs of the children?

Conclusion

A commitment to the development of pastoral care in schools and colleges is more than 'piecemeal social engineering'; for the pastoral work schools do is organically related to the whole mission of education. Pastoral care not only facilitates the work of the academic curriculum but is integral to that all-round development of the child as a 'whole person', which is what education, properly understood, is all about. It is about facilitating growth, fulfilment and integration of the individual both as a person and as a member of society.

It is for this reason that I have placed so much emphasis upon the models of humankind which underpin our perspectives on pastoral care as much as they underpin the political philosophies and ideologies which have shaped society throughout this century. Our acceptance of one or other model carries a moral commitment to a certain course of action.

In my view, education in the latter decades of the twentieth century has been dominated by a pessimistic view of humanity as individualistic, competitive and self-serving. Rather than promote the opposite and, I believe, highly desirable qualities of equality, cooperation and respect for persons, the authorities have embraced the market mentality and reduced much of education to 'product outcomes' and 'performance indicators'. To re-emphasise the values and practice of pastoral care in education is to challenge such a view. Improving pastoral care through action research, however modest the scale, is therefore much more than a matter of technical proficiency. It is also a moral act which re-asserts a much more positive and optimistic view of humanity.

And at the turn of the millennium, a rebirth of optimism about what education can achieve is desperately needed.

3

REVISITING THE PASTORAL
CARE SCHOOL

Úna M. Collins

I have chosen the title 'Revisiting the pastoral care school' because I intend to explore a new approach to such a visit. To contextualise this visit I will review the growth of:

1 the concept of formal pastoral care in national education awareness
2 the articulation of the term 'pastoral care' in national education literature, and
3 the perception and experience of pastoral care in the Irish secondary school.

  In 1994 there took place what has been described as 'an unprecedented democratic event in the history of Irish education' (National Education Convention Secretariat 1994: 1). A National Convention was convened and representatives from forty-two educational bodies, and parents' associations, along with the Minister for Education and her Department officials, came together to engage, in a structured way, in a discussion on the key issues of Irish educational policy. 'It reflected a nation discussing what is probably one of its clearest core values, education' (Collins 1998). When preparing a paper for the first European Conference on Pastoral Care at Warwick University in 1994 (published in Lang *et al.* 1998), a quotation from Drudy and Lynch struck me as crystalising the Irish value for and preoccupation with education:

> If the mythical Martian were to arrive in the Republic of Ireland to investigate the dominant activity of its citizens she or he might be forgiven for assuming that its principal industry is education. The figures show that nearly one third of the population (968,457 people) are engaged in full time education (Government of Ireland 1992). In addition to these, a considerable body of workers provide a service to these students, teachers, lecturers and others in the administration of the educational system. When one takes into consideration that for each of these students there are also parents and often family members supporting or monitoring their progress through the system, one can reasonably

conclude that education is a central institution in Irish society.

(Drudy and Lynch 1993: ix)

The Education Convention in 1994 was a milestone in public awareness of and (for the first time) clear articulation in national policy of the term 'pastoral care' within the 'central institution' system.

> This [reorganisation of middle management structures] would free [teachers] to concentrate their energies on academic and pastoral work. . . . Similar posts could also be created in other sections of the school, such as in curriculum development, pastoral care, and staff development.

(National Education Convention Secretariat 1994: 53).

It was also significant that in 1994 the newly created National In-Career Development Unit within the Department of Education listed pastoral care as one of its priority areas. I would argue that this event indicated the raising of awareness of the significance of pastoral care: the statement in the official report of the Convention reflected a twenty-year process to develop a formal pastoral care system in secondary schools.

There are many aspects of pastoral care to be considered. One is conscious that the term itself creates difficulties. During sessions of inservice provision during the past twenty years, I have heard the often repeated comments and questions about 'care' being the task of professional social workers and not of teachers. One hears the questions about 'pastoral' and the perception that it conjures up images of shepherds and sheep. The etymology of the term, its definitions and descriptions as well as the history of the development of pastoral care in the British context have been well documented, among others, by Michael Marland (1974); Ron Best, Colin Jarvis and Peter Ribbins (1980); Peter Lang and Michael Marland (1985); Anthony Clemett and John Pearce (1986).

There is not a similar body of literature on pastoral care in the Irish context. This book is one of the first contributions. The experience of formal pastoral care in Ireland dates back to the 1960s and 1970s, and to the development of comprehensive and community schools. This development reflects a similar development in Britain with the growth of such schools in the 1950s and 1960s. It is interesting to note that the term entered British official literature in 1974, and comes into Irish official statements in 1994! The first handbook on pastoral care in Ireland was published in 1980, and recognised that the title, though not the practice, was new – 'Pastoral Care in education is a relatively new term for a concept that is as old as education' (Collins 1980: 1). The practice of formally developing roles and structures to support caring education grew, and with it grew the need for teacher inservice education and re-training. The first postgraduate course in pastoral care was provided by the

National University of Ireland, Maynooth, and Marino Institute of Education, Dublin, 1992–95, and this course has subsequently been developed into a School Guidance Counselling Course in a pastoral care context. The founding of the Irish Association of Pastoral Care in Education (IAPCE) in 1995 was the direct outcome of these postgraduate courses, and it is now a national body providing inservice education and resources for secondary schools in Ireland.

The revisiting, in this paper, is within the frame outlined above. I am conscious that there are as many perceptions of what constitutes a pastoral care school, as there are experiences of school. If I could weave together all the perceptions and all the experiences, my fantasy is that I would have a pattern in which one sees a network of relationships in a community of learning which values all its members, with special value for the most vulnerable; and which is structured in a systemic way to support what the school community values.

Some years ago when I was attempting to describe the 'pastoral school' I was challenged by a professor of education who said to me, 'Surely you are describing the "good" school. Why do you use the term "pastoral"?' This challenge sparked an ongoing reflection and evaluation of my own concept and of the theories which were being generated by my own experience.

First of all, the concept of a 'good' school. Again there are as many concepts as there are experiences. For some the 'good' school is the school which ensures top academic results. For others it is the school which provides a wide range of learning experiences. Some even consider that the school which serves the middle-upper socio-economic class is 'good', and there are some who believe that the school which has caring teachers deserves the label 'good'. Having reflected on why I continue to use the term 'pastoral' rather than 'good', I am convinced that it challenges me to consider certain focused values related to the education of young people. The ambivalence about the term 'pastoral' is a challenge for each school community. All members of the school need to articulate what is understood for their school, own its meaning, plan and evaluate in relation to it. I am going to revisit the 'pastoral care school' within my present understanding of that term, and from a systemic or holistic perspective. I do not intend to get caught in a definition of pastoral roles or outlines of pastoral programmes. My visit could take any one of a number of routes (see Figure 3.1) which are holistic in outcome, such as:

- the students' experience in the network of relationships
- a systemic overview of school
- teachers' concepts of and experience of school
- leadership vision and practice
- theoretical foundations.

In line with my attempt to identify how conceptualisations of pastoral care have changed, and continue to change, I am choosing three of the above routes, and I invite you, the reader, to revisit the school with me.

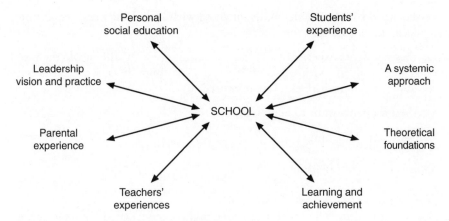

Figure 3.1 Pastoral care school: possible routes for revisiting

My first revisiting route is through the students' experience in a network of relationships that is called school. One might argue that this is the only valid route to revisit a school, whether or not it claims to be 'pastoral'. This will be our main entrance in revisiting; and then we shall proceed to 'fly' over the school in a systemic overview; and finally we will look at the foundations of the school in pastoral care theory.

I want to take a fresh look in this visit, and review learning, empowerment and community, concepts and values which are integral to a pastoral care school.

Students' experience in the network of relationships which is school

Let us now visit the school by trying to imagine the students' needs and how the pastoral school would know these needs and respond to them. I will do this by asking some key questions, and will endeavour, through both my imagination and my experience, to project the students' feelings and the school's response. The questions will be focused towards the students who might be termed most vulnerable. I would argue that the practices of identifying the students who are most vulnerable, and agreeing values and structures to meet the needs of these students, are at the heart of what we call a pastoral care school. The strength and effectiveness of our human communities, family, school, local, national or international communities is rooted in how the most vulnerable members are included, supported and engaged meaningfully. My revisiting is primarily and centrally through the experience of the 'most vulnerable' students.

The key questions, therefore, in this visit are:

How do the least academic students, or the students who seem limited in personal and social qualities/skills, or those with least family and social support, experience school?

Do these students experience a culture of learning which will enable them to move into adult life with self-confidence, questioning minds, social skills and the ability to commit themselves to others?

Do these students want to be in school?

Can they enjoy learning?

Some consequent questions might be:

Does the student feel they belong in this school?
Belonging is a fundamental human need and consequently, I would argue, a fundamental right for each young person in school. It will remain a vague aspiration of well-intentioned adults unless the school engages clearly in reflecting on, discussing and planning how this 'belonging' need can be met. In this visit we would expect, for instance, to find a school which relates with feeder schools before the students' arrival at school. Significant staff members, such as the principal and/or guidance counsellor, and/or pastoral staff, meet the future students, their parents and present teachers. New relationships are made for these students, the communication process begins, and the difficulties of transition are addressed. The process of belonging, then, begins before the student arrives. The significant adults who will continue that process have spoken to, and, most importantly, have listened to the new students and to their parents. Questions about subjects, choice of subjects, streaming, assessments, books, costs, and so on are answered within new relationships and communication modes. Belonging, necessary for all students, and essential for the most vulnerable, has begun. We will meet students who can tell us how their anxieties were reduced when they met and could question some teachers from their senior school. They looked forward to their new school, and were relieved when the adults they had met were there to introduce them to senior students who would have responsibility for them as they settled in to a new environment. Without having all the words to express how they are feeling, these vulnerable students are able to tell us that they belong in this school.

Does the student experience school regulations as supportive and in their interest?
We will ask the principal and the pastoral staff about school rules and regulations. We will ask the students, our special group of most vulnerable students, the same questions. We will expect to find that the school has few rules and regulations, and that those it has are rooted in the values of human dignity and respect for adolescents who are becoming adults. They are simple rules. They are clearly student-centred, and are regularly evaluated with students. Teachers are clear, and of one mind, about the values underlying the rules, and each teacher helps their class to 'own' the need for a group of people to have agreed

regulations which support them. The students will tell us that they generally keep the rules, and recognise that these rules make school safe for all. Teachers see themselves as experienced adults who manage the school experience for the good of the students. The students tell us that they understand and own the school rules, and they are regularly involved in evaluation and re-planning.

Does each student experience success related to their individual abilities?
In our visit we will ask what success means in this school. Is it a narrow, confined space into which only a small percentage who have linguistic and mathematical abilities fit? Does school celebrate success only in the context of results? We will ask the students if they have experienced a success which is open to all. As visitors to this school we will discuss with the principal and staff the significant impact in recent educational history of Howard Gardner's (1983) theory on multiple intelligences, and of Daniel Goleman's (1996) work on emotional intelligence. These we know are sources of strength for teachers who have constantly experienced 'intelligent' students who nevertheless could not succeed in the narrow, officially approved sense. We will be confident that the staff of the pastoral care school will be comfortable with these theories and will be developing programmes influenced by them. When we talk to the students they will show us their work with pride, and it will be obvious to us that they enjoy their learning. Success in this school is a pathway open to all students.

Does this school address the dignity of each person?
Dignity of person is, we believe, a key learning and therefore a key experience in the school. We will expect to find that 'dignity' as a value has been named, and that a consensus exists about how it is expressed and experienced in the processes and programmes provided in the school. When we are talking with the students, we will know by how they behave with each other, speak about themselves, and describe various activities, that the value of human dignity is real in the school.

Is there a network of appropriate relationships in the school?
We know that our visit is to a pastoral care school, so we will be conscious of the appropriate network of relationships we expect to find. We will have heard from the students about the principal, the guidance counsellor and other adults and students whom they met on entering the school. Now we will meet the middle and senior students and hear them speak about school relationships, formal and informal. We will want to hear about, and even experience, the whole network of these relationships: students with staff, students with students, staff members with staff members, management with school members, parents with school, school with local community. We will situate our interest in the network in the context of life's network of relationships, and we will expect to find structures and programmes which develop and train young people for such relationships. Therefore we will hope that students can tell us

about the support of tutors and year heads, and about a creative and systematic developmental personal and social education programme.

Does each student know that being different is all right, and even encouraged in this school?
At this stage, reader, we will know our school fairly well, and so can engage more closely with the students, especially with the most vulnerable ones. We are now focused on creativity and difference, and we need to know if this school encourages these gifts. We will be very aware that there are students whom other institutions might label 'disabled', and we will be asking how these students are included in all aspects of school life as 'differently abled'. We will expect to find an integrated body of students, all with different abilities, gifts and limitations, in a learning community which serves all well.

Are students challenged?
The school we visit might well believe that our visit does not take account of the need for firm boundaries and behaviour codes (including sanctions). Life is not easy or soft, so we will not fail to engage with students and staff about the 'shadow' side of school life – those who do not respond, those who are selfish and demanding, those who upset others, those who just do not want to learn at this time. . . . How does this school deal with those 'shadow' experiences? Has the school learned that young people learn from their mistakes and their failures, and that it has a responsibility to challenge students consistently and fairly so that they take ownership for these outcomes? A pastoral care school is a place where justice is experienced. Can the students reflect this to us, and propose how the school might continue to allow light into the shadow? Are there life lessons in this reflection?

Through these seven questions, posed to the students and staff of a school, we have revisited the pastoral care school through the experience of its most vulnerable members, those students who are at the heart of the school community. My argument is that if these students are accommodated, supported and engaged in learning and in meaningful relationships then school staff and management can be confident that all students are engaged effectively in learning.

Systemic overview

I will now take a 'helicopter' or outsider's perspective, and offer a systemic overview of the pastoral care school (see Figure 3.2).
    This implies that:

• There is a whole-school approach: school is perceived as a whole rather than a sum of parts.

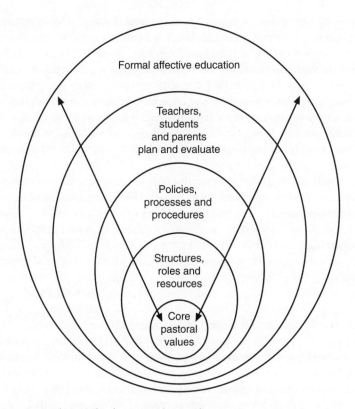

Figure 3.2 Pastoral care school: a systemic overview

- All members have agreed to the core values of the school, and there is a common ownership of and responsibility for these values.
- Roles in the school system are clear, and are related to the agreed values – student, prefect, teacher, tutor, year head, pastoral care coordinator, guidance counsellor, special learning staff, school chaplain, principal and vice-principal.
- Structures support students and teachers, and facilitate communication through regular meetings, regular evaluation, and ongoing planning.
- Policies, practices and procedures reflect the school's values. The school reflects clearly in its written (and agreed) policy what all members of the school value. A common example of this practice will be found in the school's Behaviour (Discipline) Code. A systemic approach sees the school's values in its policy, in its practice, and in its procedures for dealing with students.

A healthy system (in this case, school) is open to its environment, and is therefore open to on-going renewal, and to engaging all who ought to be involved in that process. A significant development for Irish secondary schools in recent years is a systemic approach to whole-school planning. I came to be involved in the development of a process for such planning because I experienced that schools which had shown enthusiasm for small pieces of development, such as pastoral roles (tutors, year heads) and Personal–Social Education programmes, did not, in many cases, sustain the enthusiasm and the innovations. Revisiting these schools and being invited to 'jump start' the original initiative, I found that what was missing was a systemic/whole-school approach partnered by systematic 'small-piece' development. It is both possible and desirable to engage all the school members and keep all the pieces moving in such an approach to planning.

> The challenge is in the fact that healthy organisations (in this instance schools) plan by collaborative processes. They aim to achieve clarity and ownership of vision and of values. They develop goals and objectives, and they implement and build in the criteria and processes for evaluating. Thus they are developing a growing, learning culture within which continual improvement is the norm, and shared responsibility is the practice.
>
> (Collins 1996: 3)

Formal affective education is part of the national core curriculum. Affective Education or Personal Social Health Education (PSHE) has been the most tangible and 'need'-identified aspect of pastoral care in schools. In many schools PSHE provision is called pastoral care. Some excellent work has been done by the national Department of Education psychological service, by regional health boards and by IAPCE in the provision of training for teachers and of actual programmes for classes. The school experience of Affective Education/PSHE, however, can be quite fragmented. Many schools have a pastoral care coordinator responsible, with a team of teachers, for the organisation and provision of the programme within a pastoral care system. Many schools have no formal provision, and are confident that PSE requirements are met within religious education or another curriculum area. In revisiting the pastoral care school from the systemic helicopter I would expect to see Affective Education/PSHE timetabled for all classes, but, more importantly, recognised as central to values, ethos, culture and experiences of a school as a learning community.

Systems thinking, I believe, generates healthy questions, and in this instance I would be hoping that a constant question in the collective staff mind would be 'What is this student learning about himself/herself in this experience?' There will be positive outcomes in a systemic approach, including:

- All members are agreed on the core values around which behaviours are shaped. Members think 'whole' rather than 'part'.
- Members of the system are more likely to ask questions about events, pleasant or unpleasant, rather than make judgements.
- The weakest link in the system is more likely to be addressed. 'One way

of changing a system is to look for the weakest link' (O'Connor and McDermott 1997: 225).

- Pastoral roles are clear, and professional relationships and responsibilities are clearly identified in relation to roles.
- Communication is valued and structures are put in place to support it.

'Systems thinking is a basis for clear thought and communication, a way of seeing more and further . . . it is an essential tool in helping you to manage yourself and others more effectively' (O'Connor and McDermott 1997: xv).

Theoretical foundations

To conclude this visit to the pastoral school, I will situate my thinking in some key theorists in the field of pastoral care.

Michael Marland saw the school as civilisation's choice for the adolescent's 'crisis of identity'. He goes on to say that educating the adolescent through this phase 'is the core of the Pastoral Need' (Marland, 1974: 2). Marland claims:

> in secondary schools to-day we are all, in our piecemeal, amateur, and contradictory ways, creating a new kind of school experience. It will be an experience that is based on the realisation that secondary schooling for all means that a secondary school is not merely a preparation for life, but actually part of life.
>
> (ibid.: 220)

Douglas Hamblin, writing at about the same time, focused on the classroom:

> if it [pastoral care] is to be an effective agent of socialization, in the fullest sense of the term, then the pastoral team must invest considerable effort in the task of understanding and harnessing the subterranean life of the classroom, and of the informal groupings amongst pupils which are as significant as those formally imposed upon them.
>
> (Hamblin 1978: 146)

One of the significant contributions of Douglas Hamblin to the development of pastoral care in schools was this recognition of the importance of the life of the ordinary classroom experience, and of the need for teacher and tutor training and support.

Keith Blackburn in the introduction to his much used work *The Tutor* (1975) situates the concept of pastoral care in the context of societal change: 'This development in schools is taking place in the context of a rapidly changing world . . . the development of Pastoral Care in schools is taking place concurrently with changes in society which are increasing the need for it.'

Within these earlier writers on pastoral care one can see three key elements emerging:

- adolescent needs
- a changing society
- the role of the school.

Wall (1977) concentrated on the psychological goals and tasks of adolescents, and saw a challenge for the school 'to be aware of the task' and 'to seize the chances offered'. The adolescent tasks, according to Wall, are:

physical: coming to terms with dramatic bodily changes
sexual: coming to terms with sexuality
vocational: finding an occupation
social: discovering clear and differentiated roles in adult society
philosophical: developing a set of ideals, principles, and interpretations of life.

Wall's work on adolescence is deeply challenging for the school. A systemic approach, developing the core values of the system (school), would be informed about these adolescent tasks and concerned to provide an education which supports them. An integrated and systematic programme in Personal Social and Health Education, well resourced, would be required.

Another strong challenge for school is found in the work of John Bazalgette and Bruce Reed of the Grubb Institute. In their paper 'Becoming Adult', they write:

> A psychological characteristic of adult sociological institutions is that people relate to each other as persons in their own right so that, though new members may be young, they are treated the same way as others . . . see themselves as recognised . . . can contribute . . . [and] begin to take authority as adults.
>
> (Bazalgette and Reed 1971)

John Bazalgette (ibid.) argues against encapsulation: 'The teacher tends to become encapsulated in the classroom and the classroom in the school. The process for the young adult is of moving outwards, cutting through encapsulation.'

Reid *et al.* (1987) looked at how research seemed to suggest that effective pastoral care is related to some or all of the characteristics of the effective school. These include:

1   the disciplinary orientation in the school
2   the degree of pupil participation

3   teachers' expectations of pupils
4   size of school and size of classes
5   form of institutional control
6   the psychological environment of the classroom
7   the academic environment of the school
8   the professional outlook of staff.

(Reid *et al.* 1987: 77)

Essentially Reid *et al.* are concerned about the influence of those relational factors which one does not quantify, but which are at the heart of the matter of pastoral care in schools.

> Schools are different. Some are lively, some are happy. By contrast, others are dour and somewhat forbidding. . . . Schools have their own tone, their own vibrations and soul that set them apart and make them unique. This tone or culture or ethos or climate as it has been variously called, is a result of the way in which individuals in the school interact, how they behave towards each other and their expectations of one another.

(ibid: 3)

I find it interesting that John McGuiness gives the title 'No opting out!' to his final chapter in *A Whole School Approach to Pastoral Care*, and his final sentence reads 'no one in education can opt out' (McGuiness 1989: 173).

In this section of revisiting the pastoral care school I would draw attention to a recent publication, *Education, Spirituality and the Whole Child*, edited by Ron Best (1996), which engages us in a reflection, a conversation, hopefully a debate, on the spiritual dimension of the school. Engaged in my own reflection on this subject I look forward to an ongoing debate, and I conclude this 'visit' with an extract from the publication:

> The School's contribution to spiritual development is not the preserve of Religious Education, and does not happen only in assembly. It can/should be happening in every subject/classroom/school activity and relationship. It is not knowing something different, it is a different way of knowing; it is not doing something different, it is a different way of doing; it is not being something different, it is a different way of being.

(Rodger 1996: 60)

Our revisiting does argue for a new way in concept and in practice. First, we focused on the strength of the school, the learning community, in relation to its most vulnerable members. Second, we looked at the whole school in its valuing, owning and practice of pastoral care. Last we rooted the practices of the school in some theories of pastoral care.

Of its nature pastoral care defies rigid definition. We use words to try to explain concepts such as human, adolescent, learning, relationships, community, becoming, spiritual, but each explanation is incomplete and unsatisfying.

Let us continue to visit the experience, engage in conversation, and, especially, listen to the most vulnerable members, and we shall continue to re-define and to wonder.

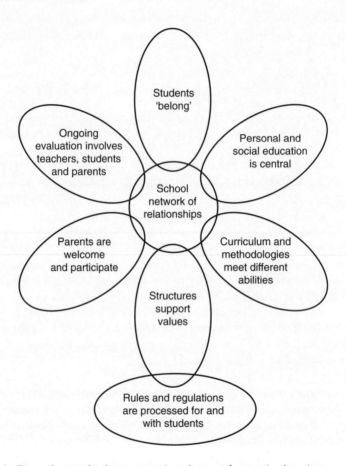

Figure 3.3 Pastoral care school: a community where students enjoy learning

4

ACTION RESEARCH, A
METHODOLOGY OF CARE

Jean McNiff

Some things defy definition. As soon as we try to define them, they are somewhere else. Sometimes the attempt to define itself distorts the thing we are
trying to define.

So it is in acts of love, and despair, in acts of compassion and acts of care.
The acts speak for themselves. They are the meaning we give to our lives as we
live them. The acts elude definition, the capturing in linguistic form of the
actions we do in relation to each other. The iridescent butterfly in flight is
pinned to the board and becomes a crusted mockery of itself; the letter is a
fragile bridge flinging itself across the chasm of absence, staying connected.

There should be more poetry in science, says Chris Langton (in Horgan
1996: 201). There should be more poetry in teaching and educational research,
say I, and tactfulness (Van Manen 1991), and care (Noddings 1992). There
should be more feeling, and multiple kinds of language to voice that feeling,
expressive forms to show the reality of lived experience at all levels of the self.
Yet, as soon as we try to pin the words to paper, communicate the complex
transformative experience of living in the linear format of well-formed grammatical utterances, we are at risk of losing the awesome wonder of life as
experience, and aim to transfix it as a phenomenon to be described and
explained away. We cling to philosophy as analysis, not as a means to understand existence; we speak about, rather than do as we say.

This, for me, is one of the major dilemmas in writing about subjective
experience – finding a way to communicate non-linguistic and non-sequential
experience through the use of words that of grammatical necessity follow a
linear, well-formed sequence. The dilemma is acute in the field of educational
research, for research is held to be scientific, and dominant views say that one
particular form of science is legitimate, and its methods must follow strict
rules. I do not hold such views: this kind of thinking is outdated, as is the concept of science it celebrates, as the literature of the new science tells us. The
methods of science in the natural and physical sciences have moved on, as have
their forms of enquiry and their modes of expression. It is time for the social
sciences to catch up, and for educational research, both as an art and a science,
to point the way in which existence might be understood and expressed at the

level of lived experience – a form of living theory (Whitehead 1993) that shows the reality of flesh and blood people in relation with each other and the earth that supports them.

Science and accountability

There are probably multiple methodologies of care, and there is a growing movement in the research community to identify and articulate them (eg., Beck 1994; Bowden 1997; Christiansen *et al*. 1997). Here I want to investigate how action research might be one of them – possibly a major candidate – and why.

A methodology is more than a method. Put in a simplistic way, method might be seen as the steps involved, whereas methodology would include the values and attitudes that the researcher brings to their work.

One of the purposes of doing research is to generate new theory, which then needs to be tested against existing theory to check the strength of its authenticity in making claims to knowledge and understanding. If a practitioner claims that they have done such and such, they need to show how and why that claim can be taken seriously, by producing validated evidence in support of what they are saying. This is responsible practice. If the practitioner cannot produce such evidence, the research community could rightly require this to be done before they took the claim seriously.

Theory helps us to produce descriptions of our practices – what we are doing and how we are doing it – and explanations – why we have undertaken research and what we hope to achieve. These constitute the methodologies and epistemologies of our research, our ways of doing, and our ways of knowing. We state our reasons, purposes and intentions for our research; we give an account of ourselves. This is not the case for all kinds of research, nor for all researchers. Empirical research, which has traditionally been seen as the 'correct' way, has stopped at the level of description; and many researchers working in this tradition do not see any need to offer real-world accounts of how the research influenced their own situation or that of the participants in the research. Such a view has significant implications when it is applied to educational research. I am not saying that this approach has not use value; but I think the extent of its use value is in serious question.

The rise of empirical research, and 'the scientific method', associated with Newton and his contemporaries, taught us that events in the world were linear, contingent on each other, and discrete. We live in a clockwork universe. Descartes taught us that it was possible to discover absolute truths. While no reasonable person would want to diminish the legacy of the scientific achievements of this time, I think Magee (1997: 464) is right when he complains that this was the beginning of a fool's errand in search of certainty from which the scientific community has ever since suffered. For three hundred years or so we have believed that reality is constituted of a series of separate events which happen sequentially; that events stand in a causal relationship with each other (event B happened because of event A); that reality has an existence of its own, independent of the observers who are describing it; that once researchers produce descriptions of phenomena which are approved by peers on the specific criteria of replicability and generalisability, these descriptions become the Truth. It is assumed that there is an external body of knowledge, that this knowledge is true for all time, and that it exists independent of knowers. In this tradition, research has been viewed as a value-neutral activity, its objective being to contribute to the generation of new knowledge. Professor Sir Ernest Chain (1970), for example, writes:

> Science, as long as it limits itself to descriptive study of Nature, has no moral or ethical quality, and this applies to the physical as well as the biological sciences. No quality of good or evil is attached to results of research. . . . No quality of good or evil can be ascribed to studies aimed at the elucidation [of such questions].
>
> (in Midgley 1989: 74)

This is a sad depiction of science, saying that it has no further use value than to offer descriptions of natural phenomena and to accumulate knowledge of facts, and with no moral or ethical intent. It is also a sad view of scientists, who in this case are encouraged to stay outside the field that they are investigating and not to contaminate outcomes by their personal engagement. Fortunately, there are scientists who disagree with the establishment, and insist that the purpose of science is to help us understand the nature of the world we live in, and how we are to live together (e.g., Bohm 1980; Appleyard 1992; Prigogine and Stengers 1984). These scientists also say that science should not limit itself to the descriptive study of Nature, but move beyond, offering explanatory accounts of what it means to be human. Exciting and problematic issues arise here: How do people interpret 'humanity'? What kind of evidence can they produce to show this humanity in action? What standards are to be used in judging the quality of that humanity?

In the latter half of the twentieth century, a new paradigm has been emerging steadily that not only challenges the old-mind view of science, but has focused on finding new ways of doing research, and imagining new ways by which its findings might be validated. These new ways celebrate the idea of science as a quest for knowledge that will help us understand our own existence more fully (Popper 1985). This understanding, it is hoped, will enable us to address seldom-asked major philosophical questions such as 'How are we as people?' and 'How do we live better together?' (Magee 1997). This approach has been based on new models of science that began with the work of people such as Einstein and Bohr, in the 'upper echelons' of science, and has now spilled over into all areas of human enquiry, in fields such as economic theory (Fukuyama 1995; Henderson 1978), theological enquiry (Capra *et al.*

1992; O'Murchu 1997a, 1997b) and management theory (Senge 1990; Wheatley 1992). What is particularly important is that these fields are no longer held to be separate fields of enquiry, but are linked by the deep-level strands of commonly held commitments. These commitments are towards exploring how healthy and life-giving relationships might be nurtured for all people, and how these relationships might contribute towards people's current and future well-being. Importantly, the aim of investigating the nature of relationships is conducted in a relational way; the object of study itself becomes part of the research methodology. Responsibility and concern are anticipated features, and these are investigated within an ethic of responsibility and concern.

Until quite recently, and ironically, the methods of much social scientific and educational theory have lagged behind those in the natural and physical sciences. Educational research has traditionally been located within social scientific research, and its main commitments, methodologies and epistemologies have been those associated with empirical research. In other words, the main aim of research is to find out facts about the world; the way to do this is to conduct experiments; such knowledge is validated using the criteria of replicability and generalisability. People, in this view, are variables, and what they do can be predicted and controlled. When this view is applied in real-life education settings, the outcomes are, not surprisingly, adequate as descriptions – activity lists – but quite inadequate as explanations for human interactions. This approach to research can show what is going on, but can only guess as to why that activity is going on, let alone suggest how it might be improved. This is a sorry state for researchers who hold commitments towards the betterment of the contexts and quality of human life; and, since betterment is the major aim of education, it is not surprising that the major thrust for reform has come mainly from the educational research community, by placing the search for reliable information within a broader humanitarian, politicised view of human endeavour.

In my opinion, this shift needs to be extended. Educational researchers need to make a conscious leap away from the traditional methods of science, and embrace new forms of research (Eisner 1993) that enable us to address issues of what it means to be human and how we should live together (a humanitarian conceptualisation of curriculum); and we need to develop new metaphors and analogies to help us describe and explain our practices as educators. Nor is it enough to claim science as the ultimate rationalisation for educational practices; for science might help us to understand the world, but it is our responses as people to those facts that help us to give them meaning in our lives. Science gives us facts; faith gives us meaning. Faith may or may not be theistic; faith constitutes a commitment to something; and faith, commitment and the will to care are beyond the purview of science, sometimes beyond cognition, and, often, beyond words.

Science and spirituality

One of the inevitable spin-offs from the reductionist and behaviouristic view of traditional science is that people have come to expect research to generate specific outcomes, in a cause and effect way, and these outcomes are seen as objects and structures. Such outcomes and structures are bounded, wrapped up as certain answers or packets of truth. So, for example, when we want to understand the nature of violence, we look at statistics or sociograms to give us facts and verification of the facts; when we want to understand spirituality, we first define it (NCC 1993) and find that it is some thing different from, say, personal and social education or personal development. It is tempting to settle for glib answers and structured outcomes; and these would reinforce the ways of thinking that led to such answers in the first place. We are in danger of expending time and energy in finding the right way to talk about problems, rather than tackling them in a thoughtful and creative way; of directing our commitments to thinking about and describing problems at the level of conceptual analysis (which does not involve putting ourselves out personally), rather than feeling about and tackling problems at the level of lived joy and misery (which does).

New approaches to research encourage us to shift our gaze from anticipated outcomes (very often they do not come out as we expect, nor do we know what to do about them when we have them), and to focus instead on what happens in between. The new science descriptions that we have of space are that it is not a vast emptiness in which planets and stars exist in splendid and remote isolation from each other. Space is filled with teeming activity, full to the brim with potential matter that is in vibrant and continual interaction, new forms constantly coming into being and transforming themselves into and within an infinite seamless unity. The same is true of human interaction. People do not exist separate from each other. We are all in some way in relation to each other. I am alone as I write, using a pen that someone else produced, on a table, in a house, that other people made. Yet I am inextricably bound to those others in the activities that we share and our influence on each other, albeit at a distance in time and space: they made the pen and constructed the house that I use, and I write the words that I hope others will use. We are all part of the field of action and influence in which we live; and, as responsible people, we need to ensure that the quality of our relation with each other is the best it can be, otherwise we limit not only the other in our potential for responsiveness, but also ourselves.

As researchers, we need to break away from the mental security of faith in bounded objects and outcomes, and make a commitment to faith in unbounded processes and relationships. We need to move from an objectivist view of knowledge and experience as separate realities, to an epistemic view, where we see knowledge and experience as interrelated and interdependent, each contributing to and transforming the other within a unified reality. In our research we need to see ourselves as practitioner–researchers, in relation to others, and they to us; we need to see what we are doing not so much in terms of what we are aiming for but in terms of how we are with each other. If we can get the relationships right, the aims and outcomes will look after themselves. Futures research teaches us that if we can concentrate on getting today right, we are already contributing towards a good tomorrow; for tomorrow never comes, but today is here and is all that we have. So we need to commit ourselves, as responsible human beings, to finding ways to understand ourselves and others better, and learn how to live together for a sustainable good society.

There is a substantial and growing literature on spirituality. Throughout, there is a deep connecting strand saying that spirituality is about relation. Two books especially have helped me to understand what this means (and these books have not only been part of my experience, but have also constituted moments of grace, appearing at times when I most needed them). One is *Belonging to the Universe* by Capra *et al*. (1992). The authors share their ideas that belonging is a reciprocal act undertaken in faith and trust; living forms belong to each other, to the earth, and ultimately to the universe. Humans are made of the same stuff as stars; the earth may be seen as a living organism, constantly in transformation. This view is rooted not in metaphysical lyricising, but in hard-nosed scientific investigation. The other book that has helped me to understand the nature of my relationships with myself and others, and also my work with them, is Bradley J. Macdonald's (1995) collection of the essays of his father, James B. Macdonald, entitled *Theory as a Prayerful Act*. James Macdonald wrote of response as a key element in dialogue and interaction. (I am reminded of the words of Jean Clandinin as they appear in the conversation in the final chapter of this book.) Macdonald spoke of

> [t]he act of theorizing [as] an act of faith, a religious act. It is the expression of belief, and as William James clearly expounds in *The Will To Believe*, belief necessitates an act of the moral will based on faith. *Curriculum theorizing is a prayerful act.* It is an expression of the humanistic vision in life.
>
> (Macdonald 1995: 181, emphasis in original)

He spoke of the need for educators to *profess:* 'to reveal and justify from our own viewpoints what we believe and value' (ibid.: 159), and this, for Macdonald, constitutes an act of faith, of prayer (some might say of meditation or reflection), and concentration on the serious responsibility of giving an account of our lives as good, responsible lives.

Here is a link with our newest kinds of theory in education: the idea of a living educational theory. Jack Whitehead of the University of Bath, UK, is its acknowledged major theorist. The kind of theory, says Whitehead (1989; 1993), that qualifies for the term educational (in that the process of theory-making itself demonstrates the growth of educational understanding by the researcher) has its roots in a view of human development that, as Macdonald notes, focuses on 'human potentials that center upon the developmental aspects of personal responsiveness' (Macdonald 1995: 17). While learning may be seen as an individual activity (being that which goes on in the individual mind–brain), it needs always to be situated within a socio-historical context. No learner, no human being, can be separate from their own situatedness, both in space and time; nor for that matter can they ever transcend their own perceptions of that situatedness, as Kant and Schopenhauer emphasise. Not one of us can see 'reality' as it is, if it exists at all; everything we perceive is mediated by our perception. The most we can ever hope to know is that process of perception, and to know that we know that. This constitutes a major task for educators, for the contexts of our situatedness arise from interpersonal activity, people in relation with each other. Whatever reality we know arises from the quality of the relationships we have with each other, and from our perceptions of those relationships. It is the quality of those interactions and relationships that influences the nature of the responses to each other of the participants in the dialogue. Educative relationships are those in which the responses are life-giving for all, and enable each person to develop those potentialities of humanity, in a way that is reciprocal and danger-free to all participants. Such relationships have to be worked at. They require intention, purposeful morally committed action; and they constitute a praxis of thoughtful response in relation.

This is why I call action research a methodology of care. It is not the only such methodology: others include listening, counselling, supporting – the caring practices, which call for a commitment by practitioners to care and be held accountable. Action research, however, seems to be a major candidate (if not the only one) among research methodologies that holds this commitment as a necessary condition.

Action research as a caring practice

There is a vigorously developing literature about action research – its characteristics, use value in social situations, and different approaches. To some extent Úna Collins and I have discussed the characteristics of action research in Chapter 1. Here, I would like to point to some major elements in action research, and show how it meets the challenge of the commitment to care.

Action research above all is a methodology that requires practitioners to accept the responsibility of offering a public account of their own educational journey, of how they grew in understanding. This is, however, not a solitary journey, since no meaningful research in the human sciences can be conducted by one person separate from others. Action researchers acknowledge that they are undertaking their research with the aim of improving the quality of life for themselves and others, and that their research will inevitably involve others in a variety of ways: as participants in the research, as validators of its findings, as new researchers who will carry the research forward, and so on.

This aspect is neglected in the old-mind paradigms I discussed above, where researchers adopt a neutral stand to doing research. Neutrality is not a feature of action research. Action researchers make a personal decision not to leave an unsatisfactory situation as it is, but to work towards improvement.

The focus of action research is the self, the living 'I', to use Whitehead's terms (Whitehead 1989; 1993). It deals with real-world work undertaken by real people in real situations, such as you and I and the practitioners whose stories are told in this book. The aim of the research is to improve the social situation of others. This raises some key issues about the ethics involved in the methodology of action research, and about the personal responsibility of the practitioner–researcher, and how far this responsibility extends.

No one person can accept the responsibility for the thoughts and actions of another. To try to do so is as pointless, says Chomsky (1995), as trying to accept the responsibility for something that happened in the eighteenth century. A researcher cannot claim that they have 'brought about' change within human interactions, since such a claim cannot be justified. There are too many considerations, not least the fact that we can never know another person's consciousness, and will never know exactly why they acted as they did. Consider the 'what if that had happened' game that we all play from time to time: it takes us into a permanent regress of possibility, and we end up with thought experiments that cancel out our own existence. It is impossible to say what led to what in human interaction. All we can do is recognise that we are in relation to our situation, including other people (and these may also be distant in space and time); and recognise that what we do will affect them, as their actions will affect us, just as the beat of the butterfly's wing may have unforeseen effects in other spaces and times (Lorenz, in Casti 1994). All we can do is accept that, by nature of our very humanness, we are in relation to each other and the rest of creation; and because we are in relationships of influence, we have to accept the responsibility of constantly changing ourselves for the better, and try to make our influence count for good in the wider scheme of things.

By the same token, as responsible researchers, we need to produce accounts to show our commitment – as Macdonald says, to profess what we believe in and value. We need to show the nature of the change we have begun in ourselves, and how we hope that might impact beneficially on others. Public accounts are vital to show the real-life action of what people do when they say they care. The more real-life accounts that appear in the public domain, the stronger the case for encouraging this kind of practice, and the stronger the case for such accounts to be legitimated by academic bodies. The business of producing accounts of our own self-studies applies to all – managers, practitioners, students.

This is a far cry from the idea of 'bringing about change', a phrase that implies sequential cause and effect, separate bodies existing in a fragmented reality. As researchers we make a commitment to investigate our practice, not with a view to impacting at first hand on others, but on our selves. This is a personal undertaking, a desire to transform oneself into the best of available potentials, for those potentials are, in Macdonald's words, potentials of response. We take care in our own way of being, knowing that we must embrace our connectedness with each other and the rest of creation, knowing that it is our responsibility as educators to respond with thoughtfulness and compassion. While action research might begin with the commitment of the individual 'I', this is an 'I' who recognises her or himself in relation to others; *and this is a reciprocal commitment enacted collectively.* It is not a case of one individual over against the rest; it is a case of all individuals acting in the best interest of each other.

This is, of course, the message at the heart of many religions and beliefs. For it to work at its most effective, all members of a community should share the same kind of commitment (though this would probably manifest at diverse levels). In real life this is frequently not the case; yet it is sometimes so. Nor should the fact that it is not always the case deter us from trying. The trying is as much part of the endeavour as the outcome; for commitment given when future success is uncertain works towards a more sustainable vision of relationship than commitment given when the future is assured.

It begins with individual persons, you and I, recognising that we are in relation with each other – I with you, and you with me – and we care enough to take the trouble to do something about our own personal practice for the benefit of each other. Such recognition of personal accountability is an act of devotion, a prayerful act of care.

5

TRANSITION YEAR STUDENTS AND PERSONAL DEVELOPMENT

Joe Lynch

Reflection

It has become clear to me that the quality of educational experience that I provide for my students depends on my competence as a teacher. This means that, at all times, I must be looking at my professional practice, evaluating, imagining alternatives, re-evaluating, as a continual action–reflection cycle.

During the school year, 1994/95, I was involved in an action research project, as part of my Higher Diploma studies, which gave me a new way of looking at what I do. Doing action research has shown me that if there is a change in me, there will be a change in the situation I am in. The individual and the context influence each other. This has helped me to understand more clearly how I might realise my values in education:

> it is largely up to teachers to give the initiative within their academic community by strengthening the explanatory power of their accounts of professional practice.
>
> (Whitehead, in McNiff 1988: x)

I am willing to offer a description and an explanation for my practice by inviting any person to talk about my work or see me in action. My critical friend who visited my class during the course of the project has stated her belief, in her written validation, that there was a positive progression both in my approach to the classwork and in the students' feelings of being more 'at home' in my class.

Do I feel I am making a positive difference in the lives of others?

I wonder can anyone make a sure claim to making a difference for good in other people's lives? I do believe, in my own way, that I made some contribution to helping many of the students at least feel more accepted and valued in Personal Development class during the course of our work together. The written statements from students clearly showed an increased level of ease with fellow students in their class. They contained expressions of confidence: 'more open and less intimidated by others'; 'it is now much easier to give my opinion'; 'I feel more comfortable now than I did at the beginning of the year'; 'during the class, I am now relaxed'. Some students expressed, in my opinion, a sense of personal growth. This, I believe, was also evident in their comments: 'I am now more confident and sure of myself'; 'asking questions was good for me'.

As teacher researchers we have to recognise the problematics of drawing a direct relationship between our own actions and the learning of others. We can say we influence, but we cannot claim to cause; and we always have to recognise that others influence us as much as we believe we influence them. I am clear, however, about the influence on me of intervening critically in my own practice. Doing the project made me acutely aware of the way I behaved towards students. I became increasingly aware of how my words and actions could have an effect on individuals and on the class as a whole. I learned to take care, recognising that my words and actions could influence the lives of others, often in subtle ways below my level of awareness.

As a teacher I should really care for my students. This is what pastoral care means to me. The pastoral dimension of a school needs a structure, personnel and time allocation. However, if the people involved do not care for the students they deal with, there is no real relationship present.

Doing my action research project has brought my values in education alive. It has also alerted me to the fact that every contact with a student, or indeed my colleagues, has a pastoral dimension. Of course I make mistakes on a daily basis. However, I am now aware that I am no longer walking blindly. I am now acutely aware of the potential impact that I can have, both negative and positive, on the lives of those I teach. This has made me different.

Action research is a method that will bring relatively immediate insight into a problem along with creative ideas of how to deal with it. It means that those using it must look at themselves in relation with those they teach, the situation they are in, and how it might be improved. I believe that we can often get into a rut as teachers unless we are open to change. Society, in schools and in the wider domain, changes quickly. We ignore this at our peril. There is no single answer to new problems that arise. They will be different for different schools and different groups of students within the same building.

Action research as an approach to in-career development has the advantage of sowing the seeds of 'being open to change' in teachers. This was certainly my experience. In traditional forms of in-career development, teachers are presented with information that they are supposed to bring back to their own classrooms and use to bring about improvements in their situations. This approach does not encourage teachers to consider how we might effect change ourselves, and how we might use our own experience and talents. The methodology of action research ensures that teachers decide what kind of changes are appropriate to their own real-life situations, and how that process of change might be managed. It awakens in us the power to change ourselves and our situations, and it puts the responsibility for success on us. It gives courage to its users.

I believe that I am now more open to change. I see change as something desirable and challenging. New ideas come to mind more easily, and I see possibilities everywhere.

I can now more fully accept that I am responsible for myself.

Background to the project

Currently, and as indicated in the appendix to circular M31/93 from the Department of Education, it is now official Department policy since the beginning of the academic year 1994/95, to introduce a three-year senior cycle in post-primary schools in the Irish Republic. The Transition Year is recognised as a first-year option for this three-year senior cycle programme. According to Department of Education Guidelines the Transition Year should:

> offer students a broad educational experience with a view to attainment of increased maturity before proceeding to further study and/or vocational preparation. It provides a bridge to help pupils make the transition from a highly structured environment to one where they will take greater responsibility for their learning and decision making.
>
> (Department of Education 1993a: 3)

In January 1994, I was appointed Transition Year coordinator at St Joseph's Christian Brothers School with responsibility for developing a Transition Year programme together with a working group of eight teachers. This programme was to be implemented for the first time in September 1994. As well as having overall responsibility for coordinating this new programme, I had responsibility for devising a Personal Development syllabus to be taught to students for two double periods each week.

I have had various experiences of 'pastoral' roles in my eight years in St Joe's: year head, form tutor, students' council liaison officer and others. Very often I felt inadequate in my role to deal with problems that arose both with individual students and in my efforts to develop a relationship with my form classes. I therefore undertook some formal courses of study in order to equip myself with the skills necessary to improve my ability to develop the kind of classroom relationship which I believe is essential for fruitful communication with students. I used my newly acquired skills with some success.

Then along came Transition Year!

The Association of Secondary Teachers Ireland comments:

> In a sense the whole Transition Year Programme is aimed at the personal development of students. It is a year in which students are encouraged to acquire a better knowledge of themselves and the society in which they live. . . . Personal Development through Social and Health Education will, it is hoped, provide students with the social skills which are appropriate to their status as young adults.
>
> (ASTI 1993: 31)

Identifying the research issue

I identified the following research question:

'How can I improve my effectiveness as a teacher of Personal Development with a Transition Year group, with a view to assisting their growth in maturity and confidence?'

The philosophy of Transition Year greatly excited me. Phrases such as 'the whole development of the student' and 'taking greater responsibility' appealed to me. 'The general aim of the Transition Year is the preparation of young people for their roles as autonomous, participative and responsible members of society' (ASTI 1993: 2). It was sentiments such as these that first attracted me to the idea of providing a Transition Year programme in our school. I have always been aware that the education system through which our students pass did not always provide them with a truly valuable 'education for life'. I believe that the chains of failure continue to permeate the fabric of the society which is our schools.

In coming to my research question I had to clarify my educational values for myself. Ongoing reflection led me to the understanding that the core issue for me as an educator is that students will learn who they are through their relationships and interactions with others in their school context; and that includes their dealings with me, and how I respond to them. Therefore, the core value for me is the quality of the relationship between the student and myself. I needed to ask myself, 'Is my classroom environment one that is safe, free from fear, ridicule, failure and coercion?' 'A teacher may unwittingly or otherwise engage in or reinforce bullying behaviour in a number of ways: using sarcasm or other insulting or demeaning forms of language when addressing pupils' (Department of Education 1993b: 8). How could I ensure that such behaviour was not part of my repertoire, and that I made every effort to aim for a quality educational experience both for myself and for my students?

The Transition Year philosophy seemed to me to provide a way through. I perceived the whole philosophy of Transition Year to be pastoral in nature and it allowed me to design a programme suitable to the students whom I taught. It emphasised students as responsible people in terms of their own development and learning. This view called for new approaches and method-ologies by my colleagues and myself to explore how we could support the development of Transition Year in order to realise its potential as a valuable curriculum initiative. In short, I felt excited about 'what could be' and I com-mitted myself to making it work.

Planning the project

I spent a number of weeks planning my project. At the time I had just started my duties as Transition Year coordinator. The students and I were enthusiastic, but I was aware that there was something missing. The group of students were quite closed and reluctant (and often afraid) to say much about themselves. I wanted the Transition Year to make a positive difference in their lives, and if my values in education were to be realised I knew that both the group and I had a lot of growing to do. I wanted them to be more confident about themselves and their ability to express themselves. I also recognised that my practice would impact on theirs, and that I would need to monitor myself as much as them. My research project gradually crystallised in my mind as a period during which we could attempt to show that process of confidence building by monitoring what we were all doing, gathering the data to show our actions, reflecting on those actions, modifying our practices in line with our identified aims and showing what we hoped would be an improved situation.

I therefore drew up the following action plan for my project. I was aware of the need to limit the scope of the project within the logistical constraints of time and resources.

Action plan

October 1994 – Assess the situation

1 Taking stock of the students as I find them at the beginning of Transition Year, and of my own practice.
2 Collecting data to show the current situation.
3 Data collection methods:
   - questionnaire
   - class discussion
   - my own reflections – keeping a journal
   - making a video.

November 1994 – Validation

1 Analysis and interpretation of data.
2 Validation by my critical friend.
3 Alterations and amendments to my account of the data in light of my crit-ical friend's analysis.

December 1994 – January 1995

STEP 1 HOW CAN I IMPROVE THE SITUATION?

1   What steps should I take to try to improve the situation?
2   Continuing intensive reading.

February 1995 – Taking those steps

1   Carry out strategies that I believe could improve the situation.
2   Keep an account in my journal of what happens.

March 1995 – Evaluation of step 1 – How?

1   Collect second set of data.
2   Methods to be used:
    •   student questionnaire
    •   my own reflections
    •   class video.
3   Validation of data:
    •   my own reflections
    •   analysis by critical friend.
4   Amendments and additions:
    •   in the light of consultation with my critical friend.

April 1995 – New action reflection cycle

•   Where do I go from here?
•   How can I improve the current situation . . .?

May 1995 – Write up the project

Doing the project

The project adopted an action research methodology using key questions to provide a structure.

What are my concerns?

I met my Transition Year class during the first week of September for their first Personal Development class. I asked them to sit in a circle, rather than the traditional ranked seating arrangements that they were used to, and invited them to start speaking about issues that were important to them. Very quickly, I realised that this was not working. Speaking about themselves seemed quite alien to the majority of the students. I felt and saw that they were very uncomfortable about being asked to comment on 'how they felt' about issues. Their body language made this quite clear. I was aware, even then, that almost without exception they had not experienced such methods or classes in their previous experience in school.

Because I sensed the unease among the students, I also became uneasy. I felt that I had to support and help them by asking more questions, such as, 'Why do you feel uncomfortable?' In hindsight, I realise that such questions only made matters worse.

I had studied group facilitation skills the previous year. I thought that I knew it all! 'We will sit in a circle and have a heart-to-heart discussion and everyone will love it!' However, the situation did not evolve like this. Such progress with students did not 'just happen'. I needed to be aware that this kind of work had to be introduced gently, and that they could opt out if they wished.

At the time, one aspect of the class that annoyed me particularly was that some students *did* opt out. They just did not want to take part in the class discussion. I found this difficult and asked myself, 'What am I doing wrong? How can I get students over to my side?'

Such questions plagued me at the time. My reflection on my own practice helped me here. By monitoring what I was doing, and reflecting on my actions, I gradually became aware that I tended to focus on a particular student if I believed their comments were an indication that they were experiencing difficulties. I was aware that my nature is to be a 'helper–rescuer', which, according to the counselling skills that I have studied, should not occur. I should listen to the 'client' and forget my own agenda. My journal entry of 14 October reads: 'I need to respect other people's views. I don't have to agree with them. Just because I don't agree with them doesn't mean I should treat them differently.' I began to realise also that a class environment in the company of others may not be a suitable environment to 'probe' the student. These understandings emerged over time, however, and in the early stages of my research the situation was often quite problematic.

There were two or three students who were very influential among their peers. One student, 'John', had influence over his classmates and his comments could destroy any progress made within the group. My journal entry of 28 October records: 'I was annoyed today by John's comments – they got a good laugh from the class but it undermined the whole atmosphere. I wish I knew how to get him to go with rather than against me.' I decided to focus on this issue as symptomatic of what was going on within the wider group.

First set of data

I collected my first set of data over a period of weeks by issuing short questionnaires which I called assignments. This took the form that the students answered the questions in the assignment, I collated the results, and then designed the next assignment in response to the issues they had raised in the previous one. In this way I felt we could develop our understanding of the tasks in hand.

Assignment 1

I asked each student to give a personal statement about their experience of classes similar to Personal Development in their previous time in our school. I felt that this would allow me to see more clearly where the students were coming from.

Think back to what was your experience of Religion / Personal Development class while you were in third year. Write an account (at least one page) of what you felt like in such a class.

Did you feel it made a difference to you?

Did it help you to get to know your class better?

Did it help to develop a relationship among the students in your class?

Did it allow the development of trust and honesty in your class?

Please be honest. Mention no names!
Assignments to be given back next Wednesday.

Responses to Assignment 1

My initial reaction on reading the students' accounts of their previous experience was sadness. The written comments from the students said that classes similar to Personal Development in their past years in school were 'a doss class', a time when 'we could get our homework done'. When work was done they expressed a feeling of 'boredom' with the subject matter. Some other revealing comments included: 'At the end of three years, there were students that I knew nothing about'; 'Often my feelings were built up inside but I never got the opportunity to say them.' After reading the results of this assignment, I felt apprehensive about the prospect of bringing the students forward.

Assignment 2

Now that I had a sense of where the students were coming from, I felt that the next step was to gauge their initial reaction to their new Personal Development class. I did this by asking them to complete Assignment 2, which read as follows:

Using your own diaries, write an account of your experience of Personal Development.

What did you expect from Personal Development class?

Did you expect it to be the traditional Religion / Civics class that you were used to last year?

How did you feel at the end of your first Personal Development class? Please be honest!

How did you feel sitting amongst your friends? Was it comfortable or uncomfortable?

What were the things you liked / disliked?

Again, please be honest!

Responses to Assignment 2

In general, students expressed feelings of discomfort, fear and apprehension about their initial experience of Personal Development: 'I felt silly and strange'; 'At first I felt uncomfortable.' They felt vulnerable and insecure. One even wrote that he felt sick at the beginning of every class and was relieved when it was over. In particular, students found sitting in a circle off-putting and intimidating: 'I was uncomfortable because I didn't want to make a fool of myself'; 'I was disappointed and scared because I would have to say something.' There were also positive comments: 'Sitting in the circle gave me a relaxed feeling.' There was a variety of reactions to the warm-up exercises, from 'stupid' and 'surprised' to 'that was good' and 'I felt good'.

My own initial reaction was one of frustration. I realise that I have 'an urgent need to communicate' as typified by my personality type on the Enneagram (Riso 1988). My awareness grew from about this point that I needed to let go of 'my agenda', accept the students as they were and not have unrealistic expectations of them.

Assignment 3

We spent a number of classes discussing the students' views of their class experience. Students were honest and direct in what they had to say. I then asked them to complete Assignment 3, detailing their own personal difficulties with the format of the class. By now we were about five weeks into the academic year.

During the Personal Development class over the past four weeks, you the students have described the difficulties you have with such a class. Students have made comments like:

'What's the point of this class anyway?'
'It's very difficult to talk in front of a class.'
'You would get the sneers after the class.'

Please outline below the difficulties you find as a class member in Personal Development. Please be honest and do not be afraid that you will offend me with your comments!

Responses to Assignment 3

All students expressed the fear that they did not know anyone. Many students did not trust their classmates and were afraid of being talked about outside class. Almost every student expressed the fear of being 'sneered at' as a result of the comments that they made. Other comments included:

'The subjects we talk about are embarrassing.'
'I prefer to keep my feelings to myself.'
'I do not have much confidence.'
'I find it hard to talk about myself.'

My understanding grew about how comments such as these show that students might have difficulties in expressing themselves in ways that leave them vulnerable or with issues that require them to reflect on their own lives. My awareness deepened about how I must respect the privacy of the individual and allow them to have the freedom to decline to be involved. After all, I would expect this courtesy from adults. On the other hand, I believe it is necessary for all of us to have the ability to be insightful if we are to understand and therefore be in tune with our emotional lives, and this is what I wished for my students. How to resolve the dilemma?

Assignment 4

In this assignment I asked students to suggest solutions to the problems that they had with our class. Assignment 4 was worded as follows:

You have outlined the difficulties you have with Personal Development class. I believe that it is important as a group that we come up with some solutions to these problems in order to improve the class environment for each and every student in the class.

In view of the problems that you previously outlined, please suggest some solutions that you feel might improve the situation for you and your fellow students. Again, please be honest. Everyone's opinion will be looked at and evaluated by the class.

Responses to Assignment 4

Over half the students mentioned some form of 'contract' that would respect confidentiality, the views of others, everyone's right to have their say and not to answer questions. Some students mentioned the importance of warm-up exercises to make them feel relaxed, while others asked that I explain questions more clearly. There were suggestions that they could be paired with members of the group that they did not know so well; and others critiqued my own practice of questioning the views of students with which I apparently disagreed. This assignment certainly gave me a lot to think about, particularly in respect of my own approach to students.

The video

On Tuesday 30 October, I recorded a video of my Transition Year's Personal Development class. On analysis, this video identified a number of concerns for me, particularly in relation to my own practice.

I think I started out all right in that I introduced the concept of 'my talents' well and gave examples to ensure that students understood what I required from them. However, watching the video revealed that I jumped in too quickly and did not allow them sufficient time for reflection. I tended to direct rather than facilitate.

I think many people might be surprised when they listen to their own voices or see themselves in action. For me, 'surprised' was an understatement! I thought that my instructions were unclear at times, and I got tongue-tied on a number of occasions. In fact, I said to the group a couple of times, 'You may not understand.'

As I observed the video, I became aware that the focus of the lesson was not always easy to see. I felt that I was grasping at straws: when a response was not forthcoming I latched on to any comment made by a student. The questions that I asked were all similar. I said, 'You are all very quiet' on several occasions. This probably made things more difficult for them. I feel that I flew around a lot but never actually landed. The same pattern occurred when any student volunteered a comment. I reflected back what he said, asked him to expand on it, and brought my ideas forward to elicit answers that I thought would be relevant.

I watched my students' reactions on the video. Their heads were down, with their faces covered. They sat forward in a posture that suggested that they were protecting themselves. Two or three were biting their nails. Comments by and large were monosyllabic. The silence was deadly on occasions, and as the video progressed it was quite clear that many students were becoming increasingly restless and were withdrawing mentally.

I could go on. I realised that I needed to develop strategies to bring life into the group process and the students. I needed to bring a variety of activities into the class, and help the students to feel that the class was theirs rather than the teacher's. I needed to develop ownership strategies.

My assessment criteria

I now had a realistic overview of what the current situation was like, and some ideas about how to improve it, mainly by changing what I was doing. In order then, methodologically, for me to have some idea of how I might check whether I and the students were making progress, I had to isolate a number of criteria by which I would be able to gauge improvement. I therefore decided to narrow the focus to the following four assessment criteria:

Student behaviour

1   Do the students feel more at ease in class?
2   Can I help the influential student, John, currently having a negative influence over the others, to feel less threatened?

My own personal criteria

3   Can I become less of a helper–rescuer, and help the students to help themselves?
4   Are my classes more structured? Do they have a beginning, middle and end?

Validation 1

Gathering the data from the assignments helped me to make an assessment of what I needed to change. I also needed to have this data verified, so I invited my critical friend to observe a lesson, and also to review the video that I had made the previous week. My critical friend was Mary Adamson, the Guidance Counsellor in our school. She offered comprehensive comments. Her overview reads:

I sat in on Joe's class on Tuesday, November 14th, and assessed the video that he had made the previous week. He asked me to validate the situation as he saw it from the analysis of the data.

As I have stated already, student behaviour showed clear discomfort with the class format/topic. I agree with him that this is an area that requires improvement to allow for successful class cohesion and development.

It was also clear to me that, as Joe suggested, there was a student that appeared to be particularly hostile to the class and this was evident from his comments in the last video and from his reaction in the class period that I observed.

As regards Joe's personal criteria of assessment, I have also stated that I believe that a more planned approach on Joe's part is required. As he puts it himself, 'a beginning, a middle and an end'. There is need for variation of stimulus and some form of 'warm ups' to make the class feel more at home.

What can I do to try to improve the situation?

I reflected on the comments of the students and those of my critical friend. They were right. I felt that I needed to do some thinking in the areas of:

* the philosophy behind action research
* group processes
* a look at myself.

Action research

Doing my project was increasing my awareness that the focus was primarily on me. I began to realise that I am involved in change; it is not something that happens external to me. This is as true for my work as it is for my life in general. 'Action research approaches education as a unified exercise, seeing the teacher in class as the best judge of his total educational experience' (McNiff 1988: 1).

How I experience a relationship with a class will be different from the experience of another teacher. The methods I use and the way I deal with issues will be particular to me. I must be personally responsible for looking at problems in my own class, as they will always relate to my own practice. Action research is about improving the situation by changing its features, and these changes involve me. The situation is not external to me; I am part of it, and improvement means action by me as well as by others. We are in a relationship of influence with each other.

As I write this report in hindsight, I see that the most lasting benefit from action research for me is that I realise how my research is a continual process whereby I have become aware of my everyday practice in the classroom and indeed in my life in general. It has allowed me to embrace personal change which is essential for growth. I have learnt that organisations grow through the willingness of their individual members to grow.

Another added attraction of action research is the systemic approach to the process of personal and professional change. This framework provides a logical set of steps towards dealing with concerns that we may have in any aspect of our lives. 'Having identified an issue, the practitioner then systematically sets about proposing possible solutions and working them through to a possible answer' (McNiff and Collins 1994: 11).

In my original thesis I have written about how beneficial I found the process of engaging in action research. Here I would briefly summarise by saying that this approach is right for me, because it is educational for me. It is not only about educating my students, but also about educating myself into an awareness of my own personal and professional development, which, I hope, will then in turn lead to better learning situations for the students I teach. Since I first came to these ideas I can honestly say that I am now much more aware of my teaching. I may not always do the right thing, but I am aware when something goes wrong that this is not what I want to happen, and I immediately question how I might take action for improvement. This process gives me energy that constantly brings things alive. I feel I have control over my educational outcomes, and that things can be different. It is up to me, and that feels good. I would like to see this awareness grow within the Irish teaching profession, in that practitioners are authorised to influence their situation in their own time and within their own experience. 'Action researchers need to be insiders, researching practices integral to their work. The imperative to intervene distinguishes action research and the researcher's professional values should be central to the investigation' (Lomax 1994: 4).

A look at group processes

Until I began my research I had never questioned the traditional teacher-directed methodologies I was using. Interaction was mostly of the student–teacher form and rarely student–student. As soon as I began my research I became aware of the dynamics that occur when a group forms. My reading supported my learning about how trust in relationships takes time to develop, and that groups develop organically (Senge 1990).

I examined my role within the group. I became conscious of my own 'drive' to push an issue forward rather than allowing it to evolve in accordance with the comfort level of the student group. My research further confirmed that the model of active, participative learning which I wished to use is generally accepted to be the most effective when dealing with issues related to self-esteem and confidence building with students: 'The pupils through questionnaires and interviews stated that they felt better able to express them-selves and discuss issues . . . in general, pupils felt that they and their friends were more mature, happier and less moody' (Parsons *et al.* 1989: 13).

My resolve strengthened. I would revitalise my own practice by introducing new attitudes and methodologies.

What did I do to try to change the situation?

I thought long and hard about possible courses of action before deciding what to do.

First, at a practical level, I assigned 'posts of responsibility' to all members of the class. These posts included a student coordinator for each subject being taught, and the student had to liaise between me and the subject teachers. Coordinators also assumed responsibility for a school exchange with a Dutch school and also in the setting up of a mini-company. Every student had respon-sibility for some aspect of the year. This was part of my effort to ensure that they felt ownership of who they were, and for the practice of the group as a whole.

In relation to my identified criteria, I took the following actions.

To begin with, I made an effort to prepare classes more thoroughly. It took extra time the night before but it was worth it. I decided that the class should commence with an energiser, followed by an introduction from me about the topic for the class and a round-up at the end. What happened in between depended on the students. While I would facilitate the progress of the class I would not dictate it.

I became more relaxed in the class. This in itself seemed to make the stu-dents feel more at home. I also started to encourage the students to get more involved in the discussion by using interactive techniques such as, 'David, what do you think about what James just said?' The degree of student activ-ity visibly increased.

Overall, I found that the students became more reliable in themselves. They would now take on the responsibility for making phone calls, writing letters, and so on, rather than asking me to do it for them.

The 'reluctant student', John, remained difficult. The local bank wanted to start a school bank and I asked John to apply for a position. To his surprise, he was appointed manager. During the following couple of months, he did a huge amount of work with the school bank. In fact he seemed a different stu-dent in class. He began to speak quite openly and honestly in class and came to me on two occasions during the year with quite serious problems.

I began to listen more. At the beginning of the year I was obsessed with doing what I thought was best for the students. As time progressed, I became increasingly aware of my own agenda, my need to help people. It was a huge lesson for me to shut up and listen to what the students were saying, both directly and indirectly. When I really listened to them, that was when I really got to know them.

Was there a change for the better? More data gathering.

I used the same methods to collect my second set of data as were applied when collecting the first. I gave the students two assignments as follows:

Assignment 5

It is now the end of February and you have had Personal Development for six months. You will remember, in one of your first assignments, you gave an account of what your feelings were about the class, given that you had not experienced such classes before.

Now six months later, I would like you to give your opinions on what Personal Development is like for you now.

Do you feel more comfortable than at the beginning of the year?
Is there a greater class spirit present in our class?
Do you find it easier now to give your opinion?

Please be honest!

Responses to Assignment 5

The majority of the class stated that they were now 'more at ease' and 'felt more comfortable'. Many students said that it was now 'much easier to give my opinion' and 'I am now more open and less intimidated by others'.

The general response was very positive to the question of whether or not they now felt more comfortable. There was also general agreement that students felt a greater trust with each other which made it easier for them to speak out thereby giving them increased confidence: 'I am confident that what I say will be kept confidential'.

In my first round of data gathering, I identified one student who found the nature of Personal Development so difficult that he felt like leaving Transition Year. However, in this assignment he said, 'During the classes I am relaxed. I even like the classes now which I think is good because I have come a long way since the beginning of the year when I hated the classes.' I put this transformation down to the fact that I do not make demands of my students. He continued: 'I feel more comfortable now because there is no pressure on anyone to say anything if they do not want to whereas at the beginning of the year we would go around in a circle which put more pressure on people to say something.' I feel this student's comments are symptomatic of the changed attitudes of the class towards my more democratic and considerate method-ologies.

Assignment 6

Please give reasons why you feel better / the same / worse in the Personal Development class now as compared to the beginning of the year.

Has the way I have done things in class helped / not helped?
Is there anything about the class that allowed you to get to know the class better?
If you found the topics dealt with difficult at the beginning of the year, why do you feel / not feel more comfortable with them now?

Please be honest!

Responses to Assignment 6

In general, students felt the class was better because time had elapsed, thereby allowing them to get to know both their fellow students and me better. My 'no pressure methods' also seemed to have a significantly positive impact in allow-ing students to feel more relaxed. Many students expressed the importance of the 'increased confidence' that they now had; however, most did not outline reasons for this.

John's story

I referred to John in my assessment criteria as a problem in his capacity as 'leader' of the group. In his assignments 5 and 6, John said, 'I think Personal Development class is the best of the week and I know that everyone looks for-ward to it, even Joe.' He claimed that the class had helped him 'mature in my thoughts and actions' and that it had 'helped me to come out of my shell that I had been hiding in most of my life'. I had seen John mature a lot over the year. He has proven himself to be a very perceptive, sensitive and caring young man.

The second video

In line with the methods that I used in my first set of data collection, I decided to do another video recording to see if there had been a change for the better.

Video 2 showed a very different class from that recorded back in October! The students were relaxed and their body language clearly showed this. They seemed more at home in the situation and with the discussion. There were fewer silent students. They spoke about themselves and their own experiences in a subjective way: for example, 'When I get angry, I . . .'

Validation 2

Again, my critical friend, Mary Adamson, assisted me in validating my data.

On my second visit to the Personal Development class I was struck by the number of changes that had taken place. The atmosphere was warm and friendly. A large number of students were willing to offer their viewpoints and a number were prepared to argue their corner. Joe has developed in his role. He was both at ease and in control. The group now seemed to be more comfortable with itself and individuals 'felt free' to explore personal problems and bring personal concerns into the open.

Possibly most significant:

It would be important to stress that the fore-mentioned behaviour was not the norm in the Personal Development class I attended. The pervasive mood was one of quietly determined purpose; discreet yet firm management by Joe and an evident sense of camaraderie among the students involved. The students had adapted to the discursive, informal style. In conversation afterwards, a number of boys confirmed to me that they always looked forward to the Personal Development class and considered it to be the highlight of the week's classes.

So what have I learnt . . .

. . . about my practice?

During the past nine months I have been involved in action research which has given me a new way of looking at what I do. Completing the project has alerted me to the following:

- Every problem has some solution. There is always something I can do to improve my situation. These solutions are specific to me, in my classroom with the particular group of students with whom I am working. The experiences that are reality for me are unique to me. As a result, it is up to me to do my research and come up with my solutions.

- I now realise that I am an able, confident researcher. I am not an expert by any means but I am improving the expertise when it comes to making changes for me. I know this because things have happened in my class due, I believe, to my own intervention.

- I believe that I am now more open to change as a person. I now see change as something that is desirable, positive and challenging. I now see possibilities more easily in all situations.

- I strongly believe that action research has helped me to enhance the quality of education that I offer my students in their Personal Development class. Such classes are, I believe, essential to allow adolescents a forum for self-expression and development of their confidence. In the past, I believe that I would have just drifted along, hoping for the best. Now that I have become critically aware, it can never be like that any more.

. . . about myself?

In the past year, I have journeyed a little, reflected a great deal, and discovered many new things about myself. I believe that I have developed many insights into my personality and my way of life. Becoming involved in my own professional learning has acted as a catalyst for my personal growth.

I have learned that change is always painful. This is true for both students and myself. It calls for balanced reflection and ownership of my vices and virtues and recognition of habitual thought patterns that can distort reality for me.

I am often enlightened by the freshness and spontaneity that young people can bring to my professional life as a teacher working with young adults on a regular basis. I believe that contact with young people has a huge potential for growth for both them and me, and I have evidence to demonstrate this from the last year.

Improvement is about being educated. While I would have known this in the past, I am now consciously aware of it. It has become part of me. The research methods involved in action research require a large element of self-reflection, of identification of my motivations and of my values. During the year I have had to address the issue of why I do the things that I do. As a result, action research has helped me to synthesise many elements of my professional life. With this synthesis has come a new perspective, a new way of looking at my professional practice and the way I am with students.

Can I realistically make a claim to knowledge?

Can I really say with conviction and evidence that I have gained knowledge about my practice during the past year?

The short answer is 'Yes'.

I have outlined the way things were, what I did to change things – particularly myself – and the way they are now. In moving from A to B, changes occurred. I learned to do things differently. Doing things differently has led to different kinds of outcomes from those I would have expected in previous times. I have learned to:

- let go of situations more easily
- organise my classes better
- prepare my classes
- deal more effectively with a difficult student
- include the shy student more
- not push students too soon
- encourage openness in the class in order to allow some 'skeletons in the cupboard' to emerge. I have therefore learned to be more cautious.
- use energisers more effectively.

I have also learned how to:

- evaluate my own practice
- become more aware
- attend to my own needs as an individual in being a 'helper'
- be aware of the group process, the stages of group formation, and group dynamics
- how to make a class feel more at ease by using appropriate non-threatening approaches
- become more open to change.

The authenticity of my own knowledge generation is tested and demonstrated through:

- the quotes from my journal
- the written statements of my students in their ongoing assignments and monitoring of their own practice
- the video recordings of my class at intervals throughout the period of the research that show learning on the part of myself and the students, as manifested in our changed behaviour and attitudes
- the validation of my critical friend
- the freedom that I now have to welcome others to visit these students and assess their level of maturity for themselves.

6

THE SILENT MAJORITY

Pauline Grenham

Reflection

I believe that undertaking my research project has greatly enhanced my capacity to exercise professionalism as a teacher, as well as facilitated my personal growth. In saying this, I am aware of my own developing understanding of professionalism as rooted in an individual's caring practice.

I came to understand more clearly that subject matter expertise is not the only determinant of success in teaching. As teachers, we need to reach out to students as individuals and recognise their uniqueness as persons. One-to-one encounters are central. Doing my research helped me to understand that students are nurtured through the guidance of tutors, very special teachers, and enabled to reach their full potential for good.

I have learnt many things. I have learnt to see and listen more keenly, not only with my tutor group, but also with all my classes. Perhaps I have grown to be more in tune with my own creativity, and, like the artist, I have developed the capacity to see beyond 'the ordinary' and help its latent beauty to emerge. I have gained confidence to move in this direction, and am more deeply aware of nurturing a greater sense of worth, respect, reverence and sense of responsibility for all creation in students.

The rewards are endless. There is a great sense of joy and celebration as teacher–student relationships develop. It is in the sharing and experiencing of one another that the teacher can become an 'adult friend'. This is reciprocal and mutually rewarding; teacher and students mature and grow together in all areas. The richness and authenticity of young people's responses to me as their teacher privileges my practice.

I am affirmed in the positive results of inviting students to plan their health education programmes, and prioritise the topics and issues for their work. There is need for constant evaluation; I know that none of us can ever become complacent.

As a consequence of my research project, our school was selected to take part in the North Eastern Health Board's 'Healthy Schools Project'. To date, twelve teachers are involved in the Health Board's inservice training. The tutor system has improved but high student–teacher ratios still present difficulties. It is imperative that the Department of Education and Science recognise these issues and encourage further development in this area.

More than ever I am convinced that we teachers cannot work alone. We must work outwards into the community. Currently our school is liaising with the Garda, with parents and the Health Board, with a view to addressing some social difficulties in our area. We are hopeful that this kind of partnership will strengthen a deeper awareness in all of us of the dignity of each human being.

I feel that as a teacher and tutor I am honouring my profession, and in so doing may also help to preserve the dignity and integrity of humankind.

Background

A mythology has grown up around the concept of the 'problem student' in school cultures. This has greatly facilitated the development of pastoral curricula in schools. 'Problem students' are generally held to be students with identifiable specific learning or personal–social needs. Such needs are catered for within the school system, to a greater or lesser degree. Needs and difficulties are recognised and clearly identified. For example, students with low academic ability are usually identified at the entrance assessment or by individual teachers, and are excellently cared for and supported by the remedial teachers, who in turn are often supported by the remedial support teacher. Similarly, students whose overt behaviour might be seen as contrary to the school code of discipline receive individual care and attention; those in need of counselling have access to the guidance counsellor or a person with appropriate responsibility. The existing system of pastoral care in most schools has arisen mainly out of an effort to address these students' needs; it helps the students to adapt to school systems, and helps the school's system to accommodate them and their needs.

My concern is for the students who are not 'problems', in the conventional sense of the word: the silent majority, who go through their school lives not saying a word, not causing any trouble, not drawing attention to themselves. While they may not be 'problems', they constitute a problem for teachers, for they are invisible, and their invisibility invites teachers to overlook them in favour of other, more pressing concerns.

Let me draw a profile of a typical student of the silent majority.

She is fairly quiet in class, but she is not seen as 'shy'. She is well dressed and clean. She is always punctual. She smiles, is reasonably sociable, and behaves well. She answers questions in class, does her homework neatly and on time, and behaves generally as a 'good student'. Her academic achievement is satisfactory, and the teachers have no complaints.

She appears to have support from her parents, although they do not come to school except when necessary. From their feedback on school homework books they seem satisfied with her work; they are always present at parent–teacher meetings. They are usually quiet, pleasant people, and are always supportive of the school and its policies.

> *Student, my student from the silent majority: what goes on inside your head? You and the others can pass through our present school system without being recognised and known as an individual, with no expression of your dreams, aspirations, achievements, anxieties or hidden talents. You carry your hidden agenda on a solitary journey, drifting from class to class, with a sense of 'nobody really cares'.*

It was awarenesses such as this that prompted me to undertake my action enquiry, a concern that the school was not addressing the needs of the 'average' student. I needed to investigate the current pastoral care system to identify whether it did cater for her needs, and if not, what I could do to improve the situation so that she and all other students felt they were valued and cared for. While our school definitely addresses the needs of the more vociferous and demanding students, do we cater for the needs of the less demanding ones? Are we even aware that they have needs? Are we failing the majority of our students, because their needs are invisible, their voices unheard?

My context

At the time of my research (1994) I worked in a single-sex girls school consisting of 767 students, 45 teachers and 8 auxiliary staff, in a small midland town in Ireland, population 3,400. Approximately one third of the students lived in the town, and two thirds travelled in from a wider rural catchment area. There was considerable divergence in the socio-economic background of the students, parents ranging from the unemployed to millionaires. The main body of students came from the middle class.

The aim of the school was to enable all students to pursue academic, spiritual, social and sporting interests in an environment and ethos that promoted Christian values, mutual respect and responsible citizenship (as on the school's mission statement).

The school had a clear and well-functioning management structure; academic and pastoral curricula were well established. A year head system operated well; the principal had reduced teaching hours for year heads which allowed time for year head meetings, and for year head interaction with students. The role of the year head was perceived as addressing pastoral and disciplinary issues.

The principal was unreservedly supportive of pastoral efforts, along with her broader commitment to a holistic education with particular recognition and respect for each individual. Her commitment was apparent in the following:

- Her own practice of caring for teachers and students.
- Her collaborative way of working with staff in organising workable structures in the school.
- The inclusion of health education classes on the syllabus – each class from first year to Junior Certificate level was allocated a forty-minute class period once a week for health education; a core group of seven teachers were involved on this programme; a module on health education was included on the senior catechetical programme.
- the liaison officer, a previous principal of the school, had a reduction of teaching hours to facilitate her visits to families in need. She had the inspiration to set up a bereavement group in the school.

My role

I held the combined roles of coordinator of the health education department and also head of my subject department. I was also the form teacher for a fifth year group and a member of the team implementing the catechetical programme. This senior programme operates on a small group basis, with fifth year and Leaving Certificate students organised into groups of twenty-four. The fifth year team of six teachers rotates with six groups; the Leaving Certificate team of teachers rotates with four groups.

One section of the programme is an extension of the health education programme; it is this section for which I hold major responsibility, and which is the location of my research with third year Junior Certificate students.

My concern

My concern, as stated above, was focused on issues to do with 'the silent majority' of students. I recognised that the school did not address their needs, simply because no needs were evident. The students seemed happy enough; there were no obvious problems in terms of behaviour or academic achievement. The system seemed to be accommodating the students adequately.

Yet my studies on the Higher Diploma course, and my activities as an action researcher, raised my awareness of the need to deconstruct our social realities, to question taken-for-granted assumptions, and to look carefully below the surface to ensure that things really were going well, as most of us thought they were.

> *Student, my student, are you as happy as you seem to be? Why don't you speak to me? Why do you stay so unobtrusive? How can I help when I don't know what you need? Why don't you say what you need?*
>
> *Why don't you say what you need?*
>
> *Ah. Is this a clue? Am I beginning to understand?*

My values

I hold deep values around the rights of students to speak and to be heard. I believe that all students should be able to express their wishes, their desires, to share their enthusiasms and their sorrows. I believe that teachers should encourage responsible behaviour by helping students to articulate their thoughts, to find the confidence to express what they are thinking, in an atmosphere that rejects ridicule and diminishing practices, and holds each person to be of equal worth and to have their ideas acknowledged as of worth. I believe in freedom of expression, for each and every student, and I believe that students should have the confidence to speak out.

But where does the confidence come from? If our students have not the confidence, how do they exercise their right to speak? It is no use having a right if we do not know how to use it.

Here was my concern, clarified at least for myself. What does it matter that I believe in the right of all students to have their needs met if the students are not confident enough to articulate their needs in some way, if they are not confident enough in their own sense of who they are to speak for themselves? How can I as a teacher ensure that all students can speak for themselves?

So I rationalised my concern in terms of how I could help students to raise their own level of confidence, so that they could speak for themselves and have their voices heard, so that they could share their wishes and anxieties, and find people who would share with them and help them along their own journey towards maturity.

Intervention

I decided to initiate an intervention within the health education programme that would focus on raising students' self-esteem, and, I hoped, their confidence.

Initially I had to find out what the situation was. This is in accordance with the action research methodology of establishing what the situation is like so that we can intervene in a way that we hope will influence the situation for good. Elliott (1991) speaks about this as a reconnaissance phase; McNiff (1988) and Whitehead (1989) speak about a situation in which a researcher sees that values are denied in practice, and subsequently carries out an intervention that aims to resolve the dilemma, at least partly, so that values can be lived out at the level of real-life experience. At this stage, then, I was hoping to find out what the situation really was like for the silent majority.

I undertook a good deal of reading, both substantive and methodological. Two books especially helped me to foster a deeper understanding and appreciation of adolescence: Erikson's (1968) *Identity, Youth and Crisis* and Coleman and Hendry's (1991) *The Nature of Adolescence*.

I set out to gather data around the issue of how students were supported in school. I organised rounds of meetings with various groups: with the core group of health education teachers; form teachers, year heads, the vice-principal and principal. I carried out a random check of students' perceptions and experiences of pastoral care in our school's system (this included junior and senior cycle students, past and present). I captured the data using a variety of techniques: field notes, diaries, tape recordings (see Hopkins 1993).

My initial findings were not as I expected.

First round of meetings

Health education teacher

Students come to me via the health education classes, and disclose many personal problems. These problems cover a wide range. Minor problems include conflict with parents and friends; how to communicate with boys; exam pressure; feelings of isolation. Major problems also exist, including sexual abuse and sexually transmitted diseases. I am disturbed that many students seem to reach Leaving Certificate level feeling 'there was no one I could turn to'. This heightens my awareness that young people are constantly reaching out for direction, affirmation, and a sense of belonging.

The core group of health education teachers

G: I fear we miss students on the way. The programmes are good, but we do not have sufficient contact with students. There is a lack of self-esteem and a sense of loneliness in many students, but it is difficult to address. This has a lot to do with the time factor.

B: We are working within the constraints of a crowded syllabus, exam pressure, and limited time. The health education programme seems to be the only forum for listening to students and discussing problems.

K: There is lack of clarity of role and responsibility; is it just the form teacher who is responsible for the pastoral care of their class?

Or are we all responsible, I wonder?

My colleagues and I seemed to agree that

- The silent majority needed more attention.
- We had to find ways of including units on self-esteem in all programmes.

- Existing health education programmes needed constant updating.
- The role of the form teacher needed clarification.

Meetings with form teachers

Findings from interviews and meetings with form teachers revealed that the form teacher system was not functioning as well as it should, apparently because of:

- *Lack of time*: given the administrative nature of their work, and other pressures, form teachers simply do not have time to get to know all their students or develop close professional relationships with them.
- *Existing curriculum structures*: the revolving nature of the organisation of the programmes prevented form teachers from carrying out many pastoral responsibilities: spending an average 12 weeks with a group of 24 on a revolving basis cannot facilitate a caring relationship.
- *Subject divisions*: divisions of classes to accommodate subject choices, and pressure to complete exam courses, militated against the development of personal encounters and caring relationships.
- *Allocation of form teachers to classes*: there were some serious anomalies in the system – one group of students had no form teacher assigned to them; a new member of staff is responsible for a class that she does not teach and disturbingly has not met them yet.

Year heads

The year heads are generally clear about their roles and responsibilities. These include administrative and disciplinary aspects. The year head for the fifth year is aware of the potential for 'trouble' with his group. He already knows potential 'trouble-makers' (all teachers would be familiar with this scenario). The pastoral curriculum structures appear to be working well, and areas have already been identified that need attention, such as increased liaison between year heads and form teachers, and the tensions that exist between full and heavy teaching hours and the implementation of a caring pastoral role.

Vice-principal

Every vice-principal holds a key role in the pastoral structure of a school, having responsibility to support teachers and students alike. Our school vice-principal acknowledged the kind of tensions that this creates. She also raised the issue of how senior students could accept more responsibility for their own learning and preparation for their future lives in work and society in general.

Students

I tape recorded interviews with a number of students from different year groups. Comments included the following:

Third year students:

> Form teachers will deal with things like if your desk has been van-dalised or if you lose a school book. They can be very impersonal. It's like going through a legal system. You felt though that there was no one there to care or help you with the little things.

> I don't know who our form teacher was in second year . . . Most of the time those of us who don't have a teacher for that subject don't have any contact with her at all, unless there's a problem or something like that . . . It would be nice to have someone there that will help with the little things, not just the academic side.

First and second year students:

> My form teacher, I don't know who it is.

> She is nice really. I have her for a subject, but we are busy in class and I'd feel too shy to talk to her.

Senior students:

> I have never had a casual chat with my form teacher or any teacher. It is only this year that I find I can. We worked with teachers for the bazaar, and I got to know them better. It's nice. I feel more accepted as a person.

> Form teachers only come to the class when there is trouble.

> I dreaded school all the way. I felt teachers looked down on us and just told us what to do.

> Yes, I would go to my form teacher. I think she is a caring person and will at least listen.

Past students

In the first three years I felt they were there to 'fix' things. It never occurred to me to talk about things that worried me. Nobody ever said we could. Things improved in fifth year. I got to know some teachers better, and I felt more secure in the school surroundings.

No, I did not experience warmth from my form teachers. I must say, though, there were others I could go to. I did talk to a health ed. teacher and also one of the religion teachers about a problem.

What can I do to change the situation?

There cannot be a pastoral care system or programme working effectively without the tutor or special class teacher.
(Collins 1980)

I came to the understanding that it was the structure of the form teacher system that I wanted to change. The existing structure had inherent inadequacies that were in fact obstructing the implementation of a caring ethos that would embrace the silent majority. Dermody (1986) says that '[t]eachers are the immediate interface between the student population and the school as an institution'. If this is so, it is essential that the pastoral curriculum is working effectively. In my case, I was in a key position to address the inadequacies of our then system, and I set about doing this on a systematic basis.

Implementing a new tutorial system

Meeting with the principal

I presented my findings to the principal, and we immediately began to explore ideas to improve the situation. I also proposed introducing a tutor system, possibly initially on a limited scale, but over time as a whole-school structure. The principal shared my concerns, and agreed that a tutor system could enhance the pastoral provision of our school. However, we recognised that this was a huge undertaking and needed to be introduced and taken forward gently, so as to aim for maximum participation by all colleagues, thereby encouraging their sense of ownership of the ideas and avoiding potential alienation. We also discussed how we might introduce short-term measures to address immediate concerns, and how to develop longer-term plans involving the whole staff.

An immediate concern was our 'wandering' third year group without a form teacher. The principal said that she would approach teachers to try to resolve the problem. We also agreed that I would become a form tutor, in order to pilot the idea of a tutorial system. I had already met third year classes for health education, and I could be assigned to one of these. The principal and I recognised that much of what we hoped to do would proceed on a trial and error basis, but we would at least begin.

By the following day she had confirmed the new arrangements: she had arranged with a colleague to be form teacher for the 'wandering group'; another colleague would assist in the fifth year 'revolving' form teacher system; and I would be a third year form tutor. The principal and I agreed that we would meet weekly to update each other on progress. I need to place on record my indebtedness to the principal for her warmth, interest, care and support that leave me with a sense of appreciation and affirmation. It also reinforced for me the awareness that any school improvement initiatives rely heavily on the foresight, creativity and openness of the principal.

Making progress

I already knew the class for whom I was to be form tutor from our involvement in the health education programme. To get to know them better, I decided that I needed background information on each student, so I spent some time reading their previous school reports and consulting with colleagues who had taught them. The reports revealed that there were no major problems: overall they were good academic achievers, and no student appeared in need of remedial help. Comments on their capacity for study ranged from 'Excellent' to the inevitable 'Could try harder'. Behaviour in general was very good, and no problem behaviour was recorded.

Colleagues reported that they were 'a good class; you'll have no problem there' and that they were 'lovely to go into', although three or four were 'getting a little cocky'. Other comments included: 'They have really grown up this year; I've noticed great interest in the boys!'; 'Some girls never say anything. I think they are embarrassed or afraid of each other'; 'There is a child under great pressure to do well in her exams. It seems to come from her mum.'

At this stage I decided to discuss with immediate colleagues in the health education programme how I was investigating the introduction of a tutorial system into school, of course with full support and approval of the principal, and how this constituted my action research project. I invited my class group to be pioneers with me in this project. They appeared to be happy with the proposals, and there was even a little exclamation of 'Oh, great!' I explained how I felt one-to-one communication was beneficial, and how I would like to meet each student and have an informal chat. Colleagues were highly receptive, and we made out a rota for the meetings. These interviews would take place mainly at breaktime. Building a relationship takes time, and I did not want to rush the process. I also talked with colleagues throughout the school, to raise general awareness, and people were receptive to the ideas; but my focus for these initial stages was with the health education teachers .

I also turned my attention to the general third year programme, and invited the health education teachers to a meeting to discuss it.

18 October – Meeting with third year health education teachers

I updated colleagues on my findings. We discussed the idea of the introduction of a tutorial system in some detail. They were supportive.

> G: It certainly appears that we are on the right track. I feel our school is tilted slightly in favour of academic achievement. This tutorial system has the potential to balance and bridge the gap between the pastoral and academic dimensions.

> K: It's a great idea. In the present social context there are so many external pressures that it is difficult for young people. They need genuine care, and this caring also enhances their academic achievement.

G had earlier attended a National Conference on the Health Promoting School and reported to us that themes throughout the conference had emphasised:

- the need to listen to young people
- the importance of building self-esteem among young people and a sense of responsibility for their actions.

This had significant bearing on the planning of our programme.

Planning the development of our health education programme

We agreed the following points:

- We envisaged a programme based on a self-empowerment model.
- We needed to listen to young people actively, and involve them in the process of planning their own programme.
- We needed to meet regularly ourselves.
- We looked at the possibility of introducing peer tutoring where Leaving Certificate students could take on such a role for Junior Certificate students.

The aims of the programme would be:

- to improve understanding and awareness of self
- to promote the development of a positive self-image and self-esteem
- to help deepen their spiritual awareness.

Objectives included:

- to enable recognition and affirmation of positive qualities
- to build confidence
- to develop an orientation of self-help and self-reliance
- to develop communication skills through participation and dialogue
- to engage in self-evaluation techniques to improve personal capacities to deal with life situations.

This programme was designed to raise implicit issues of self-exploration to an explicit level, and make visible the process of how individuals grew to value themselves and each other.

We agreed that, although we lacked training, we would support one another in the belief that 'we could only do our best'. I felt alive to the tasks that lay ahead.

Actions

20 October

'Interviews commenced. It will be a slow process. To date I have spoken with two students. It was good to get an insight into their background. Both were at ease and I certainly have a better sense of them as persons' (journal entry).

21 October – Survey

I prepared a questionnaire to raise issues concerning:

- areas/issues students wished to address
- self-perceptions
- parent–teenager relationships
- levels of self-esteem.

K (a teacher colleague) wanted to help. We carried out the survey with all Junior Certificate students. We took care in ethical issues, reassuring participants of confidentiality and anonymity at all times.

The results of the survey showed that students enjoyed a relatively good relationship with parents, with only small amounts of conflict with one or both parents. Levels of self-esteem varied. All students wished to raise their levels of self-esteem.

Issues that interested students were predictable, and included:

- boy–girl relationships
- behaviour in relationships

- child sexual abuse
- substance abuse – alcohol, drugs, smoking
- bullying
- communication
- body language
- conflict with parents
- coping with shyness
- how to build self-esteem.

I shared this information with the students, and asked for their assistance in prioritising issues to be addressed. They divided into lively groups, while I watched to observe dynamics and personalities. I noted particularly students who remained silent, those who interacted well, and those who dominated.

Their first choice was, not surprisingly, boy–girl relationships. I invited them to bring in any materials they thought might be useful; this definitely captured their imaginations. They also decided that they would like classes with boys to discuss relationships, visits from outside speakers, and classes on make-up. I said I would see what I could do. Definitely a bond was forming between them, and I noticed more spontaneous chatter and a friendlier atmosphere all round.

3 November – Responses to questionnaire

Here are some randomly selected questions and answers which I feel are indicative of the mood:

Q: How do you see yourself?
A: I think I am a friendly person but I don't share my personal life with others easily.
A: I get shy, very embarrassed and self-conscious.

Q: How well do you cope in school?
A: I cope fairly well with school and homework, but I can't answer questions without feeling embarrassed and stupid.

Q: How well do you get on with your parents or guardians?
A: Very badly. I can't get on with one of my parents. It's impossible to live in my house. I'd like to learn how to cope with pressures at home, because I think a lot of girls are under pressure from their parents.
A: We get on well. They don't seem to understand sometimes and they are always telling me to lose weight.

Q: Do you think there is a connection between how we feel about ourselves and how we behave?
A: Yes, definitely. The lower your self-esteem the shyer you can be or like me

you put on a false personality so that people will like you, and soon you forget when the act should end and it becomes a part of you which is for everyone else. In private you can be a totally different person.

Student X

One student signed her name to the answer sheet. It was discreetly tucked away in a corner, barely legible. Tones of alienation and loneliness seeped through the lines. I arranged to see her in the afternoon. She is a lovely, lonely young person.

An intelligent 15-year-old, X comes from a wealthy background. She is bright, attractive, well groomed and very pleasant. Although she gets on well with her class group, her self-image and self-esteem seem low. Dad died a few years ago, and she does not seem to communicate well with Mum. She says she hides behind masks: 'I once considered suicide to get attention but I talked myself out of it. I don't have anyone I feel comfortable talking to.'

3 November

X was awkward as we talked for the first time. I stayed with her gently and listened.

11 November

This time she was more relaxed. I suggested she might like to speak to the guidance counsellor, and possibly attend the bereavement group. She said she would consider this.

When I spoke with the liaison office she was surprised that X was not on the list for recently bereaved students; clearly her name had been missed. There was need for greater awareness and communication.

I reported my concerns about X to the principal, and I spoke with the guidance counsellor. We were aware that we were being jolted into unfamiliar territory. How many schools face the same dilemmas? We urgently needed to develop our own strategies for advising, educating and supporting students.

X and I met regularly over the next weeks. We stopped on corridors, even for a 'How are you?' She contacts me frequently whenever she feels like a chat.

Self-esteem for students

I was deeply concerned about the lack of self-esteem among the students. I felt strongly that the way students feel about themselves very deeply influences the way they relate to others, how they learn, and the choices they make for their future lives. To enhance my own effectiveness as a pastoral tutor, I read widely. Lawrence's book *Enhancing Self-Esteem in the Classroom* (1987) was particularly helpful in the development of some initial theories. Lawrence offers a theory of the self as constituting three aspects: self-image (what the person is); ideal self (what the person would like to be); and self-esteem (what the person feels about the discrepancy between self-image and ideal self). I related this to my own practice, and became increasingly aware of how teachers can influence the development of students' self-esteem: 'We all need to be liked and valued' (ibid). I became aware from my reading, and from the critical awareness that was growing through the process of doing my research, that there is a link between teachers' self-esteem and students' self-esteem; how teachers teach is as important as what they teach, and their methodologies – how they teach and relate to others, including their students – influence the quality of those relationships.

I made good progress in implementing some of the students' ideas, though not all. Interviews were slower than I had anticipated; timetable constraints prevented boys from attending our classes; I arranged a module on sexually transmitted diseases (STD); students began to raise issues about bullying in the school – it was good that they were able to articulate this; some peer tutoring was beginning to take place; students indicated that they were enjoying the new focus in health education.

A worrying episode

Two students came to me after a class on STD. Student Y is a 15-year-old, from a middle-class family, and has a tense relationship with her mother. Student Z, also 15 and from a working-class background, has good family relationships. Both had become sexually active. Neither was using contraception. Z thought she might be pregnant.

They confided in me and sought advice. This was further new territory for me and I felt inadequate. However, I spoke with the girls about responsibility and promised to refer them to more expert advice. I became increasingly aware of the needs of young people: in their search for love, affection and affirmation, and under enormous peer pressure to perform and demonstrate their adulthood, they often act in ways contrary to their own values. I wondered how many others in my class were suffering in silence.

I was deeply concerned about these issues, and consulted with a family doctor who is also a member of a voluntary team I work with outside school to facilitate life skills programmes. Our conversation included:

Q: Is there an increase in sexual activity among young people?
A: No doubt about it. There is a high increase in presentation of STD; prescriptions for contraceptives; pregnancy and the morning-after pill.

Q: What problems do you associate with young people?

A: Exam pressure. They feel they must perform because their value as a person is measured by performance. Minimal quality time with parents . . . Schools do not generally provide an education where students can be supported in 'normal living skills'. Social pressures, youth culture, media, all contribute to their sexual behaviour . . . they have no access to adult friends, someone who will listen, be non-judgemental and yet challenge them to be responsible.

Q: Is this behaviour alcohol related?

A: 80–90 per cent of cases are alcohol related. Pressure again. I believe the underlying factor is low self-esteem.

This interview particularly prompted me to seek permission from the principal for a parent–teacher meeting to discuss relationships among young people, and with their parents. The principal made all provisions for the meeting.

Parent–teacher meetings

1 December

The first meeting was well attended. Parents seemed pleased at the opportunity to speak with teachers about their children: 'This is a great idea. We need more meetings like this'; 'I'm delighted. I find it hard to talk to my daughter and I feel she is influenced by others.' X's mum did not attend.

13 December

Because of the parents' enthusiasm for this contact, we arranged a follow-up meeting. More than a third of the parent body attended (52 out of 148). The meeting was not meant as an information evening so much as an invitation to parents to reflect on the nature of their relationships with their children. Parents' comments from the small evaluation sheet included: 'This opened many doors for me'; 'I never realised the responsibility I was taking on 16 years ago'; 'We need more of this kind of thing.'

On the same evaluation sheet we invited ideas from parents about the content of future meetings. Feedback included areas of communication, listening, strategies for building self-esteem. It was also suggested that students and parents should attend the meetings together.

Development of the health education programme

23 December

I arranged a meeting with a member of the Health Board for teachers to learn about a substance abuse programme. Teachers could become more involved in the area if they wished, and depending on take-up, this could develop into a more extended programme.

10 January

I sent a letter to the Health Board requesting funds to subsidise future parents meetings.

12 January

A parent, a qualified beautician, volunteered to give make-up classes. She was swiftly timetabled.

A member of the Health Board arranged to give a talk to the group on AIDS.

11 February

I was invited by an educational psychologist in South End, London, to shadow him in his assessment of a 14-year-old boy. I learned a great deal from this visit about carrying out assessments. In my tape-recorded conversation with the psychologist I asked:

Me: Is there a correlation between behaviour and self-esteem?
Psychologist: Oh, very much so. A good pastoral care system, a perceptive pastoral system, one that is proactive, would have been able to manage this student. His own school is very caring but no one picked it up. Every school needs to have key people that students can go to on an informal basis.

19 February

Meeting with the director of Community Care (Health Board programme). The director was very much interested in what we were doing. At a breakfast meeting (!) he offered a subsidy of £200 towards future developments. This then enabled us to set up visits by an experienced facilitator to speak to each Junior Certificate class on teenage–parent relationships, and on enhancing self-esteem. It also enabled a further meeting with parents on communication and listening skills.

27 April

The facilitator worked with each class for forty minutes. Students knew that a follow-up meeting would take place with their parents in May.

Comments from students after this meeting included: 'Other students' parents say the same things as mine'; 'Could you please discuss these things with our parents?'; 'Please bring up the topic of boyfriends: this causes most arguments with my parents.'

Students shared their experience of sometimes extreme pressure from parents for examinations success and unfair comparison with siblings. There was unanimous concern about the frequent lack of listening, reasonable freedom and understanding of feelings.

3 May – Meeting with parents

Forty parents attended the meeting. I introduced the topic of communication with a review of students' comments (including those above). The facilitator introduced the idea of listening, and engaged the group experientially in listening exercises.

Comments from parents after the meeting included: 'Why didn't we have this before?'; 'This kind of meeting should be available to parents of first year students. I might have handled things better if I had been aware.'

10 June

I supplied a full report of the project, including evaluations, to the director of the Health Board. As a result, our school was selected as a pilot school to develop a comprehensive partnership programme with parents.

Evaluation

I was anxious to establish whether or not students' self-esteem had been enhanced. While aware of the potential limitations of small-scale action research, I undertook an evaluation to try to see whether I would be justified in claiming that there had been progress. I issued a small questionnaire and, recognising that questionnaires are not always the most reliable instruments for gathering qualitative data, followed this up with personal interviews. The questionnaire was administered to all students who had been involved in the programme; interviews were conducted with a selection of students, and with the teachers who had been involved.

Feedback from the questionnaire (statistics are in my original report) indicated that a very caring relationship had developed between students. The figures were supplemented by student interview comments, including: 'I'm more confident now and I can sense a situation and what to do about things'; 'We want more health education classes because we learn about life'; 'I would think now before doing something and have a look at the consequences'; 'I'd be nervous, but I'd get up now and read in class.'

Their comments about the programme included: 'It was great to make out part of our own programme. It looked at things we needed to know about'; 'I loved the part where we all burnt a piece of paper with our worries on them. There was a lovely friendly feeling. When we joined hands and sang, I cried but I wasn't sad. Cathy gave me a big hug'; 'The day we did the strengths. Everyone wrote down a positive remark about you. I still have my piece of paper and look at it often. It's a good feeling.'

Teacher's comment: 'This is so worthwhile. It certainly shows that we need to change the form structure.'

Year head: 'The new year head system works very well.'

Principal: 'Two of your group came over to my office to ask for extra classes in health education. I think that captures more than words.'

What did I learn?

I believe the intervention to introduce a tutorial system succeeded in raising awareness of the need for self-esteem, and encouraged some of the young people in the group to gain in confidence. My initial investigations revealed that twelve students had worrying problems; this was the first time seven of them had spoken to an adult concerning their problems. All students seemed to benefit; it was lovely to meet them on the corridor, and to have them wander alongside me with spontaneous chatter. They have enhanced my own sense of worth and value with their comments: 'Ah, miss, you're sound' is a great compliment from a teenager. X's mum said at a chance meeting, 'X feels she had found a kindred spirit.' Such is what makes my professional life worthwhile.

At a structural level, I have worked with others in developing a tutorial system in school. We hope that this system will of itself enable us to identify those students at risk and take appropriate measures to support them. Our school has become deeply aware of the need to make care visible throughout the structures and the relationships that constitute our school life.

At a wider level, my awareness has grown regarding the plight of the silent majority. This applies not only to students in school, but also to any social grouping. Perhaps there are teachers who are part of this largest minority group. Certainly there must be parents. How can we, in a caring society, aim to hear the silent voices? How can we raise our own awareness of the need to be attentive to them? To hear silent voices we have to listen out and encourage them to be heard. We need to be creative in developing cultures in which people invite each other to speak, so that they can be heard; in which people actively perceive each other so that they can be seen. Care needs to be made visible. In our society so many people are invisible, simply because they are there, but they do not count; and this applies not only to the underprivileged, who are often deliberately marginalised, but also to the affable, the 'normal', those who do not make a fuss. 'Ordinary' people are rendered silent because it is assumed that they are 'normal' and therefore do not need attention.

Now, whenever I am with another, I see and I listen. My awareness is high; I reach out to connect. I believe that there are no ordinary people. We are all special, and we deserve recognition for our specialness. This is what I have learnt from my research project, and it is a learning that informs my life's work.

7

THREE SCHOOLS . . .
BECOMING . . .
ONE . . .

Frances Murphy

Reflection

When Cashel Community School opened in September 1994 I was given the task of coordinating pastoral care. This role and the role of pastoral care teacher was a new experience for all of us involved. During that first year I spent my time looking for suitable material for classwork, making it available to the teachers involved, and meeting with them. It was often a case of the blind leading the blind!

I was very happy the following year when I got a place on the Higher Diploma course in Pastoral Care as I felt it would give me a greater understanding of the place of pastoral care in the school and of my role as pastoral care coordinator. Almost at once participants on the course were introduced to action research and the idea of looking at a particular aspect of one's own work using this methodology. This involves asking questions of the kind, 'How can I improve my work?' (Whitehead 1989), because action research is all about looking at my own practice. I can still hear those words 'How can I . . .?' ringing in my ears today.

My original concern was around the development of a pastoral ethos in our new community school, so I set myself the task of addressing the question, 'How can I be an animator, enabler and unifying force within the school community?' Following some work on this task, I realised that the potential scope of the research was too broad and needed to be redefined. From my research I began to see that my main concern was around the area of discipline: how it was being carried out and what real learning was taking place as a result of the discipline structure. In the light of that I decided that the theme of my project ought to be 'How can I help to establish a behaviour system that will promote growth and development in an open caring environment?' I experienced a certain sense of frustration when I had to redefine the subject of my project, but I realised that this was part of the learning process for me.

Keeping a diary was necessary to organise my reflection. This was time consuming and required discipline, yet it was invaluable to my personal reflection. Reflecting on the diary made me more aware of the many learning opportunities previously lost.

Unfortunately, because of surgery and then some time out of work during the school year I had to change the focus of my research again. The timing made it impossible to work intensively with any group of participants, so I decided to evaluate the work undertaken to date, on a broader level, of my experience of being centrally involved in the amalgamation of three schools into what is now Cashel Community School. I had in any case consistently gathered data around this process, so the refocusing was not difficult.

Researching, reflecting and writing the project has had a special significance for me and I found the task stimulating and interesting, and a valuable aspect of my continuing professional learning.

Doing the project supported me in my work, caused me to pause and reflect and then to share these reflections with other members of staff, particularly with the vice-principal. It has contributed to the development of pastoral structures in our school. Last term, in consultation with the senior students, work began on establishing and setting up a Student Council. This was something that had been highlighted while doing my project the previous year. The experience and learning involved in undertaking the project helps me to model a more open, listening approach with students which is enabling them to be more actively involved in their own learning.

The opportunity to reflect on how we prepared and planned for amalgamation and the structures we put in place made me more aware of the needs of all the different groups involved and in particular the needs of senior students. I hope this and other issues raised will benefit schools involved in amalgamations.

The methodology beginning with the question 'How can I . . .?' and proceeding through the systematic action steps of 'What is my concern . . .?', 'What can I do . . .?', 'What action will I take . . .?' and 'How can I evaluate my actions . . .?' provides me with a coherent plan for practice. It is a process that I live out of now.

Introduction

The aim of this chapter is, first, to work towards an understanding of the nature of pastoral care in the context of second-level education in Cashel, and then to examine its development in several dimensions:

- in the three second-level schools in Cashel prior to September 1994
- in the preparation for pastoral care during the planning and implementation of the amalgamation of these three schools to form a community school
- in the ongoing development of pastoral care in Cashel Community School.

I will then:

- present my vision for the future of pastoral care in Cashel Community School, remembering that 'action without vision just passes the time' (source unknown).

As part of my research I set out to gather data around these issues. The data gathering methods I used included questionnaires, personal reflections using journalling, records of informal conversations and field notes, and in-depth interviews. A questionnaire was put to staff members, parents, past pupils, and Leaving Certificate students 1995/96, and this produced rich findings, as did extended conversations with Sr Úna Collins, tutor of the Higher Diploma course. I kept a record of my own personal experience using a reflective journal. This enabled me to keep a record of the development of my own personal theory of education (Whitehead 1989), which I tested against the perceptions of my validating colleagues in school and on the Higher Diploma course. Stenhouse (1983) suggests that 'research is systematic enquiry made public'. I am making my research public, and inviting critical comment on my findings, in an effort to improve my own thinking, and also to promote the idea of practitioner research in second-level schools in Ireland. I also wish to express strongly my view of the need for ongoing teacher education provision if policy recommendations, such as those contained in the White Paper on Education (Government of Ireland 1995) are to be realised in practice.

This report is an account of how I addressed the issues in a systematic way. It must be emphasised, however, that this is only a beginning, and the research continues currently.

Towards an understanding of pastoral care

Adolescent development

In any educational environment the caring dimension of the individual needs to be prioritised. Schools have the privilege and the responsibility for providing and promoting opportunities for young people to grow intellectually and emotionally, and for putting in place a framework of care that will support cognitive and affective development. Pastoral care provides such a holistic and integrated curricular framework by emphasising the nature of the relationships within the school and its curriculum, and the wider system of which it is a part.

In most schools there are students from varied social backgrounds with different attitudes, values, expectations and behaviour patterns. These may often be in conflict with what the school promotes. Many students find the transition from childhood to adolescence traumatic. These years are often a period of change, exploration, doubt and insecurity.

However balanced children may be when they arrive in school, however secure from their previous educational and home experience, their self-perceptions of image, worth and value come under threat when they enter second-level education, and may become undermined by the need to conform to the social norms of their group. During adolescence, the peer group is of prime importance to the individual. The need to belong, identify with and be accepted by their group is more important for young people at adolescence than at any other stage in their lives.

A task for teachers is to find ways of challenging students' preconceptions and stereotyped mental models in order to help them grow, to encourage self-esteem and the development of sound judgement and to create a sense of achievement. The pastoral system in the school can often facilitate this. However, we need to understand this system and its knowledge base in order to become more effective in our work as teachers. We do not expect that students learn academic subjects without being taught; yet, until recently, we expected that 'affective' learning just 'happened' for the young person in our schools. Collins comments that '[t]he affective or emotional needs of the students require structure, control and a caring environment' (1993: 6). Teachers need to understand the nature of this caring environment to ensure that their influence in young people's lives is positive, and this development of personal understanding is well facilitated through personal exploration of practice.

Self-esteem, personal development, responsibility, self-discipline and affirmation are concepts which are central to the development of the student. The 12-year-old who arrives in our second-level school has an image of self which may be easily threatened or undermined. The insecurity is often reflected in the child's behaviour and development. I agree with Humphreys who says, 'The child's level of self-esteem will determine not only his or her educational progress but also emotional, social, intellectual, sexual, career and spiritual development' (1993: 125). Therefore, what the school reinforces and develops in the student plays a very important part in their total development. This is effectively addressed in the pastoral care system of a school. Hamblin comments: 'It is that element of the teaching process which centres around the personality of the pupil and the forces in his environment which either facilitate or impede the development of intellectual and social skills, and foster or retard emotional stability' (1989: xv). I agree. I also believe that it is the responsibility of teachers to understand this process effectively, and to test their own understanding against that of the professional community by the production of case study evidence, such as this, to show the development of that understanding in practice.

Teaching and affective learning

Pastoral care is an integral part of each teaching day and must be part of the daily work of the teacher and school management. Therefore:

- Each teacher needs to be involved in the policies, structures and decision-making processes of the school.

- Each teacher needs to become more conscious of their role and influence in the development of each student.
- Feasible structures need to be established that promote respect and care for students with the aim of enriching their development.

In school planning it is essential that provisions are made to include development of pastoral care structures. Teachers must play a major part in the decisions made relating to class contact with their students; how they interpret their role becomes central to such structures. Sharing responsibility and intentional communication in school planning help to promote staff unity and create good management/staff relations.

Teaching is most effective when the student's readiness is established. A successful motivator will create the most suitable environment in their classroom to accommodate the differentiated needs and personalities of students.

School structures which promote humanity, care and compassion need to be developed. Such an environment of care will go some way to ensuring that personal values are lived out, and that each and every person in the school community may achieve their maximum learning potential in cognitive and affective domains.

In any successful centre of learning the pastoral aim is to affirm, support, and promote the growth and development of the people in its care.

Origin of pastoral care

Similar to Britain, pastoral care was introduced in response to growing student numbers in Irish schools in the 1970s. As Irish society and family life changed, the need for pastoral care in our schools became increasingly evident. This was a period of rapid growth throughout the education system; one outcome was that higher numbers of students spent their formative years in formal educational systems. An awareness developed of the need for schools to cater for the personal and social, as well as academic, development of their young people. This is further demonstrated in the White Paper which has as one of its aims: 'to nurture a sense of personal identity, self-esteem and awareness of one's particular abilities, aptitudes and limitations, combined with a respect for the rights and beliefs of others' (Government of Ireland 1995: 10).

Pastoral care is not an *ad hoc* activity. Structures must be put into place to facilitate its effective implementation. 'It is vitally important to formalise it, . . . recognise that it needs formal structures within school to support it' (Collins 1993: 11).

Personal note

On a personal note my own appreciation of pastoral care is motivated by my way of life, my values, and that which directed me to follow the path I have chosen. Being a member of a Religious Congregation which ministers to the young, the poor and the vulnerable, I experience numerous opportunities to care for others. One of the main directives of our Order states that:

> In all our apostolates we promote the dignity of human persons, so that they can be free to develop their own gifts and to participate in the task of liberation and social transformation.
>
> (Presentation Sisters, *Constitutions and Directives*, 1986: 17)

As an educator my work is mainly with young people in school. I am clear about the need for ongoing personal reflection on my practice, and I believe that such reflection has contributed towards an enhanced understanding of myself as a person; consequently my life experience is of greater value in my work.

Summary

As 'the child's emotional welfare is the cornerstone of his or her educational development' (Humphreys 1993: ix) it has to be a priority in our educational establishments. From my own experience it is evident that the self-esteem of students plays a crucial role in their educational development.

'A child enters a classroom carrying within him or her the effects of relationships with significant adults in his or her life' (ibid: 3). Significant adults would normally be parents, family and teachers. Their image of self and self-esteem is strongly grounded in these relationships. Teachers are in a particularly influential position in affecting students' level of self-esteem. This fact is clearly stated in the White Paper on Education:

> Schools actively influence all aspects of the growth and development of their students.
>
> (Government of Ireland 1995: 161)

Therefore one could conclude that a positive self-concept is the foundation of personal and social development.

It seems reasonable to assume that a positive self-concept is the foundation of personal and social development for any person. If this is the case, schools must prioritise the development of the student's self-concept, self-image and self-esteem, and establish and maintain well defined structures of personal and social development in all our schools. If this framework is to be successful, the carers must also be given consideration. Staff unity and a sense of belonging are necessary to build a community which works for the common good and strives to create a centre of excellence in every way.

The aim of pastoral care in schools for me must include the creation of a caring, open environment, through which staff and students, both individually and collectively, experience holistic growth and development.

Developing pastoral care in our three schools

The focus of this research is to show how I worked with others in developing a pastoral care structure during the process of amalgamation of three post-primary schools in Cashel in 1994, and how we supported its continuing development in what then became the new Community School. The schools were the Christian Brothers' School, the Vocational School and the Presentation School. As a Presentation Sister I taught in the Presentation Secondary School (Scoil Mhuire) for fifteen years, for seven of those years in the capacity of principal.

Before looking at the process of amalgamation or life in what is now Cashel Community School, I would like to explore how each of the three schools viewed and practised pastoral care. As previously stated, I understand pastoral care to be the creation of a caring, open environment, through which staff and students, both individually and collectively, experience holistic growth and development.

Pastoral care is both explicit and implicit. 'Explicit' pastoral care relates to the structures which are built into the school system. These structures ensure that the school cares for the individual student, and ensure regular meeting time between tutors and students. 'Implicit' pastoral care is the atmosphere or ethos of the school. It is reflected in areas such as the quality of relationships and the commitment of teachers to individual students; and it fosters initiative, creativity, personal development and self-discipline among all.

Pastoral care in the Christian Brothers' Secondary School

Each teacher believed that pastoral care was an unspoken, permeating policy, implicitly understood by all the staff and promoted by them. The overall well-being of each student was a priority in classroom situations. While preparation for life, the importance of relationships and good communication were part of civics and religion classes, pastoral care was generally carried out in an informal way. Teachers had discussions on the problems/difficulties encountered by students, and as a group worked together to resolve these difficulties on an *ad hoc* basis. A class tutor system operated in the school and parent/teacher meetings for each year group were held annually.

The school made great efforts to involve as many students as possible in curricular and extra-curricular activities, particularly sport. The school had a concert band and also staged many joint drama ventures with Scoil Mhuire at fifth year level. The fifth year business studies class organised a Mini Company in recent years to fund the production. These activities helped to create a sense of pride and of belonging within a class, a year group, a team, the school.

From the questionnaires issued to past students as part of my research, it was evident that they felt the school had a friendly atmosphere, where everyone knew everyone else, and where pupils had a very good relationship with some teachers. They felt that emphasis was placed on academic achievement, yet the abiding memory for the majority of past pupils was being involved in sports or in the fifth year drama production. Parents held the same view.

Teachers agreed that their involvement in the pastoral aspect of school life helped them to treat the students as autonomous people, thus increasing their own levels of job satisfaction and helping them to ensure that students enjoyed a quality educational experience.

Pastoral care in the Vocational School

Because of the size of the school (approximately 230 students), their background, the traditions of the Vocational Education sector (this sector tends to service the needs of children from areas of socio-economic disadvantage), staff were always aware of the personal needs of the students. Although the pastoral curriculum was largely unstructured there was a caring attitude for the individual students. It was structured in that the school operated a class tutor system, where a teacher had particular responsibility for each student in their care. Each year information was gathered on incoming students in relation to primary school records, health, disabilities and family background.

Most of the staff were involved in extra-curricular activities, such as games and concerts, and this enabled staff and students to interact formally and informally. Each year all students were taken on school trips, both of an educational and fun nature. Involvement in extra-curricular activities was greatly encouraged, with the emphasis on fostering involvement and sportsmanship. There was a high level of cooperation between staff and students.

Parent–teacher meetings were held at night to facilitate attendance, and the principal had a very good relationship with parents. The school had an active, involved Parents Council. Parents describe the school as being welcoming to parents and sustaining a high level of care for the students. Past students felt that there was always someone to talk to and that they had been made to feel important.

The staff agreed that pastoral care was beneficial to the school, that the atmosphere of caring certainly made the relationship between pupils and teachers more worthwhile, and that the informal and non-pressured nature of the school led to a cordial atmosphere.

Pastoral care in Scoil Mhuire

There was a general awareness of the pastoral needs of the students, and this was stated frequently at staff meetings. Staff were encouraged to cover aspects of pastoral care in civics and religion classes, while guest speakers addressed students on different aspects of growing up and social problems. However, there was no structured programme, and whatever or however aspects of pastoral care were dealt with depended on the teacher involved.

The class teacher system which operated in the school was understood to be a 'pastoral' one as much as a 'discipline' one.

The school tried to cater for the needs of all students, especially the academically less able. Consequently the school became involved in the Community Based Learning Programme, piloted by Shannon Curriculum Development Unit in 1980. A section of this programme dealt with personal development, and three teachers were trained in this area under the guidance of Dr Leslie Button of Swansea University. Students were also prepared for the world of work through work experience, work simulation programmes and competency training. From this programme the school became involved with Senior Certificate, also piloted by Shannon Curriculum Development Unit. This was an alternative Leaving Certificate programme, and again development of skills in interpersonal relationships was high on the agenda. Some members of staff attended 'An Active Tutorial Workshop' run by Jill Baldwin (an associate of Leslie Button), and training was ongoing for staff in the first two years. Time was allocated to coordinate the programme and for the staff to meet weekly in order to develop a whole-school approach to the programme. After a few years, elements of both Senior Certificate and CBL were incorporated into a Transition Year Programme.

This structured programme in personal development was never formally established in other year groups. It could be suggested, however, that the teachers trained in personal development and other new approaches transferred their skills to have a greater impact on the students in all classes. One teacher stated:

> Being responsible for the personal development aspect of CBL made me see the value of such work on an organised regular class basis. I admit that at the outset I had been sceptical about its role, but as I worked on the programme I became more and more aware of its value.

A pastoral awareness of the needs of the staff was also seen as very important and each year time was set aside for staff development. Inservice education in this area included such topics as:

* coping with stress
* the Myers Briggs Personality Profile
* a different kind of teacher (Tony Humphreys programme, well-known in Ireland)
* communication skills.

The school had a good relationship with parents and the local community. The latter evolved particularly as a result of the school's involvement in local business and enterprise. Parent–teacher meetings were held annually for each year group. The school had a Parents Council and a very active Parents Finance Group who had fundraised for a Presentation Girls Secondary School prior to the Minister's decision in 1984 to establish a Community School in Cashel. The majority of parents expressed their support for the school system, which they believed helped their children to grow and develop.

The school had a strong history of sport, especially camogie. This is a traditional ladies' game, played with a ball (sliothar) and a stick (hurley) and is something like hockey, except that the ball can be played off the ground. A great sense of belonging, being part of a team, representing the school was built around this. The school also had a tradition of drama and musicals. The involvement of all students was encouraged, irrespective of academic ability or talent. The policy of the drama teacher was 'let every child have the experience of being on stage, as that is what they will remember when they leave school'. How right she was, for what do we remember but the times when we were made to feel special, important and valued.

Data exist in the archive to show that past pupils describe the school as a warm friendly school where there was a sense of being cared for as an individual, where one felt accepted and important. They felt that their contribution to school life was of value, and that being listened to and encouraged were important elements of the school.

Staff members felt that pastoral care was never stated as school policy, yet it formed an important part of the school structure and created a living ethos.

Summary

Although each of the three schools was small in number and had a caring, personal approach, I believe that a structured programme for pastoral care, with time allotted weekly to each class, would have greatly enhanced the holistic growth and development of the students. In events such as amalgamation, where among other things there is a greater range of needs, the pastoral care programme has to be formalised. It must be remembered, however, that the structures themselves are not the important factor, but the content of the programme and how it is carried out. For this to happen in any school, time has to be allocated for training of staff, planning and implementing programmes that will meet the needs of students relating to their personal and social development. This important aspect of education must not be left to chance.

Preparation for amalgamation

The amalgamation was the outcome of the then Education Minister's rationalisation programme, and no party to the amalgamation was overjoyed at the prospect. Planning and preparing for the amalgamation was obstructed by, among other things, constant changes in the date set to start the building. The start date in fact stretched over a period of years and this made the situation appear unreal and planning almost impossible.

However, in September 1991 a meeting of the three staffs took place to organise common textbooks for the Junior Certificate Programme. This meeting holds great significance, as it was the first gathering of the three individual school staffs prior to the amalgamation.

Building work began in June 1993. This left only one school year to prepare for what would undoubtedly be a major change in the lives of students, teachers and parents. The staff from each school were only too aware of the many and varied fears and problems that would be present in the amalgamation for all those involved:

- emotional trauma
- loss of identity
- teaching boys and girls together for those coming from single-sex schools
- controlling large numbers
- sense of loss/isolation for students
- teaching different academic levels
- losing the personal contact with students and fellow staff members that existed in the smaller schools
- and so on . . .

The Planning Group

An Inter-Schools Planning Group was set up, with two staff representatives and the principal from each school. The major work of this group towards the development of pastoral care in the new school was to organise and plan a day's inservice for the three staffs with Sr Úna Collins and Carmel Coyle from the Marino Institute in April 1994. Sr Úna stated in her response to my questionnaire that she was impressed by the positive atmosphere, the size of the new staff, and the fact that the newly appointed principal was present to hear what was being said and to plan with the group.

The day began with an overview of pastoral care in a systemic framework from Sr Úna, followed by an input from Carmel Coyle on the Skerries amalgamation (the amalgamation of the Holy Faith Secondary School and the De La Salle Secondary School, both in Skerries, Co. Meath). Then a representative from each school gave a presentation of the positive aspects of life in their school that they would bring to the new structure. This was followed by some input on the role of tutor, year head, the student prefect system and group work.

During the day, working groups decided that the following issues needed particular attention in what was to be Cashel Community School:

- staff values within a pastoral school

- structures that would be required in the school
- how senior students would be involved, and the procedures for appointing student prefects
- gender equity in the school
- an outline of the role of year heads and tutors
- an outline of a pastoral care programme for first year students.

A sense of optimism, expectancy, and excitement about the function of pastoral care in the new school was evident at the end of the inservice day, as well as a feeling of mutual support and challenge.

Following the day, the Board of Management agreed to the proposal to release two members of staff to follow the Higher Diploma in Pastoral Care, which was the genesis for my formal research programme. The staff and management were committed to the development of a pastoral structure in the Community School from the beginning. However, due to the many problems inherent in amalgamation and the delayed completion of the building, it was not possible to organise the release of the teachers until September 1995. It was a lost opportunity as this course would have given greater insight into the positioning of pastoral care in the life of the new school and supporting the development of sound practices.

In May 1994 the Planning Group introduced the concept of student prefects to the fifth year students in each school, and applications were invited. Thirty-five students applied, seven boys and twenty-eight girls. Interviews were arranged, appointments were made and a training day was organised for September 1994.

Pastoral care for staffs

The amalgamation sometimes meant severe personal and professional destabilisation for some members of the former three staffs. Unfortunately at no stage during this year of preparation were such issues addressed, and on reflection this was a serious oversight. Pastoral care applies to teachers as well as students; a caring community implies care for all members of the community, and there are serious lessons to be learnt from our experience.

While 'pastoral care planning' was somewhat idealistic, there was a realisation that there would be a gap between the theory and practice, and that it would take work and commitment to bridge the gap. The development of a pastoral system within a school takes time. Once the staff are open to the idea of the school needing to provide an open, caring environment in which learning and personal development can take place for all students, then the first step in consciously developing a pastoral school has taken place. Not only were these new amalgamated staff open to the idea but they also had a strong sense of ownership of the plan, and this was very important for the development of pastoral structures in the new school.

The current situation

September 1994 saw the opening of the new Community School in Cashel with a student population of 838. What follows is a brief description of the emergent school pastoral care programme.

The staff

The first few days of the school calendar were set aside for staff meetings and planning. However, the first two days of meetings had to be cancelled because the building was not ready. Sadly this eliminated a meeting with Frank Murray, Secretary General of the Association of Community Colleges and Schools, who was to address the issue of working in a community school. Some members of staff were by now suffering a high level of stress because of the constantly changing scenario. There were anxieties about not coping, of not being important in the larger school structure, losing their sense of identity, and some were finding it hard to let go of previous school experiences and to develop new perceptions. Cancellation of this meeting was particularly grievous, as it might have given some members of staff the opportunity to express these feelings of insecurity. While these issues were discussed, somewhat, on a individual basis, a major change was taking place in the lives of the staff, some of whom had been teaching in their previous school ten, twenty, thirty or more years, and an opportunity to express these feelings and hear them expressed would have been an invaluable experience for all.

School structures

The following structures were put in place.

Pastoral structures

As a result of the inservice day in April, all first, second, third, and Transition Year students were assigned a pastoral care class period on the timetable, and a pastoral care coordinator was appointed, as were tutors and year heads. Each tutor had specific responsibility for a particular class and facilitated the weekly pastoral care class for these students. This class period gave the students the opportunity to explore their world in a safe trusting environment. It was of the utmost importance for tutors to build up a profile of each student, taking into account 'the positive value as well as the limitations of the child's background' (Collins 1993: 8).

As all students were 'new' to the school in September 1994, we began by getting them to fill out a personal profile form. This form filling was not just an exercise in writing, but an opportunity for the class to begin the process of gelling, working in pairs, listening to each other and sharing in small groups.

However, the way in which this was accomplished depended on the confidence and skill of the tutor.

Following this work the tutor and class explored the need for rules and regulations, and negotiated them according to perceived student needs. This list seldom differed from the official school list, except in how it was expressed. In this way the level of awareness and responsibility was being raised and developed.

The developing pastoral curriculum involved aspects of self-esteem, self-confidence, responsibility, the process of growing up, healthy eating and lifestyle.

Pastoral care teachers described their role as including:

- being available to students, so that they could express their feelings and needs
- being the point of contact for the class within the different structures in the school
- being a point of reference for other members of staff in relation to the background and needs of the individual students in their class
- being a motivator of the students, taking into account the behaviour, attendance and progress of each student
- helping each student to grow and develop.

However, teachers had no formal training in pastoral work, and no time was set aside within the timetable for teachers to meet. These meetings had to take place at lunchtime on a monthly basis for each year group, and not everyone could attend. As coordinator, I found that I was generally deciding on the contents of the programme for each year group, in this first year of opening, because of this lack of planning time. However, as they became more familiar with the programme more teachers gained confidence. While there was a lot of goodwill, interest and enthusiasm, lack of training and expertise in the area of pastoral care was identified as an issue. Some teachers did not see themselves suited to teaching a pastoral care programme, and taught their own subject during this period. Yet invaluable work was done and this was greatly encouraged and supported by the principal and vice-principal.

The principal saw the teachers' attitude as an important factor in the whole-school approach to pastoral care. Whether a teacher occupies a role as a tutor or subject teacher, they need to care for the learning and development of the student. This involves the importance of informal class time for students in order to focus on their own interests and development.

Personal record books

These were introduced as a means of monitoring students' attendance, getting permission to be absent from school, and behaviour. It was a way of communicating with parents about these matters. Year heads were involved in checking these books twice a term. This gave them an opportunity to meet students individually. In the school year 1995/96 a page was added to the personal record book to record personal achievements of the students.

Student prefect system

A day's training was held for the newly appointed prefects in the first week of September 1994, and they were assigned the class groups for which they had special responsibility. Inevitably, as in any new system, there were misunderstandings and some confusion, so the prefect system was not as effective as it could have been. The question of a Student Council has been raised and this was explored in the school year 1996/97.

Senior students

With the exception of the first year students, and a few students in other year groups, the remaining students came from the three existing second-level schools in the town. Like the staff they had varying degrees of adjustment to make in the changeover. Staff and students were coming from smaller, more personal, intimate structures. It was this aspect of intimacy that senior students greatly missed, and in their first year in the new structure they talked about feeling lost and not being heard.

Transfer from third year to fifth year is a major step (fourth year is an optional year, usually called Transition Year). The Leaving Certificate class of 1995/96 not only had this step to cope with, but they also transferred into a new school at this time. They had to cope with a larger building, a different school structure, a greater number of people, many new teachers and co-education. Due to the pressures of establishing a functioning school these factors were largely overlooked. While structures were put in place to cater for the pastoral development of the junior students, no organised work was done with the senior students, either at the time of amalgamation or in the following two years to help them make the adjustments involved in the transfer to Cashel Community School.

The following recommendations made by the sixth year students may help us as staff in our reflection:

- A better atmosphere would be created if rules and regulations were relaxed a little.
- A strong request to abolish personal record books for sixth year students.
- Punishment can be too severe. No difference made between a mild and a major disturbance.
- Some teaching methods should be questioned, particularly those that render the subject uninteresting.

- Student Council is vital.
- Reduce student intake, as the school is overcrowded.
- Senior students need/require their own common room.
- A more personal attitude and approach to students is vital.

Structure of discipline

The question of punishment and strictness is one that I have reflected on during the past school year. While it is necessary to establish certain practices in the school, especially in relation to standards of behaviour, the emphasis was being placed on the aspect of control and students being corrected/punished for misbehaviour. No real learning with regard to acceptable behaviour seemed to be taking place.

During the period of my research, I set myself the action research question, 'How can I help to establish a behaviour system that would promote growth and development, in an open and caring environment?' (see my Reflection, p. 92 above). Other staff members supported and shared their concerns with me in conversations and group meetings. They saw the system as 'punitive' and 'impersonal', and wondered, 'What will happen when some student really does something wrong?' At a staff meeting during the school year 1994/95, some staff members felt that too many entries were being made in personal record books for trivial matters.

Even though we have a tutor/year head system, the whole area of discipline did not generally go via this structure; misdemeanours were generally routed directly to the vice-principal. Conversations with the vice-principal revealed that he chose this practice because of his own need to establish a firm disciplinary practice in the new school. Today, however, he sees the need to work through the tutor/year head system.

During the school year 1995/96 the energy level of the staff seemed to be drained by the disruptive behaviour of a few students in each year group. Following recommendations made by the staff, the year heads, principal and vice-principal introduced strategies for coping with this problem. Each teacher stated how the particular student behaved for them and this helped to build a profile of this student. Year heads and all staff members are actively involved in this ongoing work.

Parents

The school has an active Parents Council which works very closely with management in the interest of students and parents. Regular parent–teacher meetings are held. The school organises meetings for the parents of incoming first years prior to their arrival and within a few weeks of starting in the school. Meetings are also held to help parents make decisions with regard to the best option for their children, such as the choice between Transition Year and fifth year. The school is always willing to meet parents individually. The majority of parents would view the school as open and participative, and they avail themselves of this openness in making recommendations to us:

- to be more open with their children
- to treat them with greater respect
- to reconsider the punishment issued to those who break petty rules.

Summary

In this section I have presented and developed key aspects of the pastoral reality of our school. In reflecting on this reality I have become aware of some steps that must be taken if our main aim as educators is to be the development of a pastoral school, where staff and students experience holistic growth and development in an open, trusting manner.

Immediate issues include the following:

- Ongoing staff inservice education is essential.
- Student Council must be established and supported.
- Planning/meeting time must be organised for teachers involved in the pastoral care programme.
- The need to work at developing a whole-school approach to pastoral care.
- Coordinating academic and affective programmes within the school so that no aspect of development is overlooked or over-emphasised.

An issue that I would emphasise for schools entering an amalgamation is the need for clear structures that will help students to cope with and grow through the major changes involved in the amalgamation. This must be a priority for the school, especially in relation to senior students.

As previously stated, developing a pastoral school takes time. It takes continual openness, planning, implementation and reflection in order to transform pastoral values into the lived ethos of the school. I believe such a task presents a particularly difficult challenge within an amalgamated structure, where three existing schools come together, with their own particular ethos and structures. When the school begins life with a student population of over 800, without any established traditions, practices or ethos to support it, the task is of Herculean proportions. This is our challenge in Cashel Community School. We strive to meet it, and we look to the future.

My vision for the future

Let me reflect on my understanding of pastoral care – the creation of an open, caring environment, through which staff and students, both individually and collectively, experience holistic growth and development. I see this as an intrinsic element in the evolution of the pastoral care programme which we hope to develop in our school.

I would like to use 'holistic', 'growth' and 'development' as the key words. As an educator, my role is central to the formation of young minds and personalities. Playing an influential role in such tentative years suggests the need for dynamic skills in both planning and practice.

The young people in our care are the adults of tomorrow. They face the world of work, relationships, parenting and family life. Holistic growth and development, therefore, need to provide well-balanced young people with a value system that equips them to be the leaders of the future. To make this a reality, our schools must first and foremost be educationally sound, providing excellent teaching strategies and teachers for whom continuing professional learning is a priority. 'Well-qualified teachers and a worthwhile curriculum together with administrative support can be the basis for sound pastoral support' (Milner 1983: 45). My vision foresees a community of people in our school working together to create this situation.

First, continuing staff development is vital, as inservice work challenges and refreshes already established (and sometimes entrenched) ideas and techniques. My hope for the future of our school, still in its early formation, is that as a staff we develop a team spirit and a commitment that will carry and support us through the stress-filled hours which are part and parcel of our work. 'We need to remember that the feelings of staff in any organisation are crucial to its performance and success. They must be listened to, and pastoral care of staff is likely to be increasingly important' (Watkins 1990a: 4).

A second equally important factor influencing my future vision is parental participation and support. This area is one where I see great potential in Cashel Community School. I believe strongly in encouraging parents to take an active role in their children's education. Home–school liaison is a key to success in this area. School can easily become a more welcoming environment where communication and work with parents is ongoing, and goes beyond the day-to-day behaviour of their children. If parents feel alienated and unable to communicate with the school community, an air of suspicion and mystery develops. In order to gain parental cooperation, it is necessary to encourage familiarity. Vehicles for this include parent open days; parent–teacher meetings; availability of the pastoral care team; regular information; coffee mornings; an informative, caring school report system; adult education; and parent representation at formal levels within school life. 'Whatever method is used it is vital that the consultation be real – therefore preparation is necessary' (Monahan 1996: 16).

A third factor that I would like to develop is student participation in our school development. 'Involvement of students is crucial. Failure to make pastoral activities a joint enterprise between students and tutors deprives us of what may be the most potent agency for achieving pastoral aims' (Hamblin 1993: 3). While this is a difficult issue, we have to acknowledge that the relationship developed between teachers and students when planning and working together is a key factor. Student council, social liaison groups, senior and junior prefects, school shop assistants, sport leaders, school bankers and peer ministry all provide opportunities to encourage responsibility and leadership, thus giving students valuable insights into involvement in school life; such practices are pastorally rewarding. Values are established and matured, giving a positive sense of self-worth, confidence and belonging.

Summary

There are many other factors which I envisage as part of our future in developing a good working environment. Our school plan and future mission statement include our aims and objectives which are constantly developing, and each day we strive to put our goals into practice.

In my opinion our school environment is one which must cater for all aspects of our students' lives. Our pastoral concern must set out to strengthen their self-concept. 'Pupils must be treated with respect as persons. They should be accorded worth equal with adults but accepted as being at a different stage of learning and experience' (Nuttall 1988: 5). Our school must provide a network of social support and our students must be able to participate in learning in school life, developing their own values and morals.

The recent White Paper on Education (Government of Ireland 1995) provides a comprehensive outline of what our educational directives should include, promoting throughout the pastoral support of the young people in our care. It must always be remembered that '[w]e are all personalities that grow and develop as a result of all our experiences, relationships, thoughts and emotions. We are the sum total of all the parts that go into the making of a life' (Axline 1990: 194).

Conclusion

As I write my conclusion, my vision for the future is more than positive, yet realistic. Never before has the educational system been so aware of the potential benefits of caring for young vulnerable people as they struggle in their preparation for adulthood, the world of work and indeed their changing selves; nor so aware of the problematics involved. While the prize is indeed valuable, the journey to achieve it is difficult and long. If we are to realise the vision espoused by the White Paper and current educational policy objectives, we need to develop pastoral structures for community welfare and social evolution. Pastoral care is not only for students, but also for teachers, parents and other partners who support them.

I consider myself in a privileged position in belonging to a caring community whose story is told in this account. There must of course be content to our care: it must be embedded within, and permeate, professional systematic work where students feel that they are making personal and academic progress, achieving in various dimensions and being catered for in their many needs. Schools can provide the ideal environment to bring out the best in young people and develop their potential to the fullest. However, all the partners must work together, with conscious intent, towards providing this environment. We always need to remember that '[a]dolescence is a period of identity formation. In pursuit of this identity, the adolescent moves from the security of childhood towards the newly envisioned freedom that the world of the adult seems to represent' (Sexton 1991: 9).

Let me once again reinforce the need for ongoing staff development. If we the professional carers of young people are to be healthy adult role models and the facilitators of their development, it is of paramount importance that we ourselves engage in our own continuing professional learning. Pastoral care is not a 'subject' or an 'outcome'. It is a lived process through which all participants aim to live out their values of care in their practice. I re-confirm my belief that pastoral care in our schools, at individual and systemic levels, is central, so that all members of a school community can attain their human potential, that which is God given.

> Glory be to him whose power, working in us, can do infinitely more than we can ask or imagine.
> (Ephesians 3:20, The Jerusalem Bible 1968: 248)

8

SIR! SIR!

(or: How can I enable the self-image of my tutor group to be raised, the staff's perception of them to be improved, and my own understanding of my professional role to be enhanced?)

Aidan O'Reilly

Reflection

For me, teaching was becoming routine and uninspiring. I regarded myself as a purveyor of information: one who set good academic standards and managed the classroom effectively. After twenty-three years I felt that I could write the definitive book on what teaching was really all about. It would be a very short book. Or so I thought.

As I began to write the story of 2W, I realised there was a lot I did not understand about my students and my relationship with them. Now, through sharing their worries and joys and mediating between their learning and their lives, I learned that teaching is the most noble of all the professions, because it is about human beings and their search for understanding.

My attempts to make school happier for 2W opened up larger questions about the nature of effective schools, the curriculum, management structures, the role of parents and many more. A sense of urgency to explore these issues arose out of reflecting on my work with 2W. Four years later, I am still studying.

Research of this nature enriches the participants enormously as they engage with the questions. Those questions are the ones which define our everyday professional lives and the lives of our students. They probe not just our actions, but also our motives. A new consciousness, or virtue, emerges gradually in our daily practice, a sense of humility as we regard our own efforts and a sense of pride at being part of such a glorious undertaking. In my case, this has been realised in a whole new appreciation of the young people I teach.

This research has changed me, not dramatically, but slowly, imperceptibly, over a period of years. As a means of in-career development it has been hugely effective because I controlled my own input, made my own decisions and evaluated the outcome myself. It has affected the pastoral work in my school in a mould-breaking way and encouraged other tutors to attempt similar undertakings.

Of course there is a sequel to the story of 2W. The protagonists have each moved on to take up various interesting roles in life. They still keep in touch. But they left behind a changed, improved, happier teacher – one for whom the story goes on.

Introduction

Why am I a teacher?

In 1992, I would never have thought of asking myself that question. If I had, the answer would have been something smart, even dismissive.

As a teacher of Honours English and Music I had the most marvellous tools to work with. Year in, year out the awed faces sat before me, entranced, bewitched as I led them to encounter the greatest literary and musical creations of the human mind.

To me, the criterion which really mattered at the end of the day was the exam result. After twenty-three years school life was becoming routine. I was beginning to detect a lack of challenge in my work. Teaching, for me, was a one-way transmission of knowledge from me to 'them'. For years I had regarded 'them' as a great amorphous group with few distinguishing or individual characteristics. I had failed to recognise the uniqueness in each pupil who sat before me.

My concern

My primary concern was with my own unsatisfactory understanding of my role as a teacher. I discussed this with our principal, Brother O'Flaherty, on a number of occasions. He saw that encouraging the professional development of his staff was an intrinsic part of his role as principal. He suggested that I apply for a place on the one-year Higher Diploma Course in Pastoral Care, commencing September 1993. In this way, our interests coincided. He was anxious to introduce pastoral care into the school and I saw pastoral care as a means of professional enhancement.

We agreed that, in September 1993, we would introduce a structured form of pastoral care to first and second years, and I would be pastoral care coordinator.

But one major difficulty arose. Brother O'Flaherty was transferred to take up duty as principal elsewhere. Thankfully, the new principal was one of our own. Oliver Maher was a popular choice for the post and we all looked forward to working with him.

Our next task was to assign tutors to the incoming first years and to those who were about to become our second years. Each year had three divisions based on subject choice. A shortlist of six teachers as our first tutor team for the pastoral care system was drawn up. I asked specially to become tutor to one particular class – 2W.

Why 2W?

The nomenclature may be misleading. The 'W' refers to 'Woodwork', that being their subject option within the blocking system. Although the school no longer operated a policy of strict streaming, it can happen in the best regulated enterprises that you sometimes end up with what you have made a deliberate effort to avoid. So it was with 2W. I had never taught them as a group, although four of them were in my music class. While I could name only a handful of the 2W class, I certainly had no difficulty in either hearing them or hearing about them. As 1W, they had established a reputation as an unruly, ill-disciplined lot. Staffroom stories about them were legion.

I did not get to meet them as a class until towards the end of their first notorious year in the school. On the last day of the summer tests I was assigned to supervise them in a classroom.

I could not believe it. Some were standing on desks while two were involved in a boisterous wrestling match, being cheered on even more boisterously by a small but raucous crowd. One small chap was in the corner by the dustbin, slowly shredding what appeared to be a geography textbook. A portly boy sat on the floor near the teacher's desk, contentedly chewing gum while he carved some message on the leg of the table.

They were a small class, actually, only eighteen, but they looked like thousands. I called for order. Nobody took any notice. I called again. A few curious heads were turned in my direction, but otherwise they continued with their nefarious activities. I could feel my temper starting to slip. Next time, I roared. That got the desired effect.

I began to distribute the question papers once I had managed to establish a modicum of silence, because somebody, somewhere in the room, continued to make a low groaning sound. I ignored this and went ahead with the distribution of the papers, anxious always to maintain the integrity of the summer tests. I returned to the front of the room and turned to face the class. The subject being examined was maths.

Suddenly a boy on my right shouted across the room, 'Hey, Matt! I know how to do the first one.' Matt called back, 'I'll show you how to do number four.' Conversation erupted all over the room. Then some of them stood up and walked over to talk to others. I was stunned.

I counted softly to myself. Then I roared. They liked that. They sat down. But not for long. A few minutes later, the same procedure began again. This time I was not going to be so nice. I took one culprit by the arm and stood him by the wall. This caused uproar. They all wanted to stand by the wall. I agreed – and they all did their test standing up.

Before the test ended ninety minutes later I had sent two of the boys up to the principal's office for copying. Both had been sent home, much to their delight, I understand. The 'test' was a complete sham. I thought wistfully of Ken Kesey's novel *One Flew Over The Cuckoo's Nest*.

This was my first encounter with 1W. I was to be their tutor. Would it be good for me? Would it be good for them? Would we survive each other for four years? I had asked to be tutor to this group because I felt that it would be challenging for me. I needed to prove to myself that there was more to teaching than the mere transmission of information. I believed that these boys would show me the difference between being a teacher and an educator.

The voyage had begun.

The situation

My return to school after the summer holidays was delayed by minor surgery until Monday 27 September. Casual enquiries about 2W elicited the same responses as last year – 'awful', 'unmanageable', 'can't teach them anything'. It is important to remember that I was only going to meet 2W once a week in a formal classroom setting for the assigned Pastoral Care class.

The above remarks horrified me. Was the problem simply 2W's, or did the staff's understanding of them need adjusting? I decided that the staff probably did not know how to handle 2W.

My first Pastoral Care class with 2W was on Wednesday afternoon, 29 September. They came charging through the door of my classroom rather like a pack of baying hounds. But their 'baying' was not threatening or intimidating, even though they strayed around the room chatting, sometimes shouting, playing the piano, trying to get Atlantic 252 on the stereo and greeting me loudly. They were enjoying themselves.

Feeling the familiar pangs of irritation, I tried my old trick of standing silently and staring, waiting for them to be seated. It did not work – their problem, as always, was a revulsion towards desks and sitting still. Eventually I walked slowly to the back of the room. They stopped what they were doing and watched as I leaned my head against the wall. Anxiously, they grouped around me, asking if I was all right. 'How could I be all right?' I said. 'With all this shouting and movement, I feel very unhappy.'

A voice from somewhere said, 'All right, lads. Come on, let's sit down.' And they did. Not in the desks, mind you, more on top of them. One boy sat at my desk at the top of the class. I asked him if he liked sitting up there. He said he did, so I told him that he could stay there. This was Cyril R.

I told them that this was a very special day for all of us. Our aim was simple: to make 2W the most popular, most successful class in the school. This little speech was greeted by cheers – no negative reactions; at least they were not cynics.

I asked them what they would like to do during the year. They wanted plenty of sport, craic [fun], and doing things together. Clearly bonding was not going to be a major problem here. I asked them what they thought of the school and they told me it was 'OK, sir, but too much homework'. I knew that they were not academically inclined.

This group had several striking features that were new to me – a zest for life, a boundless energy and an obvious loyalty to each other. These qualities were not always so apparent in the studious Honours English classes which I was used to teaching. The fact that 2W were causing disciplinary headaches for their teachers suggested that they needed some personal attention. I felt that they needed to be addressed as individuals rather than an amorphous group. I decided that I would like to meet them individually and perhaps discover for myself what it was like to be a hyperactive teenager in 1993; so I set aside my free classes on three days a week during October.

Among the group were:

- Andrew C, tall, gangly, eager to chat. Loved soccer, Heavy Metal, school, even his younger sister. An uncomplicated young man, I thought.
- Jim K, the brightest in the class by far. Relaxed, in control of himself, he told of his home life with a riveting candour – riveting, because of the horror of that story. His father's suspended sentence for incest was due for review shortly. Jim was terrified that his Dad would be sent to prison. He worshipped this evil man.
- Cyril R had been 'grounded' by his father since the previous August. He was alleged to have burnt down a hayshed near the soccer pitch where he spent most of his waking hours. A file was being prepared for the Director of Public Prosecutions. Cyril was only allowed out of his room for his meals and for three hours on a Sunday afternoon. He suffered from alarming moodswings.
- Gene T came from a hard-working family who lived in a local council estate. Surly, suspicious and defensive, he would snap back accusingly when asked the most innocent of questions.
- Donal M also lived in a council estate. He was knocked down by a car in 1988, following which he spent a long time in hospitals being treated for brain damage. He suffered from depression and moodswings, seemed very introverted but loved repairing bicycles.
- Matt and John H were twins. Two of their sisters had had babies recently, so there were now eleven people living in the two-bedroomed cottage.
- Ger N sat alone at the back of the class, continually interrupting the discussion with arrogant, cynical remarks about the views of others. I got the clear impression that the others were intimidated by him. He also looked older than his classmates – he could have passed for nineteen or twenty. When I interviewed him, I found him utterly charming. He had various ideas for the class and offered to help in whatever way he could. He was quite ingratiating. A new arrival in the class, he had spent first year in the nearby Vocational School, 'but the teachers were no good, sir, so I came over to the Brothers'. All very plausible.

I must emphasise that the above boys were not typical of the class. There were eleven other boys in the group, each of whom seemed to be reasonably well-adjusted. With the exception of Jim K, none of the class was academically gifted.

I felt after my first encounter with them that their main preoccupation was with immediate events, the here-and-now. They lacked the ability to see beyond four o'clock. Some of them, of course, did not want to think about life after four o'clock. Each of them told me that he liked school, but hated school-work! Perhaps there was a clue in that statement.

6 October 1993: each class has its own Sixth Year prefect, so I decided to bring along 2W's prefect, Tadgh, to our Pastoral Care class. Tadgh and I had talked about organising a soccer league so that the class would do something together. When we put this idea to the class, the enthusiasm was enormous. Even Ger N was supportive, but in a strangely strident way. His enthusiasm was so overpowering that he engineered himself into being elected captain.

Then I suggested an outing. From themselves came the idea of a trip to a soccer match at Old Trafford, the home of Manchester United. I agreed to look into it, with some trepidation. I was enjoying their enthusiasm and zest for life. I was beginning to find 'fun' in teaching. At least, one of the teacher's needs was being met.

The situation develops

On 18 October I met with our principal, Oliver, to discuss progress in 2W. He had not received any complaints about them since mid-September and he felt that they 'seemed to be coming along very well'. I was elated.

This elation was short lived. We had just got a substitute science teacher, Mary G, for the year. She said that she was having to spend far too much time correcting 2W. If their disruptive behaviour continued she would be unable to complete the syllabus.

On the same day, the geography teacher, Tim F, told me that he was finding 2W 'unteachable'. 'They shout, they roar, they won't sit down. They give cheek, back-answers and their language is foul.' Tim has been teaching for almost twenty years and is also our school's Guidance Counsellor.

On Wednesday, 20 October, I heard that the soccer league had collapsed. Most of those who had expressed enthusiasm had failed to turn up. Various reasons were provided – 'the rain, sir', 'we had a late dinner, sir', 'my bike is punctured, sir'. However, there was no question of the class accepting collective blame for the collapse of the league. There was a general strong feeling that one member was responsible. 'Cyril wants to run everything – he won't agree with anybody.' General disorder followed, and, as the class ended, I felt a sense of failure and despair.

On the next day, Thursday, Tim F came to me during lunchtime. He was desperate. He said that teaching geography to 2W was 'a constant battle'. 'In fact,' he said, 'it's a complete waste of time.' Not only was homework not being done, but four of the class still had not got the textbook and they were refusing to get it. Talking out of turn, leaving their desks and hurling abuse at each other with comments like 'your mother's a whore' were commonplace. I asked for names. Cyril R, Gene T, Donal M and Ger N seemed to be the ringleaders. Donal M had a particular penchant for remarks with sexual overtones. Tim was very distressed. 'Is it me, I wonder?' he said.

What could I do?

It was now the Hallowe'en break and time for some serious assessment of the situation and the students' needs. I devised a questionnaire which I worked on with the class on Wednesday 3 November. This was to find out how they felt about each other and the level of responsibility shown by class members. The results were interesting.

Jim K turned out to be the most respected member of the class by far. Jim is good academically and, although his father had recently been sent to prison (the rest of the class thought it was for paramilitary activity), he was handling the situation with great composure. Another positive feature was the concern that they all showed for the quietest member of the class, Kevin M. They felt he 'needed a friend'.

However, everybody expressed unhappiness and stress at the level of 'messing about' in the class, and all agreed that it was caused by only a few. I detected a strong sense of genuine fear of Ger N on the part of several members. My overall impression was of a group of students who wanted to succeed at school; they showed qualities of human goodness and caring and they wanted order in their lives. They really wanted to be able to achieve something that was within their capabilities.

It was time to talk to the teachers.

Action plan 1

From my assessment of 2W, I felt that they were being denied appropriate opportunities for learning to become adults. This was borne out when I conducted a second questionnaire with the class on Wednesday 10 November. I asked them to write out their answers to two questions:

- How would you like your teachers to treat you?
- What qualities do you like in a teacher?

There was general agreement that they did not like teachers shouting. They felt overburdened with homework, not to mention all the extra homework which they were given as punishment. They had an acute awareness of their own inability to complete tasks, or so they perceived themselves. Their self-esteem was very low.

They all cried out for 'fairness' in class. All wanted teachers to speak slowly and to repeat the information. They said that they wanted 'respect' and not to be 'treated like dirt'. Interestingly, several mentioned that they liked their teacher to be well-dressed – a favourite theory of my own.

Thus, the focus of Action Plan 1 was going to be the teachers of 2W. I would speak to each one of their ten teachers informally, individually and 'by accident'. I wanted to find out the different approaches being used and why some teachers appeared to have no difficulty with 2W while others were almost at the end of their professional tethers.

I wanted to keep our principal, Oliver, fully informed about what I was attempting. As my 'critical friend' he was very interested in the approach which I was taking and, as principal, he hoped that the results would be beneficial to the school as a whole.

I asked the same basic questions of each teacher:

1   How are you getting on with 2W?
2   Who do you think are the trouble-makers?
3   How do you deal with the difficult pupils?
4   Do you give much homework?

On Friday 12 November I managed to talk to four teachers individually.

Sean D taught Irish to 2W. He was getting on quite well with them by 'keeping a firm hand on the trouble-makers'. These he identified as Cyril R, Gene T, Donal M and Ger N in particular.

Dan Q was 2W's history teacher. He had no problems with 2W that he could not handle. He mentioned the same names as being responsible for disturbances during class. He was particularly concerned about Cyril R. 'That child is very disturbed,' he said.

Ann H is a young, enthusiastic teacher with a most cheerful disposition. She taught maths to twelve of the class. The other six were receiving special maths lessons from another teacher. Ann had 'absolutely no problem' with 2W. In fact, she 'enjoyed teaching them'. I was really curious. What was the secret of her success? 'I laugh with them,' she said. 'I listen to their stories and their complaints. I let them unpack their hang-ups when they come into class and then we can get to work and I never lose my temper with them.'

The six students who were in the special maths class were, by coincidence, equally fortunate in their teacher, Edel H. A good-humoured, happy young woman, she had great empathy with the students. Among her six were the 'trouble-makers'. They told her everything that came into their heads. She listened and sympathised. She offered encouragement and hope to them. She met them at their own level and gently brought them onwards. When I asked her what she thought of them, she said quietly, 'Ah, sure, I like them.' All of 2W loved their maths classes and all of them were making some progress in this area.

Mary G felt that she was not getting anywhere. 'I seem to spend the entire forty minutes shouting and I dread to see them coming in,' she said. Jim B, Martin S and Liam D each saw Ger as a baleful influence. Tom C agreed that perhaps Cyril needed 'psychiatric attention'. Donal M had taunted Tim with remarks like: 'You're no good as a geography teacher' or 'I haven't got my homework done for you again today.' Tim was deeply upset. 'It's total chaos in there,' he said.

I studied the notes I had taken after each teacher-meeting. During the following weekend, I also read through the letters which I had asked 2W to write to me during our Pastoral Care class the previous Wednesday, 17 November.

But all that weekend I was preoccupied with a small incident which had occurred on the Wednesday evening. I had stayed on late in the staffroom talking to the principal, Oliver, mainly about 2W. He felt that they were responding to the fact that someone was genuinely interested in them and they were displaying a more positive attitude to school life. I was very pleased. I left the staffroom at about 4.45 p.m. to head home. On my way out of the building I noticed a student sitting in an empty classroom. It was Cyril R, doing his homework. I asked him why he was there and he replied: 'I like to stay on here till the school closes. If I go home, I just get told to go to my room and not to come out till suppertime. It's nicer here.' I was deeply concerned for him.

Back to the student questionnaires. I had put the following on the board:

Dear Mr O'Reilly,

When the lads in the class don't listen to me I feel . . .
When the teachers don't listen to me I feel . . .

The letters, poorly written, all displayed a great deal of frustration, both with their classmates and with their teachers. Comments included:

I feel that there is no point in coming to school because you can't learn with everyone shouting.

I feel that the teachers can't keep control of the class.

I get very annoyed with the teacher.

I could now read the situation as follows: a small group of the class were bringing the wounds of their dysfunctional backgrounds into the school. They sought attention and affirmation using the only means which they thought were available to them, disrupting the learning process for others. By challenging the teachers they sought to raise their status among their peers. The use of manipulative tactics by Ger N, however, was more sinister.

From the interviews with the teachers, I concluded that there were really only two colleagues who needed support – Mary G and Tim F. I met both of them, separately, on the following Monday, 22 November, and suggested that each forget about the syllabus for a while and try a more experiential approach.

However, on Friday, 26 November, a rather significant incident occurred. A new, young lady teacher had arrived in September and she was breaking hearts throughout the school. A highly effective teacher and a positive adjunct to the staff, especially in the area of Pastoral Care, she was clearly very popular with the students, not least because she was the trainer of the junior football team who were enjoying a series of successes. She was not teaching 2W, unfortunately. Apparently, however, certain members of 2W had whistled admiringly at her as she crossed the yard that Friday morning. She, of course, ignored them, but the incident was spotted by 2W's incoming teacher, Ann H. Ann made it clear to them how offensive such whistling was to a young woman and they talked about it. Later in the morning, during their woodwork class, a representative number of the class asked if they could go and see the new teacher. They met her outside her classroom and apologised sincerely. The spokesman was the principal whistler, Gene T. When Ann told me this I was elated. They were showing a sense of care for others as well as learning a valuable lesson about being adult.

Evaluation – step 1

On Wednesday 1 December, I met with a more relaxed 2W. As they came into my classroom John H said, 'Good week so far, sir.' I was not sure whether this was a statement or an enquiry about my health, but I was hopeful. I threw out some questions for discussion, such as, 'Now that we're getting near the end of term, how do you feel the class is going?' The responses were quite positive: 'I think the class is getting better'; 'We're all getting on great at science, doing experiments and everything'; 'Geography is boring'; 'The messing about isn't as bad as it was.' 'I got 86 per cent in science this week,' said Cyril. 'Some of the lads are being let away with murder in geography,' said Jim.

I had decided to use a working paper from Leslie Button's 'Group Tutoring' entitled 'Progress with lessons – first self-assessment'. The results were more positive than I had expected. The sense of frustration, of lacking control had dissipated somewhat since their letters to me on 17 November.

The reports gave me hope that, perhaps, the situation was improving. I knew, however, that it was not going to be resolved so simply. Clearly Mary G was making a supreme effort to change her methods and to enthuse the boys. I spoke to her on Friday 3 December and she was more relaxed. 'I'm hardly teaching them anything,' she said, 'but the class is a great deal more manageable. They seem to enjoy doing all the experiments but I don't know how long I can keep this up for. I have to cover the course.' I urged her to conduct a 'holding action' for as long as she thought possible. Once she had them on her side, she could then resume her course work, but should be prepared to change back again as the need arose.

I met with Tim F for our customary Monday morning coffee on 6 December. My casual enquiry about 2W's progress was unnecessary – he could talk about nothing else. My journal contains the word 'trapped' as describing Tim's situation. He was trapped by his age, his social background and his lack of professional learning. He was unable to manifest his great qualities of caring and understanding within the confines of a classroom. He performed best in a one-to-one situation. He was genuinely trying to alter his teaching methods to accommodate the difficulties of 2W but he was failing. The textbook was his salvation and without it he was lost.

I was beginning to see a change in my own role at this point. Earlier I would have compared myself to a fireman on continuous emergency duty, only managing to contain the situation. Now I felt that I was more in control.

Action plan 2

As I said before, the boys had indicated that they would like to go on an organised outing to a soccer match. I had agreed to look into this for a number of reasons:

1   I felt that they needed a project that would help them to identify more closely with the school.
2   One of the strengths of the class was their loyalty to each other and I hoped to build on this.
3   I was keen to get to know these boys better – they would educate me.

On 6 October we discussed the feasibility of such a trip. The boys were almost unanimous on two points:

1   Everybody in the class would participate.
2   We would go to Old Trafford to see Manchester United play.

Cyril was the most vocal proponent of the whole idea. He was also a most vocal supporter of Man. United. Ger said that he had an uncle who could get us tickets. I asked Cyril to bring in all the information that he had and Ger promised to speak to his uncle who phoned regularly from London.

Cyril was most prompt in getting all the data that we needed. Unasked, he wrote to Old Trafford, told them of our plans and received lots of literature but not much hope of getting match tickets. Ger seemed to me to be rather tardy in making contact with his uncle. Each time I met him he always had an excuse – the uncle had not phoned or, if he had, Ger was not at home when he called. By 23 November, four weeks later, I had endured enough of Ger's delaying tactics. A travel agent friend in Dublin said that tickets for Trafford were simply not available but he offered to arrange a trip to Liverpool for £64. We would be able to see Liverpool play Chelsea on 19 March.

Cyril's unbounded enthusiasm for the tour, despite being an ardent Man. United supporter, could, I felt, have a positive influence. I decided to appoint him as our treasurer. I realised that there was an element of risk in this but I was confident that he would relish the responsibility. With previous tours, I had managed the funds myself. For the first time, I was learning to delegate. I went ahead and booked nineteen seats for the match at Anfield.

Immediately after the Christmas holidays we had a series of discipline problems. On 10 January Donal M went berserk in the science room and was suspended for three days as well as having to pay damages of £55. Donal had been sitting beside Ger during science class.

The next day I was summoned from class to deal with Gene T who had called Mr B 'a f***ing eejit' during computer class. I put him on report. He lives next door to Ger N.

The following day, Wednesday, I was summoned to Tim F's geography class, where an abusive tirade, apparently orchestrated, had begun as soon as he had asked them to open their books. Tim could not say if Ger had had anything to do with the disturbances – he was sitting alone at the back.

The collection of money for the tour continued apace. Cyril was most diligent but he told me that he felt some of the class were not going to travel. I pointed out that the trip was entirely optional. He indicated that somebody was working against us. Apparently a rumour was going around the class that Cyril and I were making money on this trip. Also it was being said that the £64 fare was only the beginning of the cost. England was reported to be a hugely expensive place: you could not get a bag of chips for under £2, or so Ger said.

I decided it was time to have a chat with Ger. I met him on Friday 22 January in the interview room.

Ger told me that all the teachers were liars and that the principal was out 'to get him'. I asked how his parents felt about the possibility of him being suspended. 'They know that I'm being blamed,' he said. 'It's the other lads in the class.' He said that the only real friends he had were myself and the Juvenile Liaison Officer, who was 'trying to get me off the court case' (an allegation of burglary from a neighbour's house). I was learning that here was a case that was completely outside my competence. If the Health Board psychologist who was dealing with him could not effect any improvement, I did not see how I could be expected to achieve anything. My concern was the well-being of my tutor group and this boy was causing severe difficulties for his classmates. He told me that he would not be able to get the money for the trip. I accepted this, not without relief, I must admit. He did agree, however, that he would not do or say anything which might cause further problems for the tour. 'Sure I wouldn't do anything that would cause you trouble, sir,' he said.

Evaluation of action plan 1

I continued evaluating the effectiveness of my 'teacher-chats' and arranged a meeting of all 2W teachers during lunchtime on Tuesday 8 February. Overall, the feeling was that there was some hope for the class but that Ger N's position needed to be monitored very closely and his exclusion from the school considered. 'They're all terrified of him,' said Tom C.

I learned a great deal at this meeting:

1 Teachers were now talking about students as unique individuals. They seemed to see the class as a composition of different personalities rather than as an amorphous group. In general they spoke about the pupils with respect and with affection. This marked a change from the dogmatic 'them and us' attitude which had characterised our school for so long.

2 Just as students have a very distinct need to live out their student role, so also do teachers need to be fulfilled in the teacher role. When teachers are frustrated in their search for professional fulfilment they sometimes take out their resentment on their students.

3 The personality of the teacher as presented in the classroom is more important than their grasp of the subject material. Qualities such as patience, good humour and a sense of fair play can create a much more effective learning environment than a rigid adherence to the syllabus.

4 Although I could advise my colleagues on possible approaches to handling 2W, I could not go into each class to monitor progress and to see if my advice was effective. It was, in the end, up to each teacher to establish their own ethos within the classroom.

Action Plan 1 was certainly not the final answer.

The tour

The month preceding the tour was marked by 2W's now familiar behaviour patterns of 'highs' and depressing 'lows'. Ger had been suspended on 9 February for insolence to the principal. The class was relieved and no problems were reported until his return on 23 February. The principal was now dealing directly with Ger's parents.

Cyril continued his enthusiastic and merciless collecting of outstanding monies from the tour participants. He was highly effective in this role. His excitement was palpable as the day for departure, Friday 18 March, approached. The other group members were also very excited, especially at the three preparatory meetings which I held in the weeks beforehand. But on Tuesday 1 March we had a near disaster. I was teaching my Leaving Cert. English class when a knock came at my door. It was Cyril, looking distraught. 'I'm not going home ever again,' he wailed. Through his tears he told me how his father had beaten him during lunchtime. There were lacerations on his face and bruising on his neck. The principal was away that afternoon. I put Cyril in a small interview room and looked after him, while trying to sustain my teaching. At 4 p.m. he still was not going home. I said that I would drive him home, but he refused to let me drive him to the front door. Again I was confronted with my woeful ignorance of procedures in these cases.

A cheerful, ebullient group packed into a minibus outside the school on the evening of Friday 18 March. As we drove slowly out of town, Gene T reached forward and tapped me on the shoulder. 'Sir,' he said, 'now that we're not in school, can I call you Aidan?' 'No problem,' I replied. 'Just put "Sir" in front of it.' He pondered this for a while.

They seemed to have inexhaustible energy. Every corner of the Sealink ferry was explored and photographed, card games were played and good humour and *bonhomie* prevailed. They were extremely well behaved, not loud or intrusive. During the night, I had some interesting chats with several of them either out on deck or in the quiet of the lounge.

I tried to hide my irritation at the size of the small bus awaiting us at Holyhead, but the boys did not complain. They had a few hours sleep until we arrived in Liverpool at 7.30 a.m. The shops still were not open so I took them to see the magnificent Liverpool Cathedral with the city spread out beneath them. Then it was time to explore the shops and the rejuvenated Docks area. It was at this point, in a crowded shopping arcade, that I heard the inimitable piping shout of Gene T calling to me from somewhere in the crowds: 'Sir Aidan! Sir Aidan!' As he ran to me to show an innocuous souvenir he had bought, I detected obsequious glances amongst the crowd at discovering that they had, in their midst, a Knight of the Realm.

We were at Anfield at 11.30 a.m. to see the team arrive and all the boys got lots of autographs and some even had their photographs taken with their heroes. Then it was on to lunch at the Liverpool Supporters Club where we had a superb welcome thanks to arrangements made by a Kilkenny friend of mine.

My knowledge of soccer is not extensive. However, the atmosphere of total excitement at Anfield that afternoon was overpowering. We had very good seats at the sideline and from there we could be swept up in the fervour, the emotion and the tradition of the splendid pageantry which surrounded us. And the match was marvellous too, with Liverpool beating Chelsea 2–1. The boys were ecstatic. Even confirmed Man. United supporters like Cyril voted it the best match they had ever seen.

Bowling and ice-skating occupied the boys heartily until 10.30 p.m. at Deeside Leisure Centre. We arrived in Dun Laoghaire at 5.30 a.m., very, very tired. It was a subdued bunch of boys that I saw off the bus on our arrival back at the school. But they were very happy, filled with stories and memories that they would never forget.

And I had enjoyed it, too.

Evaluation of action plan 2

By Wednesday 23 March I was able to write the following in my journal:

> After the weekend trip to Liverpool, the fall-out has been most positive. All of the teachers, and I mean all, say that the trip appears to have had a most positive effect on the class's attitude to what school-life is all about.

That afternoon we had our Pastoral Care class. My journal describes 'a bunch of "feel-good" kids'. Several of the boys had brought in their photos from the trip. Ger sat alone at the back, cleaning his nails. The only remark he made was to the effect that he had seen Donal M with a girl up against the wall at lunchtime. Donal denied it, but I had seen him from the staffroom window, behaving quite outrageously with his willing female accomplice.

Thus the tour was an immense success from several points:

1 It established a greater sense of identity between the boys and the school.
2 They now seemed to understand that school-life had other aspects to it apart from book-learning and making friends.
3 They felt that they were being supported in their efforts to become adults.
4 They were beginning to see that authority figures, that is, teachers, were not committed simply to being in control but were willing to share responsibility.
5 Shared experiences always deepen a relationship. I could see this developing almost immediately on our return as a new openness appeared between these boys and myself.

I was concerned, however, as to the permanence of these effects. How was I to sustain the momentum which had been created?

The final term

On the last day of the spring term I had had a long chat with Tim, the troubled geography teacher and also our Guidance Counsellor. According to Tim, Cyril R was now a changed child. He participated well in class, his work was improving and he presented no behavioural problems. Other teachers made the same points to me during the week. Tim concluded that Ger was the 'puppet-master' in the class. 'He directs all the interaction and it is directed back at him,' he said. 'He manipulates the others, especially Andrew C and Donal M.' As we embarked on the last term, this assessment became painfully clear.

On 11 April, the first day back at school, I put Andrew on report for using foul language during Mary G's science class. This was the beginning of a disciplinary saga which was to last for the next five weeks. The principal culprits were always the same – Donal, Gene and, in the background, Ger.

In February I had written to Donal's parents and arranged for them to visit the school on Tuesday 1 March. I felt that they were well-meaning but not very competent parents. They did not seem to know where Donal spent his free time. 'Sure, Donal spends all night watching the television,' said Mrs M. 'Yes. He loves the television,' agreed Mr M.

I arranged for either of the parents to call to see me every Wednesday from then on. I hoped that Donal would respond to the fact that he was being monitored. But Donal's father only came to see me once after the first interview. On that occasion he had seemed to be in a hurry. Donal's catalogue of misdeeds was no longer tolerable and he was suspended on Monday 25 April. His parents did not appear at the school until Wednesday 4 May, when they were summoned by the principal.

Ger was now treating the school as a 'drop-in' centre. He would regularly disappear during the day – 'forgot a book, sir'. When challenged by the principal he was not averse to telling Oliver to 'F*** off'. His mother wrote to the school saying that she had been advised to take legal action against the school for harassment of her son.

As the term wore on I began to feel that each day was littered with crises which seemed to feature only two students – Ger and Donal.

Deep down I was beginning to feel that I had failed.

During May we distribute re-application forms to all the students. Oliver called me to the office on the morning of Tuesday 10 May. He told me that he did not propose to give re-application forms to either Ger or Donal. I feel now that, as their tutor, I should probably have protested on their behalf but I was weary of it all. I was convinced that our school did not have the resources or specialised personnel to cope with these two boys and their very demanding needs.

I distributed the forms that afternoon. Nobody was absent, unusually. I called out each boy's name and handed him his form to bring home. When I had finished there was a stunned silence as they realised that two boys had not received forms. 'Where's mine?' said Ger. 'I don't appear to have been given one for you, Ger,' I said. 'Well, the principal will hear a lot more about this from my mother,' said Ger. Donal called out: 'I don't want one, anyway. I'm going to a school next year where there's girls.'

We had no more crises in the declining weeks.

While I was chatting to our principal, Oliver, on Tuesday 24 May he remarked that 2W had 'come a long way since September'. He said that he had had to deal with fewer discipline problems from that class than from any of the second or third year classes.

During our last Pastoral Care class on 25 May, Jim K made a perceptive comment: 'You know, sir, the best class we had with you all year was the day you didn't give the re-application forms to the two boys.'

Outcomes

I completed another questionnaire with them on Wednesday 25 May. This was a self-assessment taken from Leslie Button's 'Group Tutoring'. It dealt with academic progress and should be compared with a similar questionnaire completed on 1 December 1993.

By 25 May, they appeared to have a more positive attitude to schoolwork than in the previous December. They now seemed to know that it was important to do as well as you can in school. Their ambitions, however, were stymied by several factors:

1   general feelings of inadequacy when confronted with 'book-learning'
2   misbehaviour by classmates
3   unsympathetic teaching.

I would also suspect that home backgrounds have influence.

On 7 June I returned to school to write in my comments on 2W's summer reports. I was agreeably surprised. With the notable exceptions of Ger and Donal, all the reports were highly satisfactory. Teachers were generous in their praise of each boy and sixteen of the eighteen students must have been very pleased when they received their reports.

Conclusions

Action plan 1 involved me speaking privately to each of the teachers of 2W. Teachers altered their methods, but only briefly. Within a few weeks they were again using the techniques which had failed earlier and classroom outbursts became the norm once again. The teachers were prisoners of their textbooks and syllabi.

There is an enormous cultural chasm between most of our teachers and their students. This seemingly unbridgeable gap can be brought within tolerable limits by teachers developing an interest in, and respect for, the world which their pupils inhabit. This does not have to be a patronising interest – just a simple awareness and acknowledgement of that different world.

Action plan 2, the trip to Liverpool, succeeded briefly in that it showed that when the pupils are happy in school, they will achieve. The difficulty is always to maintain the momentum which has been created.

Despite the great vision in the new Junior Certificate syllabus, it is still too book-orientated for the weaker pupil. I feel that there should be greater flexibility in the curriculum and even more emphasis on experiential learning for those who are not academically gifted.

A danger for the pastoral care teacher is that they may become too involved in the lives of the pupils. I found as early as November that I was allowing myself, unwittingly, to be drawn very closely into their lives. Disengagement is easier said than done and it requires a supreme effort to achieve it without arriving at an opposing position of callousness. My wife also works in pastoral areas in her school. 'Are we living to work, or are we working to live?' my wife asked one March evening. We seemed to be consumed with school. We began a process of mutual control which helped us through the remainder of the year. Both of us are still learning. Home is home; school is school.

Recommendations

I now know that it was a mistake to be timetabled with 2W only once a week. It is essential that the tutor have regular and frequent contact with the class.

Tutors should be aware of the dangers of dependency. This can occur quite easily when the tutor is too readily available to the students.

I would also recommend that tutors be briefed thoroughly at the start of the new school year about the disciplinary aspect of their roles. Too many teachers look upon the tutor as being the primary disciplinarian. While it is the tutor's responsibility to help the student to face the consequences of their own behaviour, the overt disciplinarian should be the year head or dean, or whatever structure the school has in place for such matters.

In my research reports, I have also made recommendations about further structures and resources that could be put in place to support teachers in developing their knowledge and skills in affective education. It is a mistake to think that competencies in such curricular areas should be part of teachers' professional repertoires without appropriate inservice provision.

Personal effects

Reflecting on this past year is not unlike trawling through the detritus of a life: all the more unsettling when it is one's own.

In September 1993 I was a confident, competent teacher. I felt that there was little left for me to explore in my profession. The experiences of the past year have taught me to see anew the privilege of being a teacher. It complements wonderfully my other role as parent. Through 2W, I met my students at a level which I had hardly experienced before in my career. I know now that I can never understand fully what it was like to be a 14-year-old in 1994. But I also know that the 14-year-olds do not want me to be like them. They prefer to see me at a distinct remove from their world. They will invite me into that world now and again and give me a tantalising glimpse of how busy, hectic and pressurised their lives can be – much more pressurised than mine, even.

From 2W I have learned to listen, and to hear. I have learned to be very, very patient and not to expect too much. I have learned to fail, especially with Ger and Donal. Most of all, I have learned the joy it can be to find the lost sheep and bring it back to the fold.

On 3 June, school was closing down for the summer. I was in my classroom where two sixth year students were helping me to tidy up when I heard an urgent knock. It was Cyril, my treasurer for the tour, the unfortunate child with the unpredictable father. 'That's for you,' he said in his too-loud voice. He left something on my desk and ran to the door. Then he turned and said: 'Thanks. Thanks for everything.' And he was gone.

The gift which he had left was a beautifully worked money bag, empty, of course. But he had remembered that day in Liverpool when I was continually mixing up my Irish and sterling change, and how I had muttered several times during the day that I should always bring a money bag when travelling. That little money bag is very special to me.

But I gained much more than a money bag from this past year. In my other classes I learned to be more understanding and patient when a student arrived without his homework. I began to think about my pupils' personal circumstances. Through dealing with 2W, I also attempted to present my material in my other classes so that the students could subjectify it. I was now more conscious of the fact that, although T. S. Eliot and Schubert might be as important as food to me, it takes a tremendous leap for a teenager to relate to it at all.

The role of educator has taken on a new dimension for me. I now see myself as being directly involved in the forming of my students' characters, not just their minds.

I look forward to next September.

9

RELATE, NEGOTIATE, INNOVATE – EFFECTIVE CLASS TUTORING

Jim Ryan

Reflection

Having undertaken my action research, I would now consider myself to be more aware, more skilled and certainly more critical in my practice. I have taken on the role of year head in the last two years and work closely with three form tutor colleagues. In my work with the year group I am implementing a pastoral care programme and supporting my three colleagues where possible.

I find I am more involved with parents in helping them to support their sons in school. I have been involved in designing an induction booklet for incoming first years over the last three years. We now have a successful induction evening for the parents of these boys. Parents are alerted at an early stage when difficulties arise, and in so doing the school is communicating that their involvement is critical. At parent–teacher meetings parents are invited to express their views and concerns, and I find the feedback to be very helpful.

I feel the process of extending a model of pastoral care is slow but it has a cumulative effect on colleagues. They are now made aware of individual and class needs more readily.

For the students, my role has changed, and I find that I am drawn into discipline situations more and more. I have consciously to avail myself of more positive contact working with them on their programme in civics class, on the Christmas magazine, and in organising to be with them on their adventure weekend later in the term. I am still very conscious of the role of the student in the school system and try to get them to internalise that as much as is possible.

I think that doing an action research project like this makes you step back and take the year's experience as a whole. Getting the overview and reflecting on it was very much a learning experience for me. The art of journalling was a revelation! It compelled me to pause in an otherwise frantic routine and to clarify and reflect on my thoughts and feelings around my experiences.

My understanding and practice of pastoral care is better since completing the project and even on re-reading it now I am amazed at how much I have internalised and acted upon.

The gathering of the information for the research was the easy part. I found the marshalling of the data and the organisation of it into a meaningful unit quite difficult. I managed this task by separating out the individual elements and then attempting to interweave the elements with appropriate references to my experiences from my journal.

This kind of research broke the mould for me. Like many other people I had grown accustomed to the idea that other people are expert and the specialists in their fields. This new mode of researching challenges us to learn from our own experiences and therefore I think it would be an invaluable way of providing inservice to other staff. It is especially effective for staff who are out of the habit of study, as it compels us to re-think and to re-focus our practice.

I am still reflecting on my learning. However, it is not nearly as structured or as comprehensive as during the project. I think the project did have a significant effect on me, as all valuable learning experiences should. It taught me the value of reflection and has made me more of a strategist when attempting to implement some facet of a programme or structure.

My concern

Throughout my teaching career I have always found my role as form teacher to be one of the most satisfying and the most challenging aspects of my work. In reflecting on this I see that satisfaction stems from having some input into the students' growth not only academically, but also socially and emotionally. The school framework and the education system often unwittingly constrain and deny this growth rather than enhance it. The weight of pressures from external sources, which inevitably filters down to the schools, is so intense that our delivery of the schooling experience often buckles beneath it and becomes distorted, and the students' needs are often marginalised. A study by Hannan and Shorthall points to the 'very high priority' given by school leavers to the goals of personal and social development and to the 'low satisfaction marks' given by the same group (Hannan and Shorthall 1991: 6). The window of opportunity allowed to teachers working in a pastoral role as tutors is unique and must be grasped to make the school experience meaningful for many students.

My concern throughout the period of research here, from October 1993 to May 1994, is to open that window of opportunity as form tutor for the class in my care. The class, Columba, is composed of twenty-six second year, mixed ability boys of varied backgrounds and with a wide range of academic abilities. It is important to me that we will create collaboratively a learning environment in which these young people can thrive socially, emotionally and academically. It is common knowledge that the transition from first to second year has often been a negative experience for many of our students, as their innocent enthusiasm gives way to apathy and disaffection. My own experience of this group in first year was action packed, to say the least, and I spent most of that year attempting to mould the class into a cohesive unit. This meant a great deal of contact with the class, their teachers, the principal and the parents. (In my school the form teacher has both an unspoken pastoral role and a clearly identified disciplinary role.) Over that first year we learned a great deal about each other. I know that much remains unresolved as we embark on the second year and that the group continues to consist of a number of individual children with special needs, such as learning disabilities, and those experiencing bereavement, separated parents and dysfunctional families. I am determined to work with the group in an effort to combat the oft-experienced slide into disillusionment and other problems that accompany the transition to second year. I want to make our journey through second year a positive experience that will involve collaboration between us and engage them in a way that will increase their sense of belongingness to the school and their sense of unity within the group.

In the early stages, over many coffee breaks, I discuss with a critical colleague the current malaise throughout the school and what interventions are possible. I am fearful that any unsuccessful intervention on my part may bury forever the potential to develop a pastoral care dimension for the school.

My school

To help you to appreciate the nature of the school I will set the context for my concern. I teach in an all-boys' secondary school situated in north Dublin. Approximately 530 boys are in attendance and are offered a five-year programme. The catchment area has radically changed in the last decade or so. Increasingly the school's intake is from working-class areas. This has greatly altered the student profile and has placed enormous stress on a school that was traditionally very academic in its provision. A recent informal survey carried out by a colleague (as part of the Department of Education Remedial Course Certificate) revealed that 73 per cent of students in our 1993/94 intake are from working-class areas, where there is a high rate of unemployment.

The parents of many students, while well disposed towards the school and seeking the best for their sons, tend not to be actively involved because they have either been alienated by their own school experience or feel intimidated by contact with the school. As teachers we are often out of touch with the day-to-day realities of our students' lives to such an extent that O'Neill calls for 'special training for teachers to enable them to understand working class culture and the problems experienced by families living disadvantaged lifestyles' (1992: 119). Prior to the introduction of mixed ability teaching in my school in 1992, children from the more affluent areas generally ended up in the top streams. This did not necessarily reflect a greater aptitude but rather a different set of expectations. Class Columba, as the first mixed ability class to move into second year, represents therefore a microcosm of all the social complexities to be found in our school intake and therein lies, as we shall see, a potential for enrichment but also one for tension within the group.

My role in the school system

As a form teacher I am described by the principal as having 'responsibility' for the class. The parameters of that responsibility are variously understood and the ambiguity surrounding the role creates its own problems. I find the Higher Diploma course in Pastoral Care helps me to sharpen my own interpretation of this role and I contact a colleague in another school which has an advanced pastoral system to compare perceptions. He shares with me his school's view: 'The tutor is someone with whom the pupil can identify and relate to in a personal way. This relationship helps the pupil to relate to the school system overall in a positive way.' The simple logic of this systemic view of the tutor's role is profound and appealing. My critical colleague summarises one day the difficulty in defining the role in our school (the following comments are recorded in my journal): 'The role seems to change from year to year depending on what's expedient.' We speak often of this over the period and he is of the opinion that: 'If a system of pastoral care is to be introduced next year I think defining, supporting and monitoring the role of form teacher is a priority.' We agree that in some cases the form teacher is perceived by students as 'just someone you give notes to and who gives out to you if you get into trouble'. At the end of the year I surveyed a first year group to find out their ideas about the perception of the job done by form teacher, vice-principal and principal. The findings confirmed my belief that ill-defined roles lead to misperceptions. The misinterpretation by students of the roles of staff members are staggeringly different from that which is intended by the school .

The emphasis on the 'roles' played by individuals takes on a whole new significance for me as I listen to practitioners in the field of pastoral care and to my colleagues on the Higher Diploma course. I discover that clarity of role definition is essential to the health of the school as a system. In journalling my experiences I grapple with some of these thoughts and I return again and again to the words 'relationship' and 'development'. The quality of how we relate ought to be uppermost in our minds as pastoral caring teachers and should direct all our behaviour in the school context. In writing of the conditions that make schools more effective, Reid *et al.* declare: 'Form tutors need to start from the basis that the quality of the relationship with their students is all important. Nothing should be allowed to endanger that trust' (1987: 105). For me that professional relationship is all about providing a point of personal contact for the students in my care. The notion of development in the educational context leads me back to the classical root of the word 'education' – *educere*: to lead out.

In leading the 'apprentice adults' through enjoyable and challenging learning experiences I hope to give them opportunities to grow in maturity.

Action research framework

The action research framework gives me the first opportunity, in a career spanning fifteen years, to reflect on my practice in a structured way. During the course tutorials the question of how to involve/invite colleagues into another perception, another way of approaching a situation, arises for me. I want this research to make a difference for good, however slight, to the climate in my own school. The importance of this was brought home to me by the international report on 'Schools and Quality', which states 'that student motivation and achievement are profoundly affected by the distinctive culture/ethos that is to be found in each school' (OECD 1989: 126).

What could I do?

My class contact time is limited to three periods of geography and one civics class per week, and I am aware in September that this amount of time would not be sufficient to accommodate my expanded form teacher role. I therefore make it my practice over the year to visit the class at critical moments such as before first class in the morning, at junior break or immediately before class begins in the afternoon. This gives me opportunities to build the relationship of mutual respect and trust that I know is needed. From the outset the civics class becomes sacrosanct as our class meeting time, and much of the routine administrative work on absences, lates and information-giving is confined to the informal contacts.

Autumn term

Identifying the needs

On 24 September as I attend the Association of Remedial Teachers Conference, I leave behind a questionnaire for my class to complete based on Baldwin and Wells *Active Tutorial Work – The Second Year* (Baldwin and Wells 1979: 76), coupled with an instruction to write on 'My hopes for second year'. That weekend I collate the information from the questionnaire. It becomes very clear that there is a certain consensus about class needs. Clearly 'anxiety about tests', 'being told off for talking in class', 'not liking subject X' and 'never seem to be chosen to do things in school', are all issues for class Columba. I negotiate with them to spend time in our class meetings on study skills. Their comments point to a lack of confidence and it is clear that much work on self-esteem will be needed. I am aware that the mixed ability group contains students who have already good study skills and others whose only experience of examinations is failure. The programme on study skills needs to be inclusive and structured in such a way as to reach everyone. I listen to the unfolding stories about other areas of need, and I realise that the most sensitive issue of 'not liking Subject X' is the most intractable. They speak passionately about this and I feel powerless to do anything. I try reasoning but they can see I am uncomfortable. It involves relationships between staff colleagues, and needs to be handled very carefully, and I transmit some of my own sense of the difficulties to my students. This issue will shadow some of our later class meetings and I will have plenty of time to regret not acting on the students' behalf earlier on.

The problem of being told off for talking in class is an all too familiar difficulty from first year where the transition from the pupil-centred, activity-based learning of the primary school gives way to the didactic subject-centred approach of post-primary. I decide to deal with this through a series of behaviour modification techniques aimed to enhance students' self-awareness.

The final issue of 'Not being chosen to do things' intrigues me. It acts as a salutary reminder of the level of childhood longing which adults so often forget is very much with these 13-year-olds. We expect and assume so much and yet their life experiences are very limited. Hamblin asserts quite correctly that 'it is the task of the teacher, as the responsible professional, to adjust to the needs of the immature pupil rather than the other way round' (1978: 9). Students need opportunities to participate in class activities as much as possible.

To achieve something in these areas I know it is necessary to create a forum for the class to discuss their concerns and frustrations openly. To this end the civics period becomes our class meeting time and we abandon the notion of a set text, preferring to work more flexibly on needs as they arise. This is a step outside my own traditional practice and means dropping some of the rigidity that stylises my approach. I am anxious both about this departure from the comfort of the familiar, and about the students' perception of my new openness.

As the weeks go by, I am given ample opportunity to take disciplinary action as complaints come in about misbehaviour. The class are very accepting of my dual role. Stuart, in his study of 'Social Perceptions and Social Skills in the Classroom', concludes, 'In many respects the attitude held by the teacher can, in a very real sense, shape the behaviour of the pupil' (1990: 61). I am more conscious now of the students' perceptions of my attitudes than ever before.

On 5 November I decide to survey class attitudes to the weekly class meetings, and I distribute a questionnaire. We are working at this stage on study skills but I need feedback to assure myself that something valuable is happening. To my delight the findings indicate that they are enjoying them!

In response to the question 'What are the advantages/disadvantages of our class meetings as they are currently being used?', they reply:

'It is a break out of 42 classes a week.'

'We talk about things we want to.'

'You can bring up your own ideas.'

To be able 'to speak out' is a common thread running through many of the comments and this release I feel is therapeutic and does a great deal to unite our group. The airing and sharing of ideas and feelings gives each class member an opportunity to gain insights about others.

The class dynamic

Some students are clearly dominant in the group while others seem less involved and connected. I want to confirm my beliefs about the social composition of the class before going further, and I conduct a sociometric test designed by a colleague, Teacher Y, who is also a form teacher for second year. The class are asked to write down the three people they would most like to work with in a group. For each student's choice I assign a 3 for first preference, 2 for second and 1 for third, and I then total the results. Accepting the obvious limitations of this instrument, I discuss with Teacher Y the results of the test. He feels it helps to objectify the social pattern and improve our understanding of the complexities in the classroom interactions.

This glimpse of the subterranean life of class Columba clearly identifies the dominants and the isolates within the group and gives me valuable insights into the group dynamic. I am most concerned about those who are chosen by no one. At the end of November I meet with colleague X, who is also my learning partner on the Higher Diploma course, to review my progress with the study skills programme and to examine the sociometric results. She remarks: 'Those isolates are in every class. I can recall many who have passed through their second level schooling with no real friends.' Without some intervention we feel that much of their social development during their time in the school will be eroded. We make a conscious decision to include the identified isolates more in our subject classes (history and geography respectively) and to involve them wherever possible in group activities. Unless we do this, we feel, we should abandon pretence at achieving our goal of personal and social development. Bazalgette, speaking about this drive to maturity, summarises the position:

> If they can learn how to struggle to make sense of their experience, relating their self-awareness to the context in which they find themselves, taking action in the light of how they interpret their relationship, they will be helped to become adult and to engage with a world which is hostile but which also has opportunities for those who can recognise and take them.
>
> (Bazalgette 1983: 3)

Further steps

Friday games

I approach the concern surrounding the sense of belongingness and the desire to be asked to do things in a number of ways. To engender class spirit I decide to run a class football league. The games will take place each Friday lunchtime. It gives me and the students an opportunity to meet each other in another context, and develop a new set of perceptions. Refereeing their games gives me a chance to observe their unselfconscious interactions. The games become a talking point amongst us and this contact further consolidates the group.

Classroom environment

The classroom itself, where students spend six hours per day, provides another arena for improving class cohesion. To encourage pride in the cleanliness of our classroom environment we negotiate a rota of people to tidy up at the end of each day, and I am pleased at the number of volunteers. I am tempted to display geographic material everywhere on the walls, but we reserve a corner of the room for the students' own achievements and experiences, and this is the one that arouses most interest. I want achievements other than academic to be acknowledged and they begin to show their enthusiasm by bringing in items of interest. The spin-off effect of this valuing of their out-of-school achievements is evident in our class meetings and the more knowledge the class develops about itself the more the class spirit grows.

Study skills programme

The main focus of our class meetings throughout the first term is study skills. From discussion with the group I feel this is their most pressing school-based need at the moment – improving their grades and reducing the anxiety they have around examinations. Hamblin (1978, chapter 3) speaks of teaching coping strategies that will help students perceive an anxiety-provoking situation differently, and increase their control over it. A sense of feeling successful is going to be important in enhancing self-esteem. To launch our classes on this aspect of the programme I select an exercise for my class to ask themselves questions about their experience of school:

1 Why are you at school?
2 Why do you study particular subjects?
3 Why are there school regulations?
4 Why are there examinations?
5 Describe your role as a student in this school.

(Collins 1993: 9)

The point which causes greatest confusion is 'Describe your role as a student in this school.' Bazalgette holds that 'Taking up a role in the systems approach is not something that can be taught but it is something that can be learned' (1979: 1). We devote a number of classes to clarifying the role of the student. One approach I take with the group is to identify all the roles they perform in their lives – son, brother, nephew, classmate, team mate, as well as student. We focus on the student role and look at what behaviours are appropriate. Throughout the year I take every opportunity to reinforce the meaning of the student's role. From my own reading, I also become increasingly aware of the need for self-motivation and acceptance of responsibility, as well as academic excellence, as features of what it means to be a student. My journal notes: 'Our teaching is so unbalanced, we spend 99 per cent of it teaching them what to learn and so little time on how to learn. The pressure to cover the course leaves little time for these necessities.'

I find myself re-evaluating the position I take on a lot of the 'sacred cows' of my own practice and begin to realise that the journal is nudging me ever more in the direction of personal professional critique. Interestingly, the physical act of recording and re-reading is a very powerful reflective mechanism.

In working through the study skills programme with the students I include the following items:

1   an inventory of strengths and weaknesses in study
2   the major obstacles to getting down to work
3   planning study.

The move to a more systematic approach to study is a revelation to some of the students. In an attempt to bridge the gap between home and school I devise a study planner, with notes, which would allow teachers to set study work for five weeks before the pre-Christmas tests. The planner is a booklet designed to include every subject, and breaks study down into manageable units of three half-hour slots per evening. At the same time as issuing the booklet I notify parents by letter. Some staff members do not see themselves involved in the study planning work. Given also that the students move constantly between teaching rooms, the impact is limited. However, some parents perceive the idea as helpful and remark on it in February at the parent–teacher meeting. It is also heartening to see the study skills scheme adopted by two other form teachers later in the year and it demonstrates how small ideas can be disseminated with potentially wide influence.

Drawing again on Hamblin's work (1978) we compile a list of how to get down to work:

•   have clear objectives
•   manage your time – draw up a study planner

- organise yourself
- don't worry about the work, do it!

Teacher Y validates

I am aware of the challenge of potential subjectivity in drawing conclusions from observations of my own practice. To avoid such challenges, and to strive towards objectivity, I use triangulation, a technique that invites interpretation on a particular issue from several different perspectives (see, for example, Robson 1993).

I therefore go to Teacher Y and outline my concerns. He is concerned about the limitations of the programme from the students' point of view. I note his comments in my journal: 'The research to improve study skills is set against an overall development of personal and interpersonal skills. To succeed the class contact time must be such as to be a dominant part of each day' (17 January 1994).

I agree with this sentiment and I feel in an ideal world this increased contact would allow such a desired outcome. However, I also feel that a great deal more is happening beyond study skills work. There is evidence of increased group discussion work, enhanced self-esteem through confidence building, deeper understanding of friendship and peer pressure, greater self-awareness and hence greater control over personal actions.

Teacher Y also observes: 'The effect on the school procedures since it is a bottom up approach would be negligible in the short term.' My own perceptions are reinforced that change happens slowly and is tempered and strengthened in the smaller arena before being adopted beyond that. I feel also that if management could be convinced of its value then perhaps the process would accelerate.

In reviewing my own journal Teacher Y remarks: 'There is a sense of the work load carried by an "active" form teacher. A sense that the difficulties/problems encountered by students are actually on someone's agenda.' I am gratified by this remark and its essence is not lost on me. I realise that my responsibility to my students in Columba is to ensure that their needs will be addressed.

Self-discipline

By the end of November I have met individually with a number of parents, at my request, to review students' progress and behaviour. From first year each student's class journal has been a channel of communication between home and school and vice versa and parents respond well to this. They know from the journal what homework is required and they and I sign the journal on a weekly basis. However, in discussions with them in November, their chief concern is about the study element and how much their sons should do. Some are concerned about disruptive behaviour, and we negotiate a reporting system, a kind of behaviour modification process. A particularly disruptive student, and one of the tallest, most physically mature students in the class, is upsetting a number of teachers by his poor work rate and his general demeanour. I place him on a daily report. Each teacher at the end of every class will make a written comment on the student's participation. I contract with the parents to sign the report booklet every night. By the end of the year another three students are voluntarily on daily report and the feedback from parents, teachers and students is positive.

These journals become an early warning device for all concerned but more importantly they challenge the students to take control of their behaviour on a regular basis. This positive growth in self awareness is to be welcomed. Glasser would define such responsibility as the ability to 'fulfill one's needs and to do so in a way that does not deprive others of the ability to fulfill their needs' (1986: 13). Eileen Hegarty's thesis on the work of Glasser points out that he believed that 'the education of a student in self discipline is possible only if someone in that school takes a personal interest in the student', and that teachers will 'lose control if they are not involved with students' (1989: 161–3). The quality of that involvement and my own interest in each student is a constant challenge to me.

Christmas magazine

To harness students' enthusiasm we take a further step forward in November. In our first year the class had published a school Christmas magazine. I had found it a worthwhile group activity and felt it would again encourage students to use all their abilities in the variety of tasks involved in such a production. 'Christmas Craicers 2' necessitates many meetings at lunchtime to decide on the editorial committee and the various tasks involved. This is an exercise in group work and decision making. Fifteen students from Columba make themselves available at various stages in the production. The class are proud of their achievements and raise £270 for their selected charity 'Focus Point'.

Spring term

Reviewing

My journal opens on 10 January as follows: 'Returning exam papers, there is a palpable atmosphere of expectation. Responses vary from elation to depression.' I know at this time that some group counselling on their results will be needed to overcome their sense of failure. Our first class meeting is devoted to some discussion of the results and a look to the future. I want to set our eyes firmly on future improvement and to do this I bring in their report booklets going back to Christmas 1992 and ask them to review their results and teachers' comments. This establishes for them the notion of progression and development from one year to another.

We look at the following sentence completion exercise:

1 When I saw my report I felt . . .
2 I thought I could do better in . . .
3 My parents feel . . .
4 I don't like . . .
5 Now I'm going to . . .
6 My summer report will be . . .
7 My first term in second year was . . .
8 I wish I . . .
9 What is the difference between the results and comments of 1992 and 1993 . . .

This exercise is designed to allow open responses and students are not required to hand it in. I want to put them in touch with their own feelings and responsibilities around these results and to give them the opportunity to think through and to make decisions about the future. Their journalled comments on the exercise include:

'My summer report will be ten times better.'
'My summer report will be better because I'm going to study more.'

Following this exercise one student comes to me and asks to go on daily report and another asks to be moved up near the front. This sense of wanting to change their behaviour is a result of their own insights into barriers to their progress.

I continue with the study planner as we approach the summer exam. I feel this type of structure provides a much needed organisational tool for the class.

The highlight of our spring term is to be a trip to Coolure House, an adventure centre, at Castlepollard, Co Westmeath on 4–6 March. I discuss with Teacher X the need for outside school activity and contact for the class and myself as form teacher. With previous classes I have always found that weekend trips away can have an excellent bonding impact on the class and opportunities arise for both students and teachers to allow barriers to fall a little.

The parent–teacher meeting

We still have six weeks before our proposed trip and our parent–teacher meeting is due on 11 February. I am hoping all our students will be able to go to Coolure, but the spring term gets off to a bad start, with a good deal of disruption happening in some classes. If such behaviour continues, I know that doubt will be placed over the participation of some on the trip.

Unfortunately, the new term begins with two of Columba's teachers absent through ill health. The substitute teachers find the class difficult to handle and the students test them to their limits. I am disappointed with them, and my journal records: 'Back to reality. Individually each of these boys is fine but together the ingredients for chaos are present. They seek and find the most vulnerable and then attack' (17 January 1994). My annoyance shows through this comment as I feel all the extra work with them is wasted.

I work on this in our class meetings and in the early part of term deal with issues of relationships, friendship and peer pressure. There are various students in the class who I am aware can be subversive if given the opportunity, and I am concerned that they are beginning to set the agenda for the class. I want to support the majority who are moving towards developing a respectful and cooperative class ethos. I am aware, however, of resistance to such interventions in the area of peer relationships and pressure. Discussion on friendship and problems regarding friends, I must admit, does little to fire their enthusiasm; and it stays at a theoretical level rather than becomes part of their own experience. I discover by chance that in religion their teacher is working through a programme on self-esteem and growing independence, and in conversation I realise that much of it parallels my own work. I write in my journal: 'There is a glaring deficit in our approach to our classes. We do not know anything about our colleagues' programmes' (2 February 1994). I feel this would have been a very enriching collaboration between form teacher and religion teacher if I had been aware at an earlier stage; and it highlights the need, in a pastoral school, for dialogue and sharing between staff, to develop an inclusive curriculum to support students' needs.

I call a meeting of class teachers in advance of the parent–teacher meeting to gather and exchange information on a more formal basis. With limited time available over a working lunch, I avoid the lengthy procedure of going through a list of names by categorising students in groups: 'Working well', 'Weak but trying', 'Weak and not trying', 'Able and not trying', and 'Disruptive'. This focuses our minds and we prepare for the PTM. I prepare a questionnaire for the parents who will attend and am invited to address the gathering to outline the questionnaire and its purpose. I feel that some opportunity should be afforded to parents to voice their opinion, even if they prefer to stay anonymous. Parent–teacher meetings have traditionally been a one-way form of communication and the school is learning very little about its own procedures and organisation from the parent body.

In reviewing the parents' comments with Teacher X, I comment, 'There is an unchallenged assumption here that exam results are the only reason why parents send their children to this school.' Teacher X agrees and responds, 'Results are always very important. The difference in recent years is that parents want much more for their children in terms of personal development.'

I collate the questionnaire returns. Some responses are most revealing. On the question 'What do you feel is the most important thing the school can do for your son?' some responses are:

- give him an education for life
- give him a feeling of self-worth
- good education, good sports, good outlook on life
- preparing them for their exams
- assist in his preparation for later life
- I would like my son to leave school with good results, confident, happy and a caring young man.

In his controversial study on the counselling needs of adolescents, Ryan identifies the problems of instability in the Irish family as the greatest contributor to the problems of the schools: 'the problems of the schools in Ireland in the late twentieth century are largely the problems of the Irish family' (1993: 25). Perhaps my class is symptomatic.

Coolure House – activity weekend

Excitement surrounding our departure is intense, and I am pleased that there are only two absentees among the students (they cannot go for family reasons). The group departs in high spirits and with great anticipation for what the weekend holds. They are mixing well and I am interested to observe the dynamic in an informal setting. I note that M, D and L are obviously on the periphery of the group, and that insulting remarks regarding these boys come from a loud, rather ill-mannered student. There are spiteful comments to D, and reference to others as 'wimps' are both hurtful and revealing. I speak to the student privately about this and I wonder at his complete lack of awareness of the impact of his behaviour.

Teachers have a very relaxed way with the students and this is excellent from their point of view. In conversation with Teacher X she comments: 'They are so well behaved when we are away and we see another side to them. It's good for the teachers to mix with the kids. It pays off when you go back to school, not in a "buddy-buddy" way but in a more human rounded way' (Journal, 5 March 1994). I agree but I sometimes wonder how far you can let go and still maintain some professional distance.

Looking back, my concerns about this are unfounded and I feel that the trip has had a very important impact on the group in terms of cohesion and co-operation. They are quick to tell me what the trip meant for them when it comes to the Second Year review:

Question: What was the high point of the year for you?
Response: Coolure House, it was a break.

144

Response: Coolure House, we had a lot of fun.
Response: Going to Coolure, it was a great experience.

On return to school I asked the class to review the weekend and I framed the questions around the key ideas of 'contact', 'cooperation' and 'conflict'. One general response from a student captures their corporate experience: 'The trip to Coolure worked out great. Everybody got on great and we had no complications at all. There was a swing there I enjoyed the most. . . . Overall we had a brilliant time. I hope we go again next year.'

I feel this has been a very positive experience for students and teachers alike and one that will sustain the group in more difficult times.

Feedback

On 24 March, in our Higher Diploma Practicum tutorial, we discussed how to collect further data to evaluate the steps we are taking. From a list of possible methods, I selected for my own class a drawing of how it feels to be in our class meetings. Armed with paper and crayons I gave the class the chance to respond in this manner, and I am pleased by their responses. Some opt to write: 'We can discuss things that are in our mind about school and about the things that are going wrong in our student role'; 'Happy, relaxed, looking forward to the next one'; 'I feel good because you can express your feelings'; 'In civics class you can relax, there is not the pressure of other classes.'

Key words to describe the drawings might include 'relaxed', 'problem solving', 'cooperation', and 'happy'. Drawing is a medium that allows freedom of expression, a much under-used instrument for evaluative work, particularly with young people. I feel the time we have spent thus far has been vindicated by these drawings and the space afforded by our class meetings is valuable. I know as the term closes that the climate in the class is one of collaboration and this must be sustained.

Summer term

In the final term, we spend time examining the issues of prejudice and stereotyping. The theme of empathising with others is high on our group work agenda.

Class visitor

The high point of the study block is the presentation made to the class on 20 May 1994 by a visitor from Focus Point, a well-known charity group which the class has chosen to support. This links in with and makes more tangible the work done earlier on the Christmas magazine. Having arranged the meeting, I tell the class that they are responsible for meeting the visitor on arrival and for conducting the whole encounter. We work as a group on a prepared set of questions. One pupil offers to bring in a cake, which I feel is very thoughtful, and two others volunteer to greet the visitor. In conversation afterwards with Miss Z, the Focus Point volunteer, she enquires: 'Are they a streamed class? They seem so bright and involved.' This is an interesting perception. Could it be that the class presents as such because they are working in cooperation with each other and are genuinely interested in the topic?

Her own presentation, the immediacy of her real-life experiences coupled with her skilled communication with the class, including listening carefully to their experiences, impacts greatly on them. It is undoubtedly one of the best class meetings of the year and they show great maturity throughout. So enthusiastic are they that I resolve to build in a more expanded visitor programme for third year.

Review

Now as the year draws to a close I ask my class, a number of teachers and the principal to respond to questionnaires regarding the year. I want to be sure that what I hoped for my class – a more positive experience of school in second year leading to personal and social development – really did take place.

The students

Overall the spoken and written comments of the students are positive. I include a selection here to indicate their feelings on our three major issues:

1   Anxiety about exams – 'I feel tense but I will go into them motivated and not negative.' The study skills programme combined with the planner has given the students a structured way of applying themselves. It has reached out to parents also and in the main this need has been met.
2   Subject X – 'Subject X hasn't got any better.' Not a great deal of progress has been made although the class are less angry about this later in the year. It seems so straightforward at this distance but the complexities surrounding interpersonal relationships among staff are not easily understood.
3   A sense of belonging – 'Everyone gets their fair share of tasks.' I have made a conscious effort throughout the year to involve the class in its own organisation. Simple things such as cleaning the board to the publication of our magazine, meeting and greeting our visitor, and preparing for the trip have all helped them to become more involved and have created a more positive atmosphere in the class.

A re-test on the sociometric assessment shows overall movement in the course of the year and it is healthy to see changing social interactions. However, there are still some that are seemingly isolated in the group.

They view my role as 'helpful' and 'working with' them, and this convinces me that my effectiveness as a form teacher depends on my own clear understanding of my role as form teacher. This research has been as much about improving my work as about the students improving theirs.

The teachers

I approach two teachers to review this year: Teacher X, history teacher of Columba, who has spent so much time with me, and Teacher A, their business studies teacher.

One of the most promising elements for me and, I hope, for the school is my appointment, albeit it on a temporary basis, as pastoral care coordinator for first year, and I bring proposals regarding the structuring of pastoral care to our staff meeting on 31 May 1994.

As part of the evaluation, I invite Teacher X and Teacher A to comment on Columba's progress – they respond positively. On the group's cohesiveness X finds: 'I am working with a unit in there. They seem to have a common identity. During the project work in history I've been impressed with the way they've cooperated with each other and shared resources.'

In assessing my role as form teacher they are both very gracious: Teacher A: 'Job done fully and very satisfactorily'; Teacher X: 'Extremely well with care, sensitivity and professionalism. The effects of your work with the class are plain to see.'

The principal

The principal agrees to respond in writing to two issues:

1   General questions about pastoral care.
2   Questions on class Columba.

The general questions have been prompted by my own need to know where the management in the school stands on specific issues. I am heartened by the positive view held by the principal and his willingness to support the introduction of a pastoral care system into the school. However, his view of it as a filtering system for problems and for reducing crises is limiting, in my opinion. His own view of being supportive to others involved in pastoral care is to be welcomed but this must be underpinned by his active involvement in creating a whole-school programme: 'Positive school leadership is a necessary prerequisite of effective schooling' (OECD 1989: 92). I feel that the catalyst for making formal pastoral care a reality in our school largely rests with the principal and the leadership this role provides. While much can, and will, be done from the bottom up, it is the principal who holds the key to accelerated implementation and long-term success.

Conclusion

Personally I found this research project had made me a more reflective person. The act of recording my thoughts and feelings in the journal has had a profound influence on how I now respond to situations. The value of it is particularly clear to me now, two years after its completion. In the act of reviewing the entire year I can trace moments when I am more in touch with my own feelings and how to control them. I have a more heightened awareness of my own limitations and strengths and a greater appreciation of the many talents of colleagues and HDPC course participants I met. It has reawakened in me some of the idealism that led me into teaching and has demonstrated to me that the dream is alive and well. If we teachers can begin to identify and respond in a concerted way to the needs of our students then perhaps we will be beginning to answer the call from the OECD report to be 'more responsive to individual student requirements' (OECD 1991: 75).

Professionally I feel I have developed and benefited from this research. I accept Jean McNiff's belief in 'the importance of critical thinking', that is, to 'de-construct' and 're-construct' our reality and in the reconstruction put it 'back together again within the new framework of my understanding' (McNiff et al. 1992: 24). The project has energised me and the notion that we are contributing to living educational theory (Whitehead 1989) makes it all the more worthwhile. It has brought me closer to some of my colleagues and has doubly convinced me of Michael Fullan's ideas around the importance of collegiality: 'the challenge of interactive professionalism is the challenge of continuous school improvement. It is a process which leads to gains in pupil achievement. No one working in and without schools should evade this challenge . . . even in the most apparently unsympathetic and unsupportive environments' (Fullan and Hargreaves 1991: 4). More of this kind of collegial work will, I fervently hope, improve the overall climate in the school: 'Good schools are good places to live in and work, for everybody' (Reid et al. 1987: 20).

The importance of personal and social development is very much recognised in the debate that has been ongoing since the publication of the Green Paper on Education in l992: 'The personal and social development of students must be a central concern of the school' (Government of Ireland 1992: 129). The endorsement of the pastoral care dimension in schools made by the Report on the National Education Convention is very encouraging. It speaks of freeing teachers from routine administrative chores 'to concentrate their energies on academic and pastoral work' (The National Education Convention Secretariat 1994: 51). This kind of support, one hopes, will be reinforced through the legislative process in 1994.

Besides drawing on my colleagues as a resource throughout this project, I must acknowledge the greatest resource and source of enlightenment for me – the students of Columba. These twenty-six young people and I travelled the road of second year together, and we have reached the destination more enlightened, more confident and above all more developed human beings.

10

CHALLENGING STUDENTS' PERCEPTIONS OF SCHOOL

Ann Marie Kiernan

Reflection

It is the responsibility of educators to lead students in a school on a journey towards fulfilment. The journey that is the educational process is more important than the destination of a particular educational outcome.

On all journeys there are pitfalls and potholes and dangerous turns. I have learnt that in a small school setting where 'failure' or mistakes are encountered the journey grinds to a halt. External advice can steer a staff on their journey, but collectively the staff must have an end vision if they are to reach their destination. Failures or mistakes should be viewed as stepping stones rather than stumbling blocks. Willingness and a concerted effort are sometimes not enough. We need a vision and a belief that we all have a part to play on the journey, and a responsibility to influence directions in life-giving ways. A team effort is necessary, with each member having a vital and positive input, remembering that a chain is only as strong as its weakest link.

I agree with what Goodlad *et al.* have to say about the process of renewal: 'Renewal – whether of ponds, gardens, people, or institutions – is an internal process, whatever the external concerns and stimulants. It requires motivation, dedication, systematic and systemic evaluation and *time*' (1990: 25, emphasis in original).

Background

The Green Paper *Education for a Changing World* (Government of Ireland 1992) states that the education system should help students to develop:

- an ability to manage oneself and to make the most of personal resources
- an ability to express one's own viewpoint rationally
- an ability to relate effectively to other people.

My experience and observations had revealed that these capacities were not well developed among the students in the school where I was teaching. This denied my educational values (see below). I undertook an action research project to see how I might encourage my students to develop these capacities. My research question focused over time to 'How can I encourage self-esteem, assertiveness and organisational skills among fifth year students in the school?' I felt that I needed to find a vehicle for students to develop these capacities; a possible solution was to establish a students' council. This report tells how the Student Council came into being, and how it enabled students to develop the powers that the Green Paper recommends.

My values as an educator

I believe that education is about the development of the emotional, physical, intellectual and spiritual needs and potentials of individuals. The needs of students must be nurtured carefully; each must be supported at their own rate and according to their own stage of progress. I agree with John Dewey that 'Education is not a preparation for life; it is life' (Dewey 1963).

Given that social demands on young people are great, and intolerance for them high, fostering positive attitudes and beliefs is not only an aim but also a vital function of education. The power of the attitudes, relationships and values that teachers encourage in their students, often in an unseen way, cannot be underestimated. I recognise that I will influence my students, and therefore I must educate myself to develop positive attitudes, and foster a spirit of equality and democratic practices in my classroom.

I am aware of the importance of developing caring relationships with and among my students. Carl Rogers (1961) notes that such relationships are characterised by acceptance, genuineness and empathy. When these characteristics are applied to education, there are significant implications for teachers.

Acceptance Acceptance refers to the ability to accept a person in a non-judgemental way. While a teacher might challenge a person's behaviour, the value of the person remains intact. This difference is sometimes not appreciated by teachers.

Genuineness A teacher must be a 'real person' and not hide behind a professional role. This means spontaneity in relationships without defensiveness.

Empathy Empathy involves the ability to appreciate what it feels like to be another person. It involves seeing beyond verbal and overt communication towards a deeper, possibly more important, emotional message.

As an educator, I try to demonstrate empathy, genuineness and acceptance in my practice. I also try to encourage my students to do the same, as well as to develop the ability to research, record, discuss and articulate well. I believe these skills can enable them to live out the values of empathy, genuineness and acceptance in their own lives.

Such values and capacities are not held in high esteem in our current educational climate. Capacities that are prized are those necessary for success in the points race – the assimilation of information and academic achievement. I believe, however, that greater emphasis needs to be placed on the development of the whole person. I am not alone in this; a number of researchers hold the same view (for example, Fullan 1993; Handy 1991). In a changing society with decreasing prospects for full-time employment we need more emphasis on social education, prioritising the need to teach students how to cope and learn how to learn. As teachers we need to learn how to help our students take responsibility for their own choices, behaviour and futures. We must inspire them with faith and confidence in themselves. However, because I hold these values and yet work in an education system that is dominated by market forces and the need to achieve, I experience many tensions in my professional life.

Context

At this point I will give a context of my school and work. This is important for the further development of my research story.

The school where I teach is a small rural second-level school with a total enrolment of 275. There are five feeder schools in the catchment area. The family backgrounds of students vary from small farming communities to large families of ten or twelve children. When I first joined the school from an inner city school environment I wondered what problems a rural school could possibly have. I was soon to learn. Many children come from broken families where the adolescent has to become the responsible adult. Alcoholism can be a significant factor in family life. Rural living has many complexities that are not experienced by city dwellers.

My concern

Ideas about students' perceptions of the values of education were high in my mind when I decided to undertake my research. I was aware that although our school would consider itself a caring school, students tended to have a functional view of the purposes of education. This was borne out by a questionnaire I administered to establish for myself what the situation really was like.

The findings of my questionnaire revealed the following:

- Students saw education as a product industry: 'Education is something you have to get in order to get a good job'; 'Education is the foundation of your life. If you have a bad education you won't have a great life'; 'Education is what will get you to college.'
- A few students seemed to understand what a 'well balanced person' denoted.

- Other findings dealt with issues of communication – most felt that they communicated reasonably well. In relation to confidence, comments included: 'I think I am confident but it's hard when some teachers put you down.' This response gave me pause for thought: do we always speak to our students as we would like to be spoken to by our superiors?
- Students tended to think that school was enjoyable. Most important to them were their friends, activities and part-time work.

My reflections on these findings were that students appeared to view their education as learning the facts, reproducing them in examinations, and getting a good job. Sadly, education appeared to be an activity that took place every forty minutes, excluding what went on in the intervals. My concern deepened about how I could try to move them away from the 'product' orientation, and develop attitudes in relation to 'whole-person development'.

I was also aware of the link between such a product orientation and self-image. If academic success is taken as a major criterion of personal value, then students who do not perform well academically will feel themselves personal failures as well. I followed through this idea with a small questionnaire. The findings revealed that the boys had a better developed self-image than the girls. This could of course be because of a variety of factors. I was alarmed, however, that, even though the boys scored higher, their scores were still relatively low.

My study of the literature of self-esteem and confidence building helped me to understand the crucial aspect that 'significant adults' such as parents and teachers play in young people's lives. I began to understand the nature of self-esteem as an affective process, an evaluation by the person of the degree to which they are not living out their own aims and values, and not realising the image of the 'self' they would like to be. I began to understand that a good deal of self-esteem is rooted in the responses of others, and, in the case of students in school, in the responses of their teachers. If response colours the way we see ourselves, then it is the responsibility of educators to ensure that the quality of their response is the best it can be. Yet teachers are also subject to the demands of a product-oriented curriculum. How can teachers ensure that their quality of response is appropriate to the needs of their students when they are equally driven by pressure for examination performance?

It seemed to me that this was the point at which I began to realise the need for systematic pastoral care provision.

Our school was a caring school, yet there were no formal pastoral structures. We had class teachers, but they had no clearly defined role. I think Marland is right when he says, 'It is the apparently very informal set up that is most frustrating for the individual. For teachers to work effectively lines of communication must be clearly but flexibly laid down' (1974). Possibly as a consequence of this lack of explicit structure, many teachers had a limited view of their own roles (see below). I wanted to change all this.

I invited colleagues to respond to a questionnaire which I hoped would promote thinking and discussion about the role of the class teacher and the need for a formal pastoral care system.

Responses to the question of how they viewed the school's pastoral provision included: 'Erratic'; 'Not particularly structured. Operates to a certain degree at classroom level depending on teacher–student relationship'; 'An unplanned system of pastoral care, but I believe a good attitude by principal and teachers. Individual teachers are aware of the system.' All teachers agreed that there was little time for pastoral roles when there was no structured system and when examinations are just around the corner.

In describing student–teacher relationships, there was a lack of uniformity: 'Best with first years, good with others, others again leave a lot to be desired'; 'Reasonably approachable with my own group. A little better with senior students.'

Responses to how colleagues viewed themselves as class teachers included: 'A register checker and disciplinarian, one whose job it is to make sure their class behaves and toes the line'; 'It's administrative and disciplinary but classes should be timetabled in such a way that a relationship can be formed through-out the year'; 'Our role is disciplinary. It should not be just that, though.'

I interviewed senior students, and asked what their relationships with staff were like. Their responses included: 'We should be trusted more. It's hard to prove yourself to some teachers'; 'Teachers should listen to students' opinions'; 'Senior students could speak at assemblies.'

I asked a colleague who acted as my critical friend throughout the period of my research to confirm my observations. She wrote:

> The situation is as described. The self esteem of students at senior level seems low. . . . I feel we encourage dependency in our school, because we tend to 'spoon feed' students of low academic ability to get them through the examinations, and this reinforces their feelings of inadequacy. We need to encourage independence and active involvement. We cannot at present offer a pastoral care and personal–social education programme because of logistical constraints, even though staff feel that this would be beneficial.

What now?

The problems were articulated:

- There were no pastoral care structures.
- Class teachers had no clearly defined role.
- Examinations were paramount, with intense pressure on students (and teachers) to succeed academically.
- There was a need to encourage self-esteem among students, while not 'spoon feeding' them.

What could I do?

I had a vision in which our school had a clear pastoral care programme and appropriate organisational structures; that there was a commitment to educating the whole person. This vision would not be realised overnight; it would perhaps take the form of a five-year development plan, and involve all members of staff in its creation and implementation. I could not realise this vision alone. It ought to become a corporate vision, and consequently should involve the community in its development. I wondered how I could involve students and teachers in developing a structured approach to pastoral care.

What did I do?

1 November

I had the idea of a Student Council. This, I felt, would help students to raise their self-esteem through involvement, give them a voice, help improve their communication skills, and develop good relationships between staff and students. All teachers were invited to participate as interested visitors.

2 November

I discussed the idea with the principal who was most supportive. I also discussed the idea with my critical friend, Mary.

Me: What do you think?
Mary: It's a good way to try and improve relationships between staff and students, and also get students to feel good about themselves. It might not be easy to motivate some of them, but most of them need an opportunity like this. It will help them to organise themselves, particularly some of the girls who are shy and have a low opinion of themselves. There's nothing to lose and everything to gain.

8 November

I already had clear ideas about the kinds of activities I felt would be useful for the Student Council, and what they might achieve. These included:

- actively participating in extra-curricular activities, to develop organisational skills
- evaluating the outcome of these activities in an objective way, to develop critical thinking
- developing an understanding of the idea of roles and responsibilities
- helping develop positive relationships

- providing a forum for the exercise of democratic practices
- helping students develop a notion of their potential as responsible citizens and valuable human beings.

I spoke with the fifth year girls during my own home economics class about the ideas. They were generally enthusiastic, but expressed reservations about how others might perceive them. After a good deal of discussion we drew up a list of aims for the Council. For example:

- to provide us with an opportunity to identify and discuss our needs in a positive and constructive way
- to help develop a civic awareness by the organisation of suitable projects
- to help us to understand the importance of teamwork
- to develop a sense of involvement and belonging
- to help in the running of the school by taking responsibility for our activities.

9 November

I arranged with a colleague to release the boys from their parallel timetabled class so that they could share in the discussions. Together we discussed what we would like to improve in our school. They drew up lists which included issues such as provision of canteen facilities, more sports, discussion classes, computer classes. There was also an explicit plea for better relationships – that boys and girls be treated the same, that discussion classes should encourage the expression of personal opinions.

Students were asked to vote who should sit on the Council.

11 November

I contacted several agencies to gather information on committee practices and structures which I would pass on to the students.

12 November

Elected members informed. Inaugural meeting scheduled for the 16th.

16 November

No student had served on a committee before. I explained committee roles such as treasurer, secretary and chairperson.

I learned a good deal from this meeting. The outcomes were generally positive, but I learned how time- and labour-intensive such exercises can be. We were always under pressure of time: lunch hours are short and buses wait for students in the evening. We did not get through the business of the day.

There were other aspects to appreciate. Two elected students failed to show up. I presumed they were absent but I met them later on the corridor. When I said, 'Sarah, I noticed you didn't come to the inaugural meeting of the Student Council. Perhaps you'd like to come to the next?' her reply was 'No, miss, I don't really want to.'

I said the same to Joe, who responded: 'I might come. I'll see.'

I was learning fast. It was only now that I realised how much I was presuming. While students might be enthusiastic in discussion it can be a different story when the situation becomes real.

30 November

Our inaugural meeting continued. I asked the students to think about their own strengths, and those of their colleagues, so that we could elect people to committee positions. I explained procedures of nominating, seconding, voting and co-opting.

6 December

Two students approached me on the corridor. 'Could we have a school Christmas disco? Can we put it on the agenda?' They were learning!

7 December

The agenda for today was (1) election of officers; (2) Christmas disco; (3) Christmas raffle.

The students demonstrated that they understood election procedures, and reasons for why they were nominating candidates.

> I nominate Ann for Secretary because she is a neat writer and very organised and therefore would be present at all meetings.

> I nominate Mark for Treasurer because he has some experience of handling money in his brother's business, and because he's honest and straight.

> I nominate Patrick for Chairman because he is a good listener. He will hear what each person says without taking sides if there is a disagreement. He is very much his own man.

I guided the students through the meeting. Next on the agenda was the Christmas disco. I asked Patrick as Chairperson to open the topic to the floor. He whispered hurriedly to me:

Patrick: What do I say, miss?

Me: Tell them about the proposal of a disco, to get their views.

Patrick: A holding of a disco has been placed on the agenda. Can we get some opinions about it?

And so it went. They were all anxious to be involved. They enjoyed the discussions. Many ideas were shared.

I spoke with students about their perceptions of what they were learning.

Me: Patrick, how do you feel as Chairperson?

Patrick: It felt unusual calling a meeting open and then closed. Trying to get people's attention is hard.

Me: Ann, what do you think of the position of Secretary?

Ann: I really have to listen and concentrate, and my writing is not as neat as it should be because I am writing so fast.

My own learning was recorded in my journal. I thought Patrick was a bit uneasy with his power. I was very happy with their participation. Each person arrived on time for the meeting. Ann had volunteered to speak with the principal on behalf of the Council.

13 December

I met with the principal to update her on progress. She said that the girls had been to see her and ask permission to hold the disco. 'They were very courteous and asked when it would be convenient to return to me to hear the answer. I was delighted with their approach.'

In the meantime I decided to approach staff to gauge their reaction to their possible involvement in the disco. The faces of those I approached spoke volumes. I shared my misgivings with the principal and asked for her support.

14 December

The principal put the idea to the staff that lunchtime. A generous response was probably limited because the staff were already preparing for a concert and many were feeling overloaded. However, this did not lessen my disappointment at the lack of interest.

The principal and I gathered the students together later to explain the situation. She spoke to them in a frank manner, clearly respecting their capacity to understand and cope. The students, though disappointed, accepted that this was a busy time and that the disco would have to be postponed until the next calendar event, Valentine's Day.

My reflections

Students left the room feeling somewhat let down. I was very pleased with how the principal had handled the situation. She had listened to the students, agreed to meet them and explain the situation. She did not leave the job to me as liaison officer, which she could easily have done if she had wished. She was positive and supportive.

I was also pleased with the students' reactions, and especially Mark's comments. He was truly trying to understand the complete situation, being positive and optimistic. I could relate strongly to the students' disappointment and general feeling of deflation. I felt the same. This was a low point for us all. I just hoped that the holidays would re-energise us.

Christmas raffle

Mr D reported that students had responded to his request to help him organise the Christmas raffle. They had been 'very cooperative and organised the raffle well'. Here I felt was further evidence in support of the influence the Student Council was having.

The new term

Term began on 11 January and the next meeting was scheduled for the 18th. The agenda was set: the organisation for the disco on 11 February.

To my delight all students attended the meeting. Formalities were quickly dispensed with – the meeting opened and minutes read. Ideas flowed freely: they discussed catering arrangements, organising a DJ, practical issues, who would have responsibility for different jobs. They were helpful to each other; communication was open and they were tolerant and supportive. There was less dependency on me; students discussed among themselves what should be done and other people they should access.

I was unsure of the degree of involvement I could expect from the staff, and was uneasy about broaching the subject again. The principal suggested an alternative: 'Perhaps we could enlist the help of some of the parents?' I felt this indicated the principal's positive attitude towards the students, and my spirits rose.

27 January

Paul and Mark approached me along the corridor.

'Miss, what do you think of the idea of a cloakroom?'

'That's a good idea. I would never have thought of that.'

'Leave it to us. I'll bring it up at the next meeting.'

They were really getting into this! Their enthusiasm had surpassed all my expectations.

1 February

Full attendance. They discussed decorations, catering, cloakroom, finance.
'One thing we have overlooked,' said Mark. 'We need a float.'
'What's a float?' asked Karen.
Mark proceeded to explain carefully.

2 February

'We are meeting here for only ten minutes,' I said. 'This will be our last meeting before the disco, to check that everything's all right. I'll now hand over to Patrick.'

He went through all the duties, and checked that we all knew what we were doing.

Reflections

They learned so much from each other. Mark's explanation of a float, Joe's thoughtfulness in suggesting that those coming from large families ought to qualify for a reduced entrance fee, Louise volunteering to communicate arrangements to staff – these were all manifestations of improved confidence and ability to develop mature relationships. They seemed to have thought of everything. I hoped the disco would go as well.

11 February – action!

I arrived at 8 pm to find some members of the Council ready for action. They were anxious to sell tickets for the draw. Cloakroom tickets were left ready, together with Sellotape, to place on coats. Students assisted the DJ in setting up the equipment. Two parents assisted on the door. Two other parents and the principal worked in the shop; they decided that as the students had worked so well they now deserved time off to enjoy the event. Supervision of toilets was carried out by students. Everything went according to plan.

There was, however, a major upset. A small group of outsiders appeared and wanted to gain entry. I was called for and explained that the disco was for students only. The outsiders left noisily. I patrolled the grounds with a parent, but after a little while there was a good deal of noise from the school pitch. On investigation we found that the goalposts on the pitch had been broken. I was devastated with disappointment, for myself but mainly for the students. After all that work. The principal telephoned the police. The intruders were still around, and there was a chase. It was all very unpleasant.

The disco finished at 12.30 a.m. as arranged. The Council members gathered up the litter and swept the area.

Evaluation

Parents were enthusiastic about the event. 'It was a very well organised night. A great pity about the damage. There are thugs everywhere. But at least the students enjoyed themselves.'

Mr D, the teacher who organised the raffle, commented: 'The organisation was a great success. The trouble was outside your control and that of the students.'

15 February

The principal and I had met during the mid-term break. She had been full of praise for the students and the work they had done. Our return to school had been full of optimism and hope for better times ahead. However, that morning the principal told me that the caretaker had informed her that a lot more damage had been done than first thought: flower beds had been ripped up and garden seats thrown into a field nearby. She said, 'We really can't hold another disco. Too much damage has been done, and calling the police is not good for our image.' She would explain this to the students.

That lunchtime we called a meeting. The principal explained the situation in her caring, sensitive way: 'The work you completed in preparation for the disco was excellent. Your cooperation with each other and members of staff and parents was just superb and I want to congratulate you on that work.'

The students were understandably bitterly disappointed. While they agreed they had enjoyed themselves, they were disenchanted at the lack of support from adults. I, too, was disappointed.

However, I have to remember that the main objective was served. Students did learn how to cooperate with each other in a kind and sensitive manner; they did assume responsibility and exercise it in a positive way; they did relate with adults and show that they were capable of making decisions and taking appropriate action. These aspects were important, and these were the ones where they succeeded.

17 February – A critical incident

Peter, a student from fifth year, approached me. 'Miss, are you in charge of our Student Council?'

'Not in charge. I help and guide, but no one is in charge. This is a democratic assembly. Why do you ask?'

'It's like this. I had an incident with Teacher X, and my glasses fell off and broke. It was his fault. Will you talk with him for me?'

Now, here was a situation. I was being asked to intervene on a student's behalf; was he trying to manipulate me? I fielded that by responding: 'It's not for me to make a judgement about this, Peter. You are a senior student, and you seem very capable of explaining your situation. You need to explain it to Teacher X as you have explained it to me. It's not the job of the Council to take sides.'

I wondered, however, whether the students did see the Council as a forum to fight their corner, to protect them from challenges of teachers or others in authority. I consulted my critical friend.

'Ah, it would only be him that would think of this. But do you have a constitution?'

'No, we have only aims and objectives. The idea of a constitution never entered my mind, to be honest.'

'Tell the students about the incident. I suppose they know already, but tell them all the same. Then draw up a constitution.'

She said that she would get a copy of a constitution for me from another colleague; in the event this was very helpful to me, and helped me to draw up a draft constitution which I would present at the next Council meeting.

17 March

Patrick called the meeting to order. Ann read the minutes of the previous meeting and presented the agenda. I read through the draft Constitution. I had made copies for everyone.

Karen: What's a quorum?
Me: Where a minimum number of students must be present so that the meeting can take place.
Louise: Why is there a liaison officer?
Me: As one of our aims is to enhance communication between staff and students, it is probably useful to have a member of staff to communicate back to them.
Mark: Can we have some time to think about this? Do we have to obey these rules and regulations?
Me: Yes, we do, once we have agreed them. Can we have a proposal from someone?
Joe: I propose we read it ourselves and ask any questions we wish the next time.
Aisling: I'll second that.

I was pleased that the students wanted time to be reflective about the Constitution. They were not jumping into decisions. They were cooperative and working well as a team.

12 April

The Constitution was passed by the students without further amendments.

They had in the meantime been involved in a variety of other activities – selling chips at lunchtime, organising an anti-litter campaign, etc. – there seemed no end to their enthusiasm and inventiveness. They even initiated a lunchtime quiz session for junior students.

An Gaisce – President's Award

At this point I would like to say that five of the students from the Council participated in the President's Award scheme. I felt this would be a powerful agency in developing their organisational skills and self-esteem. It was indeed very encouraging to see that they felt positive about their capacity to participate. Their comments included:

Ann: I knew that by participating in the President's Award it would be helpful to me when I leave school.

Karen: I learned some new skills which I probably would not have done if I hadn't taken part. It was a great feeling going up to collect your medal. I felt a great sense of achievement.

Aisling: I enjoyed it. For community involvement I worked with the sick and elderly. It made me appreciate being young and active.

Mark: I did the President's Award because it was a challenge.

My critical friend wrote me a validation statement:

> Students benefited from involvement in the Award. It opened up a whole new world for them. At first they depended on teachers to a large extent, but as time went on they gained confidence in themselves. Involvement in the Student Council was a great help, and they definitely became more organised and self-confident.

Another colleague was attracted to the Award and also to the work we were doing in the Council. She wrote me a note:

> I decided to get involved with the students in participating in the President's Award as I felt it would benefit them and also me. By coming together as a group they learned teamwork, cooperation, respect for others' views. They all claimed that these aspects had developed because of their involvement with the Student Council.

I was very pleased at her interest. I felt that the students and I were setting an example to the rest of the student body and also to the staff that showed how we felt we ought to conduct ourselves, and the steps we were taking to do that. My colleague's interest revealed to me that my work was beginning to impact on school attitudes and structures. This year only one person was influenced: who knows what the future might bring?

Evaluation of the project

So where are we now, one year on? I feel a great sense of achievement. Setting up the Council was a trial run, and I look forward to developing it next year.

Did students develop as persons? Were their voices heard? Yes, on both counts. When I asked for their feedback they were unanimous: 'Yes, it helps you to understand how to organise events'; 'It's a great idea because it give us a chance to voice our opinions'; 'You learn about procedures and how organisations are run.'

They agreed that the experience had been fun, challenging, supportive, and educational. Relationships had improved between themselves and with staff. Generally they felt that their own self-esteem had risen.

I am acutely aware that this initiative could be seen as the beginning of a formal pastoral care system in our school. It is an indication of how systematising ideas within organisational contexts can lead to enhanced practices. I like to think that this self-initiated project can lead to organisational change of an enduring kind. My work is, I believe, illustrative of such an endeavour, and shows how a small group of people can mobilise themselves to influence wider social attitudes and practices.

My own learning

I realise that I now have to widen the circle of influence, especially among the staff. This year only two members of staff and the principal were involved. Perhaps I need now to address involvement by other colleagues as a new action research project.

I have learnt that there is an answer to every problem. It may take trips down many avenues to find it, but as you go down the avenues you learn something new. 'Education is not a preparation for life; it is life.' The students taught me a great deal. They helped me to reflect on my practice as an educator. Through their influence I realised that I also was in a constant state of learning; I also have to ask questions and strive for solutions. We learned together, through our successes and through our disappointments. We supported each other and consoled each other. We learned to care with each other.

The Student Council was only one conduit for care. While it might be true that care needs a content, I believe it would also be true to say that the relationships we develop with each other themselves constitute the content of what we learn. There must be any number of other initiatives like the Student Council that would give us forums for care. As teachers we have to be imaginative in finding them, or creating them ourselves within our own contexts. It is our responsibility as educators to care sufficiently to put ourselves out to find those ways. The quality of care begins with us, the teachers, and it goes far beyond, out into the lives of our students, and far beyond that again.

11

MAKING COLLABORATION REAL

Luke Monahan

Reflection

My research was undertaken as a means of facilitating reflection on my professional practice. Although I worked as a member of a team and we regularly evaluated our work, I required something more substantial, a real examination of my educational values.

I asked myself:

- Why am I engaged in education?
- What are my hopes for the people I work with, staff, students, parents, etc.?
- How am I being accountable for my work in school?

I searched for a methodology to facilitate this reflection and discovered action research.

This enabled me to reflect on every aspect of my work in order to articulate my values, have them critically evaluated and consciously adopt a set of values that would inform my work in the future.

The whole experience has confirmed my belief in my understanding of pastoral care as a 'systemic approach to education that seeks to value and develop the young person at every level' (Monahan 1996: 5). Pastoral care is not confined to one section of the school; it addresses the whole system and invites all to be involved in creating the best environment for learning for all school members.

The research has given me a great joy and sense of purpose in education. Pastoral care as an approach, I believe, recalls education to its roots, of care for the whole person.

My specific topic of research is an examination of the role of pastoral care coordinator. This is fast becoming a key role in schools as a means of staff support. Any development in schools must address itself to the academic staff if it is to have any hope of success. Staff must be supported, trained and provided with adequate resources. The pastoral care coordinator is a central figure in this process.

My research outlines one approach to the development of this role in a school community.

Background

I am a member of a religious order, the Society of Mary (Marist Fathers). Among other concerns, we have responsibility for three secondary schools in Ireland.

Chanel College was opened in 1955. It is an all-boys school in the voluntary secondary sector under the trusteeship of the Marist Fathers. Currently there is a Board of Management (four trustee nominees, two parent and two staff nominees), a Marist principal, 490 pupils and 30 staff members. The school is located in north Dublin and has disadvantaged status. It has pupils from mixed socio-economic backgrounds. I was appointed to the Board of Management in October 1992 and to the school staff as pastoral care coordinator and chaplain in 1994.

Action research – a personal choice

In undertaking the research documented here, the choice of action research, as my preferred methodology, was quite deliberate. During my work in another school, I became conscious of the need to have my work evaluated. As the leader of the pastoral team I had put in place evaluation structures for the policies and programmes that we undertook. Nevertheless, I felt a personal need to evaluate at a deeper level, a level that enquired into the values and overall direction of the work in which I was involved. I found myself asking questions such as:

- What are my hopes for the students with whom I work?
- What values inform my role in pastoral leadership?
- In what ways am I developing and learning?
- How can inclusion, cooperation and collaboration be encouraged among all the partners in the school community?

My needs were around clarifying and understanding my current practice in order to make it more effective, and to evaluate its effectiveness; to develop my own theory of education rather than draw on theories-in-the-literature, although my reading of these clearly informed what I was doing throughout the research. With McNiff I agree that 'action research is probably more useful to the needs of teachers in the living systems of their own classrooms than theories that are often more sociological than educational' (McNiff 1988: 10).

My concern, then, was to improve my own practice, and the person most clearly at the centre of this was myself. Lomax comments: 'Action research involves the researcher as the main focus of the research' (1994: 3). I believe that if we are serious about improving our practice, we cannot expect the solution to our concern to come from another. We have to cultivate a new frame of mind that says: 'What if I . . .?', rather than: 'what do you prescribe for me to do?' (Leonard 1995). It is I, as practitioner–researcher, who identifies my needs and concerns and seeks to address them in my own context. In this way the distance between theory and practice grows smaller.

Another key element in the attractiveness of action research is its invitation to examine one's own values. If I say I wish to improve my practice I am saying that I experience my educational values being negated (Whitehead 1989). I am therefore making a judgement about what is improvement and what is not in the light of what I consider to be a good order.

Action research enables me to reflect on my values, to evaluate and articulate them. More than this, I am invited to move from reflection to action in putting my values into practice. My hopes for my research were captured in the words of McNiff:

> We are action researchers because we adopt an open, questioning frame of mind, because we are open to our own sense of process, because it is our practical intent to improve the quality of our own lives for the sake of others.
>
> (McNiff *et al.* 1992: 63)

In the above context I wish now to outline the action research I undertook, in collaboration with staff of Chanel College, over a period of eighteen months (December 1993–May 1995). Throughout we used the methodology outlined in Chapter 1 of this book.

Identifying the area of concern in Chanel College

> A systems way of thinking refers to a view of individual behaviour which takes account of the context in which it occurs. Accordingly, the behaviour of one component of the system is seen as affecting, and being affected by, the behaviour of others.
>
> (Dowling and Osbourne 1994: 3)

While engaging in this research over the last few years I have found the work on systems theory to be helpful in my own learning. My experience has been that it couples well with action research. Its basic principle is outlined by Dowling and Osbourne (ibid.). It emphasises the vitality and inter-relatedness of all parts of a system. 'System' may be taken to be a set of interacting relationships; in the case of organisations, a school would be a good example.

Using these ideas, I stated my concern for Chanel College in the following terms: 'How can I, in my role as pastoral care coordinator, become part of the school system of Chanel College in order to improve the quality of pastoral care, with particular reference to the school staff ?'

It would be helpful to tease out the elements of this statement as they have impacted upon me in my experience:

- *How can I?* – the focus was *my* learning. Any hope of my being a 'change agent' in the school community depended on *my* willingness to be open to learning and personal change.
- *Pastoral care coordinator* – it was in the context of this role (a new role within the school) that I was concerned to share my experience both in support of my own learning and, hopefully, in bringing it into the public domain, that it might be of assistance and support to others.
- *School system of Chanel College* – I recognised that I would be influenced by others in this system and that I would, in turn, influence people in the school community.
- *Improve the quality of pastoral care* – in trying to improve my own practice as pastoral care coordinator, it was my hope that the knock-on effect would be to improve the quality of pastoral care in the school.
- *With particular reference to the school staff* – from a methodological perspective, I had to select a focus for the research, in order to show the process of my own personal learning, and how that might be seen to influence my practical work. I was aware that I would have to produce validated evidence in support of any claim I might make that I had improved my work, and show how the process had evolved. Because my task was to provide support for the staff, I needed to involve them as participants in the research from the outset.

Why was I concerned?

I have been a member of the Board of Management of Chanel since October 1992. I became aware, through this and through other informal contacts with the school, that there was a high level of stress in the staff. This appeared to be around the minimal level of formal 'caring' structures in the school. There also seemed to be a significant need for improved communication among staff. Alongside these issues there was a wealth of goodwill, initiative and creativity – the building up of which was due in no small part to the tireless work of the principal. This work was acknowledged by the staff when they were consulted in 1992 by the Marist Provincial regarding the re-appointment of the principal for a second three-year term. He received unanimous support.

Was this situation congruent with my own values?

My educational values in the context of my work in Chanel were (and are):

- Each person in the school community deserves respect and the possibility of fulfilling their potential in relation to their place in the school community.

- The school is primarily a learning environment for the student at every level of the person. The notion of 'every level of the person' is a significant one. Elsewhere I have commented:

  The student is constantly negotiating his/her learning at the aesthetic, creative, emotional, intellectual, moral, physical, political, religious, social and spiritual levels. The school though not primarily responsible for all this development, has a significant role to play at each level of learning, and needs to address itself to this in a creative and energetic fashion.

  (Monahan 1997: 40)

I also propose an image of a Wheel of Integrated Learning that seeks to depict the many ways in which learning is occurring at the various levels (see Figure 11.1).

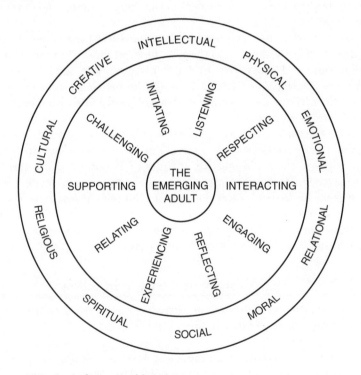

Figure 11.1 The wheel of integrated learning

Source: The Class Tutor: The Why . . . The What . . . The How . . . © Luke Monahan 1997

- I value pastoral care, as I understand it, as an approach to achieving the above in providing the 'context' for the school's policies, structures and programmes.
- The academic school staff are key partners in school development.
- The spirit and values of the Marist ethos are vital components in charting the direction for development of the school. The Marist ethos draws its inspiration from the spirituality of the Marist congregation. This spirituality seeks to highlight such qualities as mercy and compassion, inclusion, the value of community, listening and sensitivity.

Having stated my values, I can now outline how I perceived that they were not being lived out in my experience of Chanel.

Since having formally become part of the school system in October 1992 as a member of the Board of Management, I had felt that the structures were not sufficiently in place to facilitate the living out of the value of collaboration, in terms of staff involvement in the decision-making processes and development of the school.

In the context of my own personal learning I was clear about the need to find ways to put my values into practice. I looked forward to the challenge of collaboration as I strove to 'find my place' in the school community. Specifically the learning I hoped for would be inviting others in the school system to contribute significantly in the evolution and shaping of my role as pastoral care coordinator.

The values that I have outlined above had become more and more my own through my experience of working in my previous school – as much through their practice as their non-practice: at times I was not practising these values and this recognition aided my efforts to re-appropriate them. I saw my appointment in Chanel as an opportunity to live out these values consistently.

My sense was that these values were shared by a number of teachers, and these would form a basis for the development of a school community, and a shared vision of how the community might evolve.

Data to show my concern in action

In order to show the reality of the situation I gathered data from different sources using a variety of data gathering techniques:

1 Discussions at Board of Management level concerning the present climate and future direction of the school. This led to the setting up of a sub-committee. The Board adopted an approach to be offered to staff as a way forward.
2 Input to staff on this 'way forward' (February 1994).
3 Results of questionnaire to staff regarding the proposed way forward (March 1994).

These three elements form the core of my first set of data, to set the context of the situation. I will now outline in greater detail how each aspect impacted on my understanding of my role in relation to staff.

The Board of Management

The future direction of the school became a central theme for discussion at Board meetings in the Autumn of 1993. It was felt that good progress was being made in many areas, for example, the forthcoming establishment of the Transition Year. Nonetheless a broader organisational development plan was being sought. Concerns of Board members centred around stress levels among teachers and the difficulties of motivating pupils. It was suggested by a number of the Board members, myself included, that adopting a more 'pastoral' approach to the school might be a way forward. It was decided to set up a sub-committee to explore and propose a more detailed direction.

This committee, of which I was a member, drew up a briefing document. Group meetings gave me a significant insight into the school. We worked through the document and there was a strong feeling that the document represented key questions concerning Chanel College. It was clear from my two fellow committee members (teacher and guidance counsellor, who was also my critical friend) that teacher stress had much to do with needing support through the provision of class materials and other resources, and appropriate inservice training. It was also clear from our conversations that there was a great willingness on behalf of staff to be involved in school development.

We first sought agreement from the Board that our briefing document reflected the true situation of the school in relation to the staff. The Board accepted our submission as a working document. It was agreed that the next step was to involve the staff in a dual process:

1   Presentation of the 'pastoral school' option as a direction for school development.
2   Placing the staff at the centre of development through using methods such as questionnaires and discussion meetings that would access their views and set the agenda for development.

I was conscious that involvement of staff at this stage was crucial. Hamblin also comments: 'Understanding rooted in negotiation, rather than rushing into immediate action, is the soundest foundation for pastoral development' (1989: 26).

My hope was that this next step would be a further stage in gathering data to determine the 'reality' of the situation/system I was becoming part of in a new way. This data gathering stage of my research was a central part of my process of learning. Being conscious that I was involving myself in action research heightened my awareness of how it is that I act and reflect. In addition to this, what I might term 'second-level learning' was taking place: a meta-level of learning concerning the very process of the research itself, a critical reflection on my own learning in collaboration with others as we gathered and interpreted data participatively.

It was agreed by the Board of Management that I would facilitate a staff reflection process in February 1994. I was to present the 'Pastoral School' direction and to introduce the questionnaire as a means of centrally involving the staff.

Input to staff, February 1994

This was my first formal contact with the staff as a whole. At that time the negotiations regarding my role as pastoral care coordinator had not been completed. I spoke to the staff as a representative of the Board of Management. I sought to situate the development of the school in the context of the present reality, outlining my understanding of the positive aspects of the school and also the challenges facing it in the future. There was time for discussion of these, and agreement that this constituted an accurate description of the situation.

I went on to encourage discussion around the meaning of 'school pastoral care' in the light of the definition of pastoral care I have offered elsewhere: 'School Pastoral Care is an approach to education which endeavours to value and develop each member of the school community. It promotes learning at every level of the student' (Monahan 1998, p.9). I was keen to establish pastoral care as an essential feature of the whole school context, in line with the thinking of McGuiness:

> The consequences of adopting a whole school approach to pastoral care is that all teachers become responsible for it. The personal development of pupils is pursued in a professional, deliberate way by each member of staff. There can be no opting out.
>
> (McGuiness 1989: 50)

I also outlined some possible consequences of adopting this approach. A list was put together in consultation with the principal and the member of staff who was my critical friend. The report that this colleague later wrote indicated that the response from teachers was positive. Feedback indicated that:

- The staff wanted more communication as a support in their work.
- They wanted training to better equip them to face new and present challenges.
- They saw that pastoral structures would be a support in the development of the school.

Staff also gave me informal feedback about the staff input. As a further (and possibly more objective) way of inviting their opinion, I asked them to complete a questionnaire.

Feedback from staff questionnaire

I had drafted the questionnaire and submitted it to the Board of Management. They were happy with the content. I piloted it with the sub-committee of the Board of Management and several teachers before putting it out for the whole staff. The findings from this questionnaire give key feedback concerning staff attitudes, including the following:

- Teachers recognised the need for more whole staff meetings.
- Twenty-six of the thirty staff felt that the area of discipline caused most stress to teachers.
- The handling of 'difficult' students was an area of concern.
- More training of class tutors was urgently requested, together with provision of materials and suggestions for procedural approaches.

Staff were invited in the questionnaire to name what value, in their view, was at the core of the school. 'Caring' with thirteen topped the poll. 'Justice' with six, 'discipline' and 'holistic', with four each, followed. Other identified values were 'learning', 'respect', 'sport', 'numbers' and 'fun'.

I presented the collated questionnaires to the Board of Management with a proposal for action (see below). The Board members were excited at the outcome of the questionnaire and the staff inservice day. The teacher representatives were particularly positive. One of them said: 'There is a feeling that we are going somewhere and that we can get there.'

I believe that, while the above exercise was essential in terms of data gathering, it was also very useful in terms of creating a climate for positive evaluation and development. With McGuiness I hold that: 'In the final analysis staff attitudes are more important than school structures' (McGuiness 1989: 35).

Interpreting the data

The wealth of data provided allowed the sub-committee to build a comprehensive picture of the state of Chanel College, and also provided an excellent route map for me when I came to devise an action plan for my role as pastoral care coordinator. Above all the data confirmed that I needed to support the staff and provide them with appropriate resources and materials, and opportunities for training and meeting together. This process of data gathering deepened my appreciation of the value of listening and collaboration, for I realised that, without the participation of colleagues, my own perceptions of the situation and its improvement would count for nothing.

Forming and implementing an action plan

Possible ways forward

Throughout the month of June 1994 I considered possible courses of action. At this stage I knew I was to work in the school three days a week. Some of the possibilities were:

1 Take a lot of subject teaching in order to build up my own credibility with staff.
2 Teach a pastoral care programme right through the school: staff would be happy that this area was being covered.
3 Use my time to work with 'difficult' students and reduce the burden on staff.
4 Emphasise the religious and Marist side of my task as one of two chaplains in the school, so supporting the religion department who were at the centre of pastoral activity.

I discussed all these courses of actions with the principal and my critical friend.

Implementing the action plan

In my chosen action plan I wanted to emphasise the roles of supporting and provision of resources. It was my feeling that staff were ready to accept me as a resource; therefore I did not need to gain credibility through subject teaching. This perception had been reinforced through their responses to questionnaires. I was also clear that it would be an evasive step to cover a pastoral care programme with students myself. My aim was to encourage collaboration; this meant my not facilitating the programme but working with those who would be responsible. This also enabled teachers to become active collaborators in the ongoing development and revision of the programme.

Another possible course was to spend time dealing with 'difficult' students. Again I did not see that this was the optimal use of my time in supporting staff. Rather I felt it would be more beneficial to begin a debate among the staff concerning a pastoral response to these difficult students.

My 'Definition of Role' document

I drew up this document which I saw as an important first step in addressing my concern of supporting staff. The document helped me set out my aims, objectives and strategies and be able to have something to which others could respond. It clearly set out how this new role in the Chanel school system could be developed. The aim outlined in the document situated my role in the overall development of the school. The second section on objectives explained what developing towards a pastoral school might mean for Chanel and, finally, the third section on strategies demonstrated possible practical steps on the road towards realising the aims and objectives.

The final draft of this document was drawn up after consultation with the principal and my critical friend. I then forwarded it to members of the Board of Management. In August 1995, at the opening staff meeting of the year, I was given time to discuss the document with the whole staff. There was a very encouraging response to the contents. As an example, one staff member said: 'It is great to know there is someone to call on to support us' (my journal).

This staff meeting was an excellent opportunity to state my availability to staff and encourage their involvement in the development of my role. Also I informed the staff of my research work. I sought and received their permission to use the experience of working with them in this research.

Other elements to the action plan – inservice day and support structures for staff

The Board of Management met in May 1994 to review the findings of the staff questionnaire. I proposed that an inservice day on pastoral care should be held in the opening week of school, during August 1994. This would continue the work of the inservice of February by involving and positively motivating the staff at this crucial stage of the school year.

At this meeting we discussed developing communication structures for staff. The results of the staff questionnaire indicated that there was a strong desire for different forms of meetings. Marland states: 'Whatever the reason, a really successful pastoral system will depend on channels of communication being kept well open, with a constant information flow being directed to where the information will be most useful' (1974: 19).

It was agreed to propose to staff that a weekly time for meetings be put into the timetable. These meetings would take different forms – subject teacher groupings, full staff, transition year and class tutors. The weekly thirty-minute time tutors had with their classes would continue, and I would support class tutors with resources and materials concerning personal–social, health and ethos education.

Why adopt this particular plan?

The role definition document, inservice day and staff support structures made clear that I wished to adopt a collaborative role with the staff, rather than working separately to them, and also wished to encourage wider staff collaboration. The reasons for these courses of action refer back to my educational values outlined above.

Subsequent experience of the implementation of this action plan reinforced for me the understanding that, while action research initially focuses on the learning of the individual practitioner, this learning can have meaning only in relation to the experiences and learnings of the other participants in the research. In this way, I discovered, the focus of the action moves from 'I' to 'we'.

Inservice day – August 1994

My critical friend and I, as organisers, engaged a facilitator to guide the in-service day. We met with him ahead of the day to brief him on the school and its staff, gave him the findings of the staff questionnaire, and asked him to sit-uate pastoral care in the whole-school context. This would enable the staff to work towards the practical consequences for the school – its structures, poli-cies and programmes.

The facilitator was well received and put pastoral care in the context of the experience of the staff. He began the day by evoking from the staff their sense of the challenges of teaching at this time. Into that experience he placed pas-toral care, stating that it was about caring for each individual and creating the best environment possible for learning. He talked about the need to support the key basic roles within the staff – subject teacher and class tutor – outlining models of structures to enable the pastoral aims of the school to be realised. The staff moved into groups to decide on a model for Chanel.

The staff were engaged by the process and participated positively. My role, outlined the day before at the staff meeting, was located within the pastoral development of the school. The staff agreed to implement a new structure of a ten-minute slot at the beginning of each day where class tutors would be with their classes.

Developing other support structures

I was asked by the Board of Management, in response to a request from the staff, to provide class material for class tutors for a pastoral care programme. I gathered this material and put it together as folders and other handouts, but I worried that staff would become over-reliant on the folders and then be frus-trated when inevitable implementation difficulties arose. A programme, while being a useful resource, cannot be successful in isolation from other initiatives. Therefore I sought always to show the relatedness of all the pastoral efforts we were making throughout the school. Watkins and Wagner state this well in regard to a pastoral programme: 'Tutorial programmes are but one of the loca-tions of the pastoral curriculum, albeit one which is specially characterised by the tutor's extra knowledge of, and relationship with the tutor group' (1987: 164).

Nonetheless, the teachers appeared adamant about the need for such a programme. I decided that they knew best, and I would have to deal with issues of the integrated nature of pastoral programmes as they arose.

The principal and I drew up a schedule of weekly staff meetings. I had particular responsibility for organising the monthly form tutor meetings.

Monitoring the action: how my learning influenced the school system

I believe that the plan of action outlined above, as well as the ongoing introduction of further initiatives, has positively influenced the school system and in particular the staff. The following data and sources provide evidence:

1   My reflective journal – this charts my professional learning.
2   Minutes of ongoing discussions at Board of Management meetings reviewing the progress of pastoral development of the school.
3   Records of staff inservice day reviewing progress of pastoral development, January 1995.
4   Records of class tutor meetings, January–May 1995.

Data from the journal

Keeping my journal was an essential part of doing my research. I was able to record significant events and my reactions to them. I was also able to chart both the progress of the action plan outlined above as well as my own learning. Extracts from the journal include:

1   6 September 1994: a number of teachers came to see me in relation to teaching the pastoral care programme: 'I really want to give this a go'; 'It's great to have some content'; 'They'll [students] be a bit shocked when we go pastoral on them'; ' I'd love to get into this area.' Acting as a resource and support person – try and meet teachers where they're at – build on their experience – get to know them – demystify pastoral care, reduce expectations – aware of lack of confidence in staff, need to build it up gently and realistically.
2   24 October 1994: one of the sixth year student prefects/leaders chatting to me: 'What is it you do – seems like a great job, being nice to everyone. . . . I'd like to chat to you about a decision I have to make.' I was pleased that I was perceived as a positive, approachable person in the school. (To note: at this stage students were not formally perceived as participants in the research, and their comments are not recorded. However, the episode recounted here indicates that an awareness was already in place of how students contribute to the overall evaluation of the effectiveness of organisational programmes – see also later in this report.)
3   22 December 1994: meeting with critical friend to review term: 'That was

a good term's work . . . at last we're going places . . . it was impossible to do any of this over the last years.' I replied: 'This shows the value of working as a team; support for each other makes all the difference.' The value of collaboration was being recognised at an overt level.

4   21 March 1995: a class tutor talking with me about her experience of teaching the pastoral care programme: 'It's taken me a while to get the hang of this pastoral care – but it seems to be going down well now.'

5   4 April 1995: remarks from my critical friend: 'So, Luke, how do you feel the year has gone? How did you feel treated?' He went on to say that we had talked a lot about my role and the school but he wondered how I felt at a personal level. He wondered did I suffer from anxieties. I said I did, but 'I have structures in place – my community, spiritual direction, friends and relaxation.' It is important to be able to receive care as well as give it.

Data from Board of Management meetings

At each of the Board meetings during the academic year 1994/95 the development of pastoral care in the school was discussed. It was important to keep the Board of Management informed and involved in the process. They were always receptive and supportive, as when they made provision for a budget for pastoral development in the school of £1,000. This was the first time such an allocation had been made.

December 1994: during an extended review of the development of the initiative, there was a very positive feeling regarding that development. Teacher representatives reported that the staff felt more supported and most were now willing to learn new skills especially in relation to methodologies in the teaching of the pastoral care programme. There was full support for an inservice day at the beginning of the next term with training and evaluation elements.

February 1995: there was positive feedback concerning the inservice day in January. One member suggested that consideration needed to be given to training a staff member in pastoral leadership.

March 1995: a discussion ratifying key school policies on relationships and sexuality education and drugs awareness education. The Board felt it was significant that teachers and others should be fully involved in the drawing up of these policies. They saw the developing pastoral environment as central to this process.

Data from staff inservice day – January 1995

This day had two key elements. The first was further training in skills of classroom management using the work of William Glasser (1984), and the second, a review of the development of the pastoral care initiative since the beginning of the school year. The first part of the day examined the relevance of Glasser's educational ideas. The second part of the day focused on evaluating the plan of action undertaken in August 1994.

Having given a summary of initiatives during the year, I invited the staff to work in groups to evaluate these initiatives, using handouts and other resources provided. We needed to ascertain what had worked and what needed improving. The main features of this evaluation were as follows:

1   There was substantial affirmation of the value, in terms of support and communication, of the weekly staff meetings. While meetings of class tutors had been held informally, there was now a lot of support to have them structured into the rota of meetings.
2   The pastoral care programmes were more successful in the junior years than in the senior years. The pastoral care class needed to be situated earlier in the day. Regularity of contact with classes was vital.
3   Having the support of the counsellor and chaplains was helpful; further structuring of this service was needed.
4   Resources and materials were very useful.

The evaluation was positive while at the same time pointing to a number of refinements needed to the structures in place. Particularly noticeable was the goodwill with which the evaluation was undertaken. The staff appeared to feel supported, and welcomed the overall direction of pastoral development of the school.

Data from class tutor meetings – January–May 1995

Formal meetings for class tutors were scheduled into the weekly staff meeting rota. These meetings were useful in helping tutors to clarify their role. I suggested they meet in year groups, and together we drew up an agenda for their discussions. I 'floated' between the groups during the meeting.

Three examples show how this structure demonstrates development both in my role and in staff attitudes.

1   End of January meeting of class tutors: the third year tutors (Junior Certificate year) submitted a list of areas where they needed advice and resources. I responded in written form in as detailed a way as possible. The tutors appeared pleased with the response: 'This is great – just what we need' (Journal, 6 February). I recognised, however, that I had choices about how best to use my time, whether to teach the students, or continue to support the staff. I was also conscious that, while the staff appeared to value me as a supporter, I was there to support their learning. I should not assume that they could not do without me, and I should work consistently towards making myself redundant. This I believe is demonstrated in (2) below.

2   8 March 1995: meeting of second year form tutors: 'We use these meet-
    ings to choose a topic that we'll cover in the next few weeks. One of us
    gets material together and makes this available to the others – check how
    things went at the next meeting – we go to you for resources on the topic
    if necessary.'
3   End of year meeting of class tutors: the most noticeable aspect was a sense
    of greater confidence about the role of class tutor. The tutors felt confident
    to devise their own material while being supported by a programme –
    some change from the clamouring for a programme a year ago. It was
    heartening to see a request from the senior tutors to have time to plan
    their year, as they had been the group who had experienced special diffi-
    culties during the year.

How can I judge the value of my work?

The literature of educational research demonstrates the importance of distinguishing between data and evidence (see, for example, Robson 1993). In action
research projects, when we make a claim to knowledge, it is necessary to identify clear criteria by which we are willing to have that claim assessed by the
wider community of researchers, and to produce aspects of our data that will
stand as evidence for our claims. I believe that I can identify three locations in
which the data I have gathered point to improvement of the situation, and I
offer the following in summary.

1   *Attitudinal*: attitudes of staff changed towards meetings, students, the
    changing process of decision making, self-evaluation and pastoral care. I
    was aware of significant changes in my own learning and attitudes.
2   *Affective*: staff appeared more at ease in issues concerning stress, commu-
    nication between teachers and management, relationships, pastoral
    structures and new initiatives. My own feelings regarding the acceptance
    of my place in the school system were strengthened.
3   *Behavioural*: staff changed their behaviour in the light of the interventions
    that were made; for example, through the use of pastoral personnel, atten-
    dance and contributions at meetings, use of pastoral resources. My own
    behaviour changed as I developed my understanding of what it means to
    be a pastoral care coordinator.

In conclusion to this section I would claim that adopting a supportive role in
the school system has helped me to live out my educational values more fully.
I also believe that staff are more confident in their role because of the support
provided.

An evaluation of the research

In this section I want to summarise the learning from the work in Chanel from the perspective of the staff and also from my own professional standpoint. I was increasingly aware, throughout the research, that the learning was a transformative process which emerged through the interactions and critical reflections of all the participants.

Reflecting on my practice in relation to the staff

I have attempted to show how the staff have benefited from embarking on a more explicitly articulated pastoral direction for the school. I have produced data to support this idea. This data has been validated from a number of sources (see the original thesis, Monahan 1995), including the following excerpt from the report of my critical friend on his reflections of the year:

> There can be little doubt concerning the progress of staff development in this past year. Staff are more positive regarding school. They have responded exceptionally well to the new pastoral structures. . . . Luke has played a key role.

What implications did I see for my role in the forthcoming year?

1   I felt that I must build on the relationship in place with the staff, to encourage them to take increasing responsibility for pastoral work in the school.
2   I needed to encourage the staff further to see themselves as major resources in pastoral care.
3   I needed to encourage the development of the more positive relationship staff had with students to further the voices of students being included in the decision making processes of the school. With Hamblin I agree: 'Involvement of students is crucial. Failure to make pastoral activities a joint enterprise between students and tutors deprives us of what may be the most potent agency for achieving pastoral aims' (1993: 3). This is also an indication of the expanded focus of student involvement in the research – see below.
4   I hoped also, through the newly introduced home–school liaison scheme, to encourage collaboration between staff and parents in the life of the school.

Reflecting on my own learning in the course of the research

In writing up this research I have pointed to the many ways in which I have personally gained from my involvement. The most important elements in that learning were:

1   The exercise of making explicit my educational values – this helped me to focus more easily on where I needed greater consistency in my practice and how I could most usefully make my contribution.

2   The value of action research – as a means of personal awareness leading to understanding, insight, focused action and evaluation leading to re-formulation. I also learned that the methodology of action research enabled me to work collaboratively in an effective way.

3   I learned to be flexible in the interpretation of my role and to allow others to contribute to its organic development. I moved away from the instrumental model of implementing a well-defined role definition.

4   I developed a capacity to enable, to stand back and encourage others in gaining confidence and skills in their pastoral work. I increasingly resisted the temptation for short-term satisfaction in providing a 'quick fix' for immediate needs against the benefit of the longer range goals of encouraging others to take responsibility for their own situations.

5   I gained an invaluable insight into the importance of attending to my personal needs as I supported others.

6   I became aware of the value of my own reflective journal. I have drawn on it as a means of interpreting data and improving critical reflection.

7   I have learnt that success is not so much in the outcome as in the process, a process that involves, respects, challenges and supports others. As I try to evaluate the impact of the research, I refer to the criteria identified above: the data indicate that attitudes changed because of the supportive environment; feelings about areas that caused teachers stress in the past were now more positive; teachers were prepared to change their behaviour and try new approaches.

I am aware of the impact of undertaking this research on my own professional learning. I am aware that it was a process that allowed me the freedom to question my attitudes, deal with feelings of anxiety, and experiment with new behaviours. This involved adopting an open-ended plan of action that was participatory and evolutionary, significant features of educational action research in social and educational settings.

Taking the work forward in other contexts

I believe many of the lessons learned in this research project may be applied in other contexts. Those learnings include:

1   The need to clarify one's educational values: this requires the researcher to be clear about the reasons for aiming to improve their practice.

2   Involving others in the research: this has both supportive and challenging elements to it for both the researcher and research participants.

3   The staff, when accompanied in a supportive and resourceful way, will be more inclined to respond positively to pastoral initiatives. I believe adopting an explicitly caring attitude to staff will have positive outcomes. This support is essential in encouraging colleagues to become more confident in their own abilities and less reliant on an outside source.

4   Flexibility and openness are essential in developing a role such as pastoral care coordinator. There is an important lesson here for the development of any caring role in a school context, that while a role definition is important, flexibility in regard to its development is very helpful in the exercise of what that role is about.

5   When change is being proposed for an organisational system it is vital to involve as many as possible of those who will be affected by the change. I believe this was an important element in the success of the project.

6   Those in a caring role need to organise support for themselves if they are to continue to operate effectively in this kind of demanding and challenging work. This applies to all practitioners: managers, teachers, providers, parents and students. I believe this research has gone some way to demonstrating the need for support structures to be put in place as part of a caring community of learners.

And finally

A past pupil from my previous school recently asked me if my experience in Chanel was much the same as it had been in her school. I was pleased to say that it had not. The difference was that I had learned many lessons during my time in her school, clarified and developed my own educational values, and was now trying to realise them in a new way. When I began my work as pastoral care coordinator I decided that I would try to live out these educational values in a consistent way so as to benefit the school community of which I was becoming a part.

I have attempted in this paper to define my research issue, and to follow it through as a systematic enquiry: how I could become part of the school system of Chanel College in order to improve the quality of pastoral care, with particular reference to the staff. I believe that together we went a long way towards improving our situations, individually and collectively.

I am aware that this report is only the beginning of the research, and it needs to be developed. The research did not focus on the students. My concern at the time was to encourage the teachers to see themselves as the main resources in their own professional learning, and to encourage them to work collaboratively in identifying their own needs and working systematically to address them. I deliberately refrained from asking them to monitor their own practice in relation to the students, for fear of overload. However, that will now constitute the next phase of the research. How do we know whether or not we are being effective unless we ask the people whose lives we are influencing? For teachers that means the students, and, no less, the parents and carers in the home situation. I am aware that future stages of the research must focus on capturing their voices and insights, and that process is now in hand at time of writing.

I finish, leaving the final word to Julian of Norwich: 'The best prayer is to rest in the goodness of God knowing that that goodness can reach right down to our lowest depths of need.'

12

THE BULLY WITHIN

Bríghid McGuinness

Reflection

My story tells of how I discovered the 'invisible bullies' in my classes. I believe that I would never have come to the position of making such a discovery, and others like it, unless I had continued my professional learning on the Higher Diploma course, and in turn engaged in doing an action research project. I have become what Schön (1983) calls 'a reflective practitioner'. Perhaps I already was before I did the project; doing the project has raised my awareness not only of my own practice, but also of how necessary it is to reflect on that practice. My ability to think critically developed, and led to my questioning what I had previously taken for granted. Consequently I became aware of realities that had been hidden, realities that there were damaging influences afoot that I needed to tackle.

Did I influence my students' lives for good? I think I did. I have produced evidence in my work, and in this report, that my students are happier in their lives because of my intervention, and so am I. More, it was not just me influencing them. We influenced each other. I learned as much from my students as they did from me. Together we improved our collective learning environment, and that is bound to have wider influence for our school and community.

I continue to live in an action research way. Once you get into this way of thinking you do not stop. It would be like deliberately taking off your spectacles and living in a fashion that permanently distorts the reality you are part of. My critique extends not only to my work, where I now constantly question what I am doing, and am constantly on the lookout for how I can improve my practice, but also to my life in general. I am more aware of the needs of others, and of my own needs in relation to others. It is a challenging yet liberating way of life, and I love it. I believe that living and working in this way helps me to live out my values in a spiritual connectedness with others and myself.

Background to the research

If anyone had suggested to me three years ago that there were bullies in my class, I would have smiled indulgently and disregarded them. Bullies were in other teachers' classes, not in mine. I was a caring teacher, alert, positive, anxious always to identify and meet my students' needs. I monitored my students' progress, carefully evaluated my own, and maintained good records of everything that I did.

That was my perception of my own practice until I joined the Higher Diploma in Pastoral Care course, and heard a new discourse about how we construct and deconstruct our own professional knowledge, how we need to exercise critical thinking about what we are doing so that we are not lulled into a false sense of security and fool ourselves that all is well when perhaps it is not.

The idea of critical thinking was new for me, and revelatory. I had of course met the idea of challenging prejudices before, but I had always seen that in relation to other people's prejudices – never my own. Our tutor recommended that we have a look at Stephen Brookfield's work, and I borrowed his *Developing Critical Thinkers* (1987) that afternoon from the library. I learned a great deal from that book. I learned that it is necessary not only to question our own prejudices as well as other people's, but also to question the way of thinking that we use. I found this idea quite daunting at the time, but also appealing and liberating. I drew from my reading that we are never free of our own way of thinking, and we have to keep this awareness high in coming to positions and making judgements. Extended reading (for example, Carr and Kemmis 1986; Freire 1970; Young 1992) helped me to see that I needed to be aware of my own history and culture, of my own cultured context as a thinker; to see that whatever decisions I came to would inevitably be coloured by previous experience and learning.

These insights, developed through my encounter with the ideas of critical thinking, were reinforced by the methodologies of action research. As I worked my way through my research project, I became aware that I had to be accountable for my own practice. I had to show that I was acting out of a sense of purpose, that I could give good reasons for my actions, and that these reasons were rooted in the values I held as a teacher. My learning developed as I worked through the various stages of identifying a concern, stating why I was concerned, systematically gathering data to show what I was doing and whether it was having any effect on my classroom practice, and inviting the comments of my validating groups to show that my practice was authentic.

Perhaps I can communicate to you what that process was like by recounting the story of how I found that there really were bullies in my class; and that possibly the biggest bully was me because of my lack of awareness.

What was my concern?

My concern was triggered because a colleague on the Higher Diploma course said that there was a bullying problem in her class; she was temporarily at a loss how to handle it, and asked us, as her critical friends, to help her imagine ways to solve it. We invited her to describe the situation to us. She described a class scenario that might have been mine. Everything appeared to be going smoothly, yet there were some undercurrents that she was having difficulty in identifying and bringing to the surface. One of the ways in which she sensed that all was not well was the fact that some of the girls in her class were unusually quiet in the presence of another group. Our colleague worked in a single-sex girls school, and told about how the apparently dominant group had begun intimidating others in very subtle ways. She was not sure how to bring the situation out into the open. She was a caring teacher, highly professional, and the last person one would expect to have a bullying problem in her class – just like me.

I reflected on what she was saying in respect of my own situation. At the time I was working in a rural mixed school, teaching maths, and was constantly aware of the potential of the boys to intimidate the girls. As far as I was concerned, there was no bullying going on in any of my classes, yet my new reading and insights into critical thinking raised my awareness to the fact that I might be mistaken. How could I be sure that all was well? Might I be unaware of what could be going on under my very nose? Perhaps I ought to investigate, just to be on the safe side.

What could I do?

I thought about possible strategies. I could issue a questionnaire, but I was not too keen on this idea. Hopkins (1993) cautions against questionnaires: they need to be carefully constructed if they are to serve a useful purpose, and I felt I did not have the necessary skills. I could talk to various people formally and informally. That would not make things too obvious. I could observe what was going on, and closely monitor pieces of the action to get a snapshot which might be representative of other wider scenarios. Rather than monitor all my classes I could select one and concentrate on getting a good picture of what was going on there. This seemed the most practical and effective strategy, given that I was not sure that I had a problem in the first place. Perhaps this was what sent little alarm bells ringing in my head; the fact that I felt I did not have a problem was a problem in itself – at least, that is what my understanding of critical thinking was telling me.

Gathering the data

I decided to monitor the action quietly and systematically, beginning the following day. I saw my second year maths group three times a week, so I could get some kind of picture quite quickly.

The class of twenty comprised about fifty–fifty boys and girls. They were generally pleasant, high-spirited, cooperative, and academically bright. I had worked hard to engender a spirit of friendly cooperation and competition. There were no 'problems' that I could not handle.

During that lesson I did my own informal version of the Flanders Interaction Analysis. I mentally broke the class into smaller groups, and observed them during our lesson, organising my observation into sections of time and watching closely for anything that I felt might be construed as bullying behaviour. I especially kept an eye on the boys. I identified behaviour categories of 'supportive actions', 'challenges', 'aggression', 'intimidation', and tallied instances of those behaviours in appropriate cells on my observation schedules. I used a blue pen for boys and a red one for girls – how I have been conditioned by my own education and culture!

I did not anticipate that I would do any kind of analysis of my observations until after the event, but I was aware that, even as I was recording the number of instances, certain behaviours were exhibited, trends were emerging that were not according to my expectations. Whereas I had anticipated that more blue marks would appear under 'challenges' and 'aggression', there were more red ones.

So it was with a real sense of anticipation that I settled down that evening to analyse the scores. The data were there: the girls appeared to be more aggressive towards the boys than the boys to the girls. Why was this such a surprise? Why had I not seen it before?

This might have been a freak event, I told myself, so I decided to do the same exercise over the next few lessons. The results were the same: a small but clear tendency of the girls to be aggressive towards the boys. During the third lesson I narrowed the focus of the activity, and became aware that the aggression was coming from five girls in particular. They were engaging in a quite subtle game of taunting and subversion against what appeared to be a small group of boys. This was carried out in such an unobtrusive way as to be almost invisible.

My initial observations had revealed much. However, aware that this kind of informal observation was a fairly crude technique, I decided to follow up the initial data gathering with a more qualitative type of assessment, and over the next few days I informally chatted with students in the class. I chose girls and boys as the opportunity arose, and invited them to talk with me about relationships between students in the classroom. I did not refer specifically to instances of bullying, or anything that could be construed as bullying. I asked their permission to take notes as we spoke, and my observations are recorded as field notes. I was particularly anxious to speak with the groups I had provisionally identified as bullies and victims, but I was careful not to single them out in any way. When I managed to speak with them, however, comments included the following:

Conversation with two girls

Me: Do you feel that everyone in the class gets on well together?
Student 1: Yes. We have our usual groups, but there is generally a good spirit.
Me: Do the boys and girls get on well?
Student 2: Oh, yes. We have a lot of fun. There's no trouble.

Conversation with two boys

Me: Do you feel that everyone in the class gets on well together?
Student 3 Yes, generally OK, but some of the girls are bossy.
Me: How do you mean?
Student 3: They throw their weight around a bit. They like to tell us what to do.
Student 4: Not all of us. They wouldn't tell me what to do.
Me: Is this a problem for you?
Student 4: Not for me. It is for him (indicating Student 3).
Me: How?
Student 3: No, not really. He'd say that, wouldn't he.

I had an emerging sense that something was happening, but it was underground, and students possibly did not want to talk about it.

What did I do?

Clearly I had to make some sort of intervention if the problem was to be surfaced and addressed. It would not go away. Perhaps it would eventually, but in the meantime every hurtful episode would do further damage to everyone involved. It should not be postponed.

I decided to draw up an action plan. My difficulty was not only that I would have to deal with a potential problem, but also that I needed to find out what the problem was in the first place.

Defining the problem

I drew up a small worksheet which contained three very short illustrated stories of girls and boys interacting during maths lessons. Following the stories there were five questions, which invited comment about how the girls and boys in the stories might be perceived. I took ten minutes out of formal maths activities and asked the students to work in pairs in answering the questions. I asked each pair to appoint one person to write out the answers, which I then later collated. One of my concerns was to raise awareness about the need for good relationships, both by looking at the issue as a formal activity, and also through the process of working together. In organising paired work, I felt that relationships could be better cemented. Although I gathered in the worksheets and collated my findings afterwards, as part of the classroom exercise I invited students to comment both on the worksheet and also on the experience of working together. They said: 'You could have thought those stories were us'; 'I think the girls in the stories acted a bit high-handed towards the boys.' Did this happen in our class, I asked. 'No, never,' from a girl. 'Yes, sometimes,' from a boy.

The results that evening again showed that the trends were there. I needed to do something both to make the situation explicit, and also to improve it. I was embarrassed that I had automatically assumed that any aggression would be coming from the boys to the girls. I was embarrassed because of my own unnamed and unfelt prejudice.

In the next maths lesson I again arranged to finish the formal activities about ten minutes early, and invited the class to have a discussion about the way their studies were going. They were very happy to abandon maths and to talk. I explained that I believed there was a connection between how they felt about themselves and how well they were getting on in their studies; and I was anxious to make sure that everyone felt as good as possible about themselves, and also that the class spirit enabled everyone to do their best.

I have to say that arranging for a class discussion was nothing unusual. We frequently had talks as a group to check how they were getting on and to make sure that everyone understood the subject matter. This was part of my own ongoing evaluation process. However, the focus of the class talks had until now always been on maths, rather than on themselves as people learning maths. This change in emphasis was a result of my learning on my Higher Diploma course, that although care needs a content, perhaps the greatest content is in the process of developing relationships with each other; and this practice needs to permeate the whole curriculum.

I had also learnt from colleagues on the course about the benefit of developing interactive teaching methodologies, so, instead of me acting as chair, as would normally be the case, I invited two students to act as co-chairs, a boy and a girl. The boy was Student 3 (above), who I felt was a victim of sorts although he would never acknowledge this in public; the girl was one of the aggressive five.

I invited the class to talk in pairs for a few minutes, to decide on issues they felt would be worth discussing. The girl chair volunteered to write the issues on the board. Issues included:

- asking questions in class: how Ms McGuinness answers us
- how we talk to each other
- understanding the homework
- keeping up to date.

We organised the class into small groups to brainstorm ideas around these issues, and then the chairpersons invited comments from the floor.

Relationships

This was the first issue to be taken up. Comments about how I responded to questions, and how they talked to each other generated a lot of lively debate. Some people felt that we needed to give more thoughtful responses; others felt that we needed to talk with greater respect and understanding, and be less dismissive. No one said that I needed to do that; they were careful not to say anything negative about my own quality of response. I took this to mean that this might be an issue which I needed to look at myself, and I resolved to do so (this became a more coherent action research project at a later date). There was, however, a clear message that the students needed to develop a more caring attitude towards one another.

Homework and keeping up to date were also clearly issues that provoked anxiety. Some students, girls and boys, felt that they did not always understand the homework fully, and spent too much time trying to work out what was required, rather than doing the work itself.

There was not enough time that day to address how we might tackle the issue, and I invited students to think about this for our next meeting. I also suggested that we take one issue at a time and think about how we might tackle each one systematically and improve the situation for us all. I resolved to think about them myself. There was no need for mental reminders; the issues were now constantly on my mind.

Addressing the problems

The issue of bullying was still underground and was not being voiced. I reflected on this continually. Would it be productive to bring it out into the open, or might this do more damage? I gave it a good deal of thought, and I consulted with my critical colleague in school. It was also good fortune that the Higher Diploma group were meeting that week, and I could seek advice there.

My critical colleague's reaction was:

> Something seems to be amiss. You need to bring it into the open, but not in an obvious way. If you don't address it now, it will only develop further and perhaps surface in some other way and probably in an unexpected place.

Colleagues on the Higher Diploma course counselled:

Could you find some resource to help you almost force the issue to come out? Perhaps you need to get the students to acknowledge what is going on for themselves.

One colleague said she had used a video in a personal development class about a particular group of bullies. When her students saw it they empathised immediately, and some even said they recognised themselves among the bullies. This seemed like a good idea, and I began enquiring about resources through various school channels, and also enquiring direct from resource centres. About two weeks after these meetings, I found a video which seemed particularly suitable for my purposes, and I suggested to my maths group that they might like to watch it. They were very keen to do so. I also invited the PSE teacher to view it with us. He rearranged his own timetable so that he could be free to join us. I became aware at this juncture of the value of liaising with colleagues in school in pursuit of common curricular goals, and I thought how unfortunate it is that sometimes colleagues working even in adjacent classrooms have little idea what the other is doing. How much more beneficial it is for students when teachers actively collaborate, and find ways to share what they are doing, how they are monitoring their own work, and the influences they feel they are having on their students.

The video was entitled 'Me Alone' and portrayed a self-centred student who was the focus of her own world, paying little attention to the needs of others. It was well presented, and the students seemed to enjoy it. After the video, the group engaged in a good deal of lively conversation. I overheard some of their reactions: 'It made me think. The girl in the video uses other people'; 'Sometimes I think we all do that'; 'I wouldn't like to think I do.'

I regarded this exercise as another way of raising awareness of how they acted towards each other in general. However, I did not feel that I was addressing the central issue of how some boys appeared to be intimidated by some girls.

A critical incident

As so often happens, a particular incident triggered a series of episodes, and the latent situation was projected into high profile.

I tend regularly to ask students to do little jobs for me, believing that this makes them feel valued, and that it also develops a bond of friendship and co-dependency between us. Since I had become aware of the potential problem, I had asked the three boys who seemed to be victimised to work with me on developing a maths resources bank. They thoroughly enjoyed themselves, and were learning a little more about maths into the bargain. We usually did this work over breaks and some lunch hours, and often I would arrange for us to have a cup of hot chocolate and biscuits while we were working away. There was a lovely cosy atmosphere around our work together and the boys had a peaceful space where they talked quietly among the files, while I got on with other work.

Shortly after the viewing of 'Me Alone' they began discussing their reactions to the video. I deliberately stayed out of the way, listening from the other side of the classroom.

'Typical girl,' I overheard.

'Not really,' came a reply. 'She's just spoilt. She's used to getting her own way. No one stands up to her. Just like [girl's name] in our class.'

'All girls are bossy,' said the first. 'Typical. What do you think, Miss?'

I was surprised to have been suddenly included in the conversation, and in retrospect put it down to the fact that the group of boys had grown to see me as an ally. I walked over to where they were working at the filing cabinets.

'I can't agree,' I said. 'I do think sometimes all of us like to get our own way. Boys as well as girls.' Cautious lest I go too quickly: 'Is there a problem?'

'Yes. They're always getting on to us. It's not as if we provoke them. Maybe we're just easy targets.'

'How do you mean, always getting on to you? I'm not sure that I've noticed anything. Can you tell me? Can I help?'

It all came out, how a particular group of five girls, all physically more mature than the boys and far more self-confident, were systematically making life difficult for the boys, not in an obviously public way, but in subtle, almost invisible ways.

'They call us names, not loudly, but quietly when we're lining up.'

'They push us. There are five of them and three of us. They're bigger. We look like real wimps. That's what they call us.'

Taunting, name calling, unobtrusive pushing and shoving, belittling language – these were the problems that the three boys were facing on a daily basis. I thought of the Department of Education (1993b) guidelines on counteracting bullying, that overt signs of bullying are physical aggression, damage to property, extortion, intimidation, isolation, name calling and insults. This was all evidently going on; though not on a large scale, it was still having a serious effect on the victims, even more so that they were boys and so also felt trapped and humiliated by their gender roles which, while probably unwelcome, are nevertheless part of the cultural heritage of Western males.

I was extremely angry, as much with myself as with the group of girls. How could I have missed all this, when it was going on right there in my classroom? How could I have been so blind, so arrogant as to believe that everything was perfect? How could I have missed the signs? Here were three young men, systematically being unjustly treated, and, because I had not noticed, this was happening with my tacit approval.

Action!

Two days later, at the earliest appropriate opportunity, I arranged to meet the five girls together during a morning break. I put it to them that they had been treating the three boys unkindly. There was much blushing and shuffling of feet.

'Ah, miss, you can't call it bullying.'

'Oh? What would you call it?'

'We were only teasing them.'

They were not in any sense mean or vindictive girls; they were ordinary girls from the class who, because they felt the need for a target, had found easy victims in the boys from their position of corporate strength. Why do we need victims? Does it stem from a sense of personal insecurity in ourselves that we need to establish our dominance over others? I found it deeply saddening that the girls had done this for no good reason; and I said this to them.

'We didn't mean to, not really,' said one.

'Are you aware of how hurt the boys are?' I asked. Two of them were ready to cry. Don't some of us quickly become contrite when we realise how easy it is to cause pain.

One girl was prepared to brazen it out. 'They ask for it,' she cried. 'They're just goody-goodies; don't do a thing wrong.'

Before I had a chance to respond, one of the others rounded on her. 'They're good at maths. You said so yourself. You're just jealous!' She turned to me. 'Can we make it up to them?'

'You'll have to ask them,' I replied. Here was an opportunity for them to take responsibility for their own actions. While it might be the duty of teachers to help young people to become autonomous, they can never fully exercise their autonomy unless they are prepared to look inside themselves for their own answers rather than expect someone else to find the answers for them. I wonder how many adults actually achieve this; it was to the extreme credit of this particular student that she was willing and able to do this.

I felt that the conversation had gone far enough at this stage. 'Perhaps you should talk about this among yourselves,' I suggested. 'Let me know if I can help. You know where you can find me.' We parted.

I worried about it nevertheless, for the girls and for the boys. Yet teachers need to trust their students; parent birds and parent humans watch from an anxious distance while their offspring fall and sometimes hurt themselves, but they wisely judge whether or not to intervene. We all have to learn for ourselves.

Reconciliation

The following day the three boys came to find me. I was in the 'resource centre'.

'Miss, miss, wait till we tell you what's happened!'

'Oh?' I asked, all innocent.

They proceeded to tell me graphically how the five girls had approached them after English. The boys, anxious that this meant trouble, closed ranks and stood waiting for them as they approached. Instead, one of the girls said, 'Listen, we want to settle things with you. We know we've been a bit mean to you, and we didn't mean it, so we just want to say sorry. Is that OK?'

Quite taken aback, they nodded. Another of the girls produced three bags of crisps from her bag which she shoved into their hands. 'That's for you,' she said.

'Thanks,' muttered the boys, not quite knowing how to react.

'We won't be giving out to you any more,' they heard. 'We want to get on with you. OK?'

'Yes. Yes. OK.'

Then a girl's arm somehow became draped over a boy's shoulder: 'By the way, you couldn't help me with tonight's homework, could you?'

I have no idea whether the pain instantly disappeared, or whether the bruises remain. Young people constantly amaze us with their resilience. The hurt must remain in some form or another; yet they seem to bounce back, able to forgive and make friends as quickly as they fall out. What a gift that we seem to lose somewhere on the journey to adulthood.

Developing study skills

Now that the problem of bullying seemed to be getting attended to, I decided to focus on the issue of homework. Students had said that they became anxious because they did not know what to do, and the anxiety prevented them from studying effectively.

Again in class I invited suggestions from the group about how we might tackle the problem. Several students, some from our group of girls, suggested that we do as we had done last time: have a class discussion, chaired by students, and brainstorm the issue. I was delighted to agree. The girls proposed that one of the three boys should be chair. He positively grew in stature with pride, and placed himself at the top of class from where he proceeded to conduct business very competently, inviting opinion and fielding questions and answers.

Among the suggestions offered were:

- Each student should have a personal homework diary.
- All teachers would carefully explain what the homework was – no rushed 'For homework do exercise 2' at the end of the lesson. (I later discovered that one of the students, unknown to anyone, was hard of hearing and simply did not hear instructions, which got him into trouble with teachers.)

- All teachers should write down the homework on the board, and it should stay there for the next lesson – there was a complaint that some students could not write the homework down fast enough before the incoming teacher wiped the board clean.
- Parents should sign the homework diary when they felt their child had done an appropriate amount of study, even if the exercise had not been completed.

I said I would certainly adopt these practices as far as maths was concerned; I could not speak on behalf of my teacher colleagues, but I would see whether I could negotiate something on the students' behalf.

With this in mind, I met with the year head for the second year, and explained the situation to her. She was full of admiration for the courage and responsibility that the students were demonstrating, and agreed to put it to all second year teachers. This she did at the next teachers' meeting, explaining that the suggestions had come from the students themselves. All teachers felt it was a useful strategy, and all agreed to it. There were general comments about the mature manner in which the students had approached the issue and were able to negotiate in relation to their own welfare.

Evaluation

Had the situation improved? Yes, I think it had, in several ways.

The invisible bullying had been made visible, and it had stopped. The boys seemed happier, and so did the girls. Neither victim nor bully benefits in the long run. Cooperation is a much healthier situation for personal development, and a sense of well-being is certainly beneficial for the development of academic capacity. I spoke informally with some of the boys and girls after these episodes. They all agreed that they felt more comfortable in school, and that this was having a beneficial effect on their studies.

The homework diary was working. I had issued a copy book to every student which could be used as a diary. Some had chosen to get their own books, and had personalised the covers in their own style. Designer homework diaries were in vogue! Interestingly, students began to use their diary in ways for which it was not originally intended. One student was absent for five days, yet still kept her diary, copying down the homework from a friend. When I expressed interest about why she was doing this she said, 'So I know what I have missed and can catch up in my own time.'

I approached other year teachers for their opinion about whether my interventions had been effective. There was general agreement that they had. My critical colleague (see above) said:

> It was difficult to know exactly what to do in the case of the bullying, because you didn't know you actually had a problem to begin with. I

think you handled it in a sensitive manner, finding your way through one step at a time. It's necessary to trust that things will work out in delicate situations like that. Goodwill and sensitivity count for a lot.

My colleagues on the Higher Diploma course were delighted that it had worked out successfully. The other teacher who had a bullying problem said she had learnt from me – here was a reversal of fortunes! I must say I was very pleased to have benefited from the support of these colleagues, and that they had provided a kind of safety net for me to share ideas, doubts and misgivings about the advisability of my actions, and also joy in the success stories. How much we need collaborative cultures in our professional lives. How much we need the courage to share our stories of doubt as well as our victory stories.

What have I learnt?

I have learnt so many valuable lessons from this intervention.

I have learnt not to accept a peaceful situation as peaceful in an unquestioning fashion. It could be that the situation is simply inert. My experience taught me that there is potentially a lot of submarine activity going on below seemingly quiet surfaces. It is our responsibility as caring teachers to check the situation out, and make sure that it really is peaceful at all levels, deep and surface structures alike.

I have learnt to question my own assumptions. In not being alert to potential difficulties, I was in fact colluding in the bullying, perhaps not actively, but certainly by default. As a teacher, I need to be looking behind the mirror, not accepting the happy faces as real reflections of my influence, but looking a little more closely at whether the faces are real or the convenient masks that young people know so well how to adopt to avoid threatening instrusion.

I have reinforced my belief that all children are good-hearted, but that they sometimes get led astray because of their own need for affirmation, and sometimes the need manifests as victimisation of others. Our dominant social and education systems lead us to believe that one person can benefit only at the expense of another; success comes in finite packages, and when one person enjoys a piece of the package this means less for others. We need urgently to break out of this mind-set and develop newer visions of how we can live in harmony, that what is good for one will influence another in a life-giving way.

I have learnt a great deal about myself. Most importantly, from this episode of my professional learning, I have learnt that I need constantly to be open to my own process of learning. I have no final answers; and those I find are soon transformed into new questions. Professional learning is essential to keep our minds alive; we need to recognise that we learn most from those we are privileged to teach. We all have much to do as teachers.

13

MAKING CARE VISIBLE

Jean Clandinin, Jean McNiff and Úna M. Collins

Jean Clandinin is recognised as a major theorist in life history research and narrative inquiry. Her work in encouraging teachers to tell the stories of their personal professional lives is internationally celebrated.

In December 1997 Jean McNiff visited Jean Clandinin at the University of Alberta. The main purpose of that visit was to record a conversation as a response to the contents of this book. A great deal more emerged.

There was another charming context to this visit. The meeting had a focus of pastoral care. To Jean McNiff that meant pastoral care in schools; to Jean Clandinin it meant ministry in medical settings. Out of that (mis)understanding Jean Clandinin arranged a visit with the Pastoral Ministry Team at the Royal Alexandra Hospital in Edmonton. It was a deeply moving experience. Both women were received by the team, under the guidance of Neil Elford. They learned about the tireless and unsung work of the team as they supported the sick, the forlorn, the forgotten – just as teachers support children in schools who are equally vulnerable and in despair. They saw how such pastoral care can actively support those to whom few other supports are available; how genuine care manifests in relationships where people share their humanity out of the suffering that their humanity generates.

This conversation was a spontaneous event, held one evening in Jean Clandinin's office after hours. We shared our ideas, our concerns, our commitments around the need for care in all the stories and contexts of our lives. The conversation that you read is largely unedited.

Our conversation continues. Jean Clandinin explores how to encourage a public language to emerge around pastoral care in Alberta schools; Jean McNiff explores how to find ways to help teachers tell their stories in the educational communities of Ireland, and how to have them heard. We share the same aim of supporting educators, in caring ways, to create a better world for tomorrow's children. Care is the process and care the outcome. Without care, ours is a lonely planet. With care, we sing among the stars.

JM: The dilemma that I constantly experience is how do we capture the richness of experience in linguistic form.

JC: For me, the nearest we can come to capturing the richness of experience is with story. We have to pay close attention to the stories that we live out, to the stories that we tell, to the responses to our lived and told stories and then to the ways our stories are retold and relived. Narrative is everyone's rock bottom gift and we tell our stories in words, in paintings, in dance, in poetry. But at the bottom is the story. As I think about this, I am thinking about how I love to go to ballet, but what I love most about ballet is the stories that are danced. I need to be able to figure out the story in the dance. It doesn't have to be the old stories, the old familiar stories, but I have to see the possibility of the story in it, the nugget of a plotline. Stories are the closest we can come to the richness of experience. My answer is that the richness is in the stories that we live, in the stories that we tell, and in the stories that we re-story because of the responses from the communities in which we live.

JM: We create the stories as we live them, through the sharing of our experience, and the telling of our stories to others, and their response. What might be particularly significant about response?

JC: Response really can shape how we retell our stories. Right now I'm involved in a course through electronic mail. There are only four of us in this electronic conversation and so I feel a moral responsibility to respond as often as I can. On Monday night, when we met with Janice Huber and Karen Whelan, you spoke of the question and answer of dialogue. Both Janice and I were taken with your comments on that and it's just made me think about response and story again. I found myself writing this morning to Janice and to the others in the electronic mail course about the nature of responses to stories. Responses to stories almost always take the form of questions of clarification, questions of what happened next, or questions of how experiences in the story made the narrator feel or responses of trying to imagine how, if I'm narrating myself as one character, other characters felt. All the responses are ways of trying to move inside that story and of trying to live there with the narrator. What also happens is that the response sometimes is another story, for example, a story of something that happened to me. So the responses are interesting, and they are different from what we often see as the dialogue of question and answer. Janice was talking about her feelings about her research groups, and how in the principals' group she wasn't telling stories, whereas she was in the teachers' groups. She was trying to figure out why she wasn't telling stories and why she wasn't responding to their stories in the ways she was responding to the teachers' stories in the other research conversation.

JM: I wonder, has that something to do with being related to those people's experience, empathising with them?

JC: And something to do with being able to imagine yourself in the story.

JM: To be able to respond more adequately to that particular story.

JC: It's this question of response. That's what you're saying, I think. You're saying that in listening and responding to stories, it takes you to yourself and to being able to imagine yourself in that story. That's why, I suppose, we ask questions of clarification or tell a story that in some way resonates with us, in order to be able to better imagine ourselves inside the story.

JM: That act of imagination is a creative leap. And I'm wondering how does this link with the idea of care? I'm thinking that perhaps it links with the idea of care because we are committed to make that creative leap of the imagination, that we make the effort to put ourselves in the place of the other. We can imagine what it must be like to have that experience, but such imagining takes energy. Something I read recently is very high in my mind these days, that we can never know the consciousness of another person, and while I think that is probably true, we can imagine what it might be like to be that other person, to have that consciousness; and that puts us in relation to the other person. We can empathise, we can understand what their experience might be like. Would this tune in to what you are saying about response, that we respond to the person in that caring, imaginative way?

JC: Carol Gilligan writes about response and responsibility and how they come from the same word. So response and responsibility are closely linked. Responsibility for me implies care and it also implies the relational. We feel responsible for someone, we respond; so somehow response, responsibility, care and relationship get wound together. Ian Sewell (1993), an important person in my life, said that when you hear somebody's story you have responsibility for it. He has this lovely metaphor – when you hear someone's story, it sits on your shoulder, and you're responsible for that story and the person who shares that story with you. You have to think hard about the ways in which you are responsible and how you are in relation to that person and her story, and you need, carefully and with care, to consider your response.

JM: If we choose – and choice is an active thing – if we choose to respond to a story, it is an act of connection. It's a conscious choice, because another choice we would have is to talk away, to deny our responsibility to other people. And that choice of being connected to other people is an act of faith – in terms of what we've been talking about, it's a spiritual act. We're connecting at the level of experience, at affective level, not only at cognitive level. This is important, because sometimes at cognitive level we engage at a surface level only, and not always at a deep level, which involves trust.

JC: It's when you do that, when you really hear somebody's story, that it's harder to walk away. Stories engage you cognitively, affectively, morally, spiritually. It takes a great deal of trust to tell stories that are real stories, real in the sense of important stories. We each decide, in different places, what kind of stories to tell. Some stories are safe stories in some contexts.

For example, in some school staffrooms, it is safe to tell complaint stories about bad kids. In that place, that's an easy story to tell. But harder stories might be stories about how you're struggling with your teaching, or how you feel in despair or hopelessness, or even stories about being hopeful might be hard stories to tell in some places. Those stories, if you're not feeling really safe and in trusting relationships, don't come. So you do have to trust, I think, and feel a sense of safety.

JM: Relating this to the stories of the teachers as told in this book, and in the wider context of professional learning, when teachers tell their stories of how they came to know, the learning experiences that they have gone through, they are putting themselves at some risk, making themselves vulnerable to the easy, hurtful comments of people who don't share that kind of commitment.

JC: I think so. The kind of response to give is very important when people have taken that risk. One response is silence. Silence is hard to read. Silence can be, for example, 'I'm so deeply touched, I can't figure out how to respond in a responsible, caring way.' But silence can also mean, 'I don't care.' I think that's hurtful, and I think silence or other responses that are hurtful send people away from the conversation, and maybe they won't take a chance again. I think it's amazing when teachers tell stories. I think it's amazing when even you and I tell stories to each other, because it makes us vulnerable. There is a huge risk, and teachers take those risks when they tell stories because they make themselves vulnerable.

JM: And the children that they are with also run the same risk. And I wonder how we can relate this with the idea of pastoral care in schools, that when teachers transform themselves into caring tutors, who care, they are encouraging those children to tell their stories, deliberately to put themselves at risk, and it's dangerous.

JC: I agree that it's very dangerous. Children are, usually, very trusting, and they come to school at first and see the teacher as someone to be trusted. They tell these incredible stories and sometimes teachers aren't ready for the responsibility of responding to those stories. It's a huge responsibility made more so by the number of children who tell stories. How do teachers respond in a caring, educative way, in a way that opens up new possibilities?

I have to tell you a story about an amazing teacher I know called Lee Bolton. She taught drama in a Calgary junior high school and she had the students write in journals. She told the junior high girls that they could write anything, any stories that they wanted, and that they would be safe and only she would read them. And Lee said that initially the stories were superficial and she would respond to them. Increasingly the stories came to a place where the students were more authentic. One of the girls began to write her stories of abuse and Lee was struggling with how to respond in a caring way. The issue became more complicated because in

Alberta, when children report abuse to a teacher, the teacher is legally required to report it to the authorities. Lee found herself between being in a relationship with the child who said, 'Don't tell, but I have to tell you this because I know you will care', and the legal responsibility to report the abuse. That happened a long time ago, and Lee and I had many conversations about what it means when we make those spaces. Children do become vulnerable, and, as teachers, we have to think ahead to questions of how to respond. That's a huge responsibility. I don't have answers but I think about that. Yet the other alternative is that children don't tell their stories, so then there's no possibility of educative response, there's no conversation, there's no thinking about what that means or about other possibilities. What does that mean for the lives that children compose for themselves? Do we take ourselves out of them altogether? I mean, that's the option. That's why I think it's so wonderful that you have pastoral care in schools, because it makes a space. I guess it's a space for that possibility.

JM: Just go on talking about that. Why do you think it's so wonderful that we have pastoral care?

JC: I was trying to think about that last night. This is so important because it is a space. By naming pastoral care, we name something important in life. We name this as something important that belongs in schools. We name this as part of teachers' work and it's in the naming that we say, 'We value this, we see this as part of your work, it's important to name.' Helen Christiansen talks about invisible work. It's not invisible then. We name it, we say it's important, we value it.

JM: We make it visible.

JC: We make it visible.

JM: And we put a language around it, that we can talk about it, and the language reinforces the practices, and we create a practice from within and we externalise that in our daily work.

JC: Yes, that's important, that we view that process as making it visible.

JM: In your metaphors of story telling, we create stories around caring that speak to our experience, and we share those stories, we make those stories public.

JC: In my classes with students who are teachers or principals, we do a lot of story telling. The stories are almost always about children or parents. These are relational stories. Even in my curriculum class, stories rarely are stories of teaching social studies or language arts or whatever. Mostly they are centred around a child or a parent or a story of them in relationship in some way. Pastoral care makes that kind of space in schools. It allows the possibilities that those stories can be visible, made public, open for caring response. One of the things teachers and principals say when they come to class is, 'We don't have places to tell these stories.'

JM: Now, what do you think about the fact that in this book there are eight teachers who have told their stories of how they are as teachers who care? It might be construed that the events they have told are very mundane events. What is significant about the fact that they have done it, and that they are willing to share in a public forum?

JC: That's so interesting. These stories are often mundane, they are everyday, they are about how we relate, but that is what life is about. Sometimes in life we have epiphanies. Sometimes something really big and important happens. But mostly in our lives in schools and classrooms, we construct our relationships with children, we hear their stories, we respond to their stories, we hear how they are making sense of something, we respond to how they are making sense. It's very mundane. Everything isn't a big thing, a high, but this is all the stuff that makes life. Michael Connelly and I wrote a paper (1986) about rhythms of knowing around school cycles. It really is mundane, but if we don't look at these mundane experiences closely, and honour them as life, and think about how we can make those mundane moments into caring moments, we're never going to create educative experiences.

JM: I would like to think about this as an issue, a very important issue.

JC: OK.

JM: I think the act that we are sharing very ordinary experience demonstrates the extraordinariness of those experiences. So often as teachers, people in service to each other, we are so often persuaded to believe that what we have to share doesn't count for very much, and words like 'mundane' and 'ordinary' are often used as pejorative terms, but they're not. To adopt that view is almost to say that the now in which you and I are sharing these ideas is not worth very much, and yet it is all we have, it is our life experience. So I'd like to follow your ideas, and make the issue that the very ordinariness of our day-to-day and moment-to-moment experience is an extraordinary phenomenon. Every moment of my life is an act of wonder. I just wonder at the sheer privilege of being here. For me it is so extraordinary that I am alive, that I am here, that you and I are here to share this experience.

JC: It makes a lot of sense. There are some really trite expressions, like 'life is not a rehearsal', but in some ways those trite expressions also point to exactly that, that these are the moments of our lives. If we think about the time that teachers spend with children, so many hours every day, it's the teachers' lives that are being written as well as the children's lives. It's in the exchange over the report card, it's in the exchange of reading a story together, it's in how we respond to what's on the page, it's in how we respond to the mathematics class. It's in those little moments that we take for granted. The ordinariness of our day-to-day experience is extraordinary. It is life.

JM: Yes. We tend to take it for granted, but we make it visible because – and I'll return to the theme of care – we need to care about our own experience, we need to care about the experience of the people we have responsibility for. That kind of awareness-raising means active investment of energy.

JC: Knowing how we can respond at any moment, that we can respond with more or less care, or somehow with different shades of care, and knowing that it will make a difference in how part of that child's life, or our own life, will get authored in the life stories we are writing is all part of it. Knowing that there is a possibility if we yell at a child that child might say, 'I'm unworthy', and that moment of relationship could influence his/her or your life story is all part of it.

I have to tell you another story. Jan Antoniuk (1997), a teacher who just finished her masters thesis, a study of her classroom practice, came in one day at some point in her thesis journey. I started out by saying, 'Tell me about your day.' She started telling me about a little boy called Aaron. He's a little boy who is storied in the school as being a trouble-maker, a bad kid, an aboriginal, someone who didn't amount to much in the collective eyes of the school. It was in November. Jan had just read the story of *Sadako and the Thousand Cranes*. It's the story of a Japanese child at the time of the bombing in Japan. Sadako is making a thousand paper cranes as a sign of hope. Jan read the story and had the children make origami cranes. Aaron made the most beautiful origami cranes. Jan described his origami crane as the most beautiful thing he had done. Jan took his cranes and made them into a mobile. She responded to him in a positive, careful way. Then she told me another teacher had come by and wanted to know who made the beautiful cranes. Jan said Aaron had done it, and the other teacher invited Aaron to her class so Aaron could teach her children how to make cranes. She validates Aaron's new story as Jan had already done. Soon after, Aaron left the school. Jan tells this story at the start of her thesis, using themes of care and attending, and acknowledging that, as a teacher, she can make a difference by her response. She wrote the story last summer. I said, 'You'll have to take it and make sure it's all right with Aaron.' Aaron lives with his grandmother, so Jan took the story, by now at least a year later, to Aaron and his grandmother. His grandmother read it and what was so beautiful was that Aaron's grandmother said, 'That made such a difference to him. It changed how he thought about himself.' She asked for a copy because, she said, 'This is the most positive thing that anyone in school has ever said about Aaron.' It was in that little moment, in all of those mundane moments, that Jan knew she could make a difference in response. It made a huge difference. We don't know whether it will make a difference when Aaron is 30, but it made a difference in how Aaron lived in that classroom, in that school, for the month that he was there, before he moved on to the next school.

JM: In one of the stories in the book, a teacher tells of how an opportunity is made for every child to take part in the school play because that is what they take with them through life, because that is an opportunity to shine.

We remember those moments when we shine.

JC: Yes, mundane moments. They can happen every day, but it's in those moments when you can be really thoughtful about how you respond, because it can change what happens next in the story that you're authoring for yourself as teacher and also in the story that child is authoring for herself or himself.

JM: Continuing to respond in that thoughtful reflective way can be enormously tiring.

JC: That's one of the things about why I think pastoral care is so wonderful. Here, where there is no named pastoral care, what Jan did was invisible. There's nowhere to talk about it. But with a pastoral care focus, it's visible, in the sense that you can say, 'This is part of my pastoral care curriculum, this is part of what I do', and yes, it is exhausting, but it's visible, you can hold it up, and, in Jan's story with Aaron, there would be a place to say, 'This is important to me.'

JM: It raises it high in our minds, it gives us a language, it gives us words to use around the practice that we do, it helps us to name our practices and the naming of them makes them important.

JC: It is exhausting, it is tiring, and I don't for a moment want to say that it isn't tiring. Relating in this intensive way to thirty children, which is what most school teachers do each day in their classrooms, and then responding to their colleagues and responding to parents is exhausting. That kind of relational being in the world has got to be so tiring, but you know, when you can tell a story and be thoughtful about it, there's a way in which that thoughtful response can energise you, because those stories give us hope, give us possibility. I mean, when Jan was attending to Aaron, she might miss the other twenty-nine children. I think not. But in her response there is a sense of possibility in Aaron's life that wasn't there before, and in Jan's life, in knowing, in following through, at least as far as she did with Aaron, she also sees new possibility. That's a response that gives her hope.

JM: There is someone there who cares enough to listen to me and respond to me, from the child's perspective. From the teacher's perspective, there is someone there to whom I can give this care. What is there about this relationship? It's mutual, trusting, binding. It's a bond between two people, and it happens all the time in our ordinary, extraordinary lives, and most of the time we're not aware of it, so we try to name it in our public lives, we try to explain it. We try to understand the nature of those caring practices. Now, to focus on those kinds of experiences, not only at a cognitive level, head stuff, involves a good deal of energy, because it's energy from the self: it's created.

JC: It calls forth our very being. What's the cognitive practice of teaching addition in relation to this?

JM: The cognitive is much easier. There's much less engagement, and much less energy, and therefore probably is that much less tiring, in terms of helping us to become the people that we are able to become. I feel that my commitment as an educator is to help people to become more than they are. I like the analogy of Data in *Star Trek* who says, 'I can be more than I am', and I think that is so for educators, that we know we can be more than we are and we can help other people to be more than they are. I love your idea that one vehicle that enables us to do that is to share our stories, to know who we are at the moment, and who we would like to be; and we can listen to each other and support each other in sharing our stories to enable the other person to be the person they want to be. We can imagine the people that we want to be, and we can actually become those people.

J C : There are a couple of things. One is that in my stories and in my responses I see more possibilities for myself. If I tell that everyday story, it's in your response that you have the possibility of showing me something about who I am in that story that I might not have named for myself.

J M : I reflect back to you.

J C : Yes, and you can give my stories back to me in ways that are imaginative. That allows me to think about my stories differently. The other thing I want to say comes back to the tiring side. There's nothing that makes me feel more energised, and I know this is true for teachers who come to me in classes or to work on masters research projects, than being in a conversation where my story is valued, listened to, and responded to. People say, 'You must just get burned out doing this kind of work', but I don't think that's where burnout or feelings of depression or feelings of being overwhelmed and frustrated come from. When we come together and write and tell our stories, that's life-giving, that's energising, and that's, in part, because of the possibility of hope.

J M : Our teaching is to create those kinds of contexts, where we can enable each other, whether the other is a teacher or a child, or whoever, we can create those contexts, and we can generate that hope, realise that hope.

J C : That's what we do in our teaching, and it brings me back to pastoral care. With pastoral care, at least there is some time in every day, or there's some possibility of time in every day, where that's going to happen.

J M : There's an awareness, that that is what needs to be done, and as teachers it is our responsibility to influence the situation such that there is that possibility, because if we didn't do it, who would?

J C : You asked me, when I was struggling with the fact that you have pastoral care in schools and we don't, I was reminded of Lucy Calkin's (1991) wonderful book called *Living Between the Lines*, a book about writing and teaching children to write, but really it's about getting children to compose their own life stories. Janice Huber (1992) and Karen Whelan do a lot of that with children. Children write stories of their lives and write stories of what happens in their classrooms. The writing process is given that autobiographical twist, where story telling is central. Janice and

Karen bring the ideas of pastoral care into the curriculum in that way. They made language arts the place where pastoral care would be most explicit. We need to name these ideas because it is so invisible to the policy makers and administrators here.

Back in Dublin

JEAN: Is it invisible to the policy makers and administrators here as well?

ÚNA: No, I don't experience that with our Department of Education and Science or with school management. I think there is a very real awareness of pastoral needs in education as I have outlined earlier in this book. I experience not only awareness but also policy moving into action, through the various educational agencies, management bodies and teachers' unions. What concerns me is the lack of time and resources for teachers' ongoing professional learning in schools. What is needed is a sustainable organisational approach to the pastoral core of education and of school.

JEAN: This is becoming an international issue in educational debates. It is generally recognised that the quality of children's education is influenced by the quality of teachers' professional education. This is nowhere so true as in pastoral care. If teachers hold a sense of purpose, feel valued professionally, are encouraged to explore and celebrate their own giftedness, they are more likely to encourage children to do the same. In this way we encourage the development of a sustainable good society. If the self-esteem of teachers is high, there is a good chance that they will encourage the self-esteem of the children in their care.

ÚNA: Yes, I believe that support for teachers is vital to the development of effective pastoral care. It would, I believe, be true to say that the students' experience of school can only be enriched by a system that addresses teachers' needs. In current media terms one might be led to think that all societal needs can be addressed within the school by the teacher. At the other end of the spectrum it could be argued that the teacher meets all aspects of societal needs within the students. So we ask, by whom, and how are teachers' needs met?

I would return to the systems approach. A whole-school approach to planning recognises distinct roles with rights and responsibilities within the system. All are involved in the articulation and therefore the owning of the system's core values, and therefore all are involved in the policies and procedures of the system. Teachers carry the values each day in the life of the school. Teachers are the most immediate learning medium for students. Teacher–student relationships are central to a pastoral learning environment.

Questions which might be asked in the context of caring for the teacher include:

- Has each teacher been involved in the identification and articulation of core values for the school?
- Is the teacher's role, with its rights and responsibilities, clear and negotiated?
- Are teachers encouraged to be involved in a collaborative decision-making school culture?
- How are individual gifts and individual difficulties identified and integrated?
- What is the evaluation process in the school? How is accountability encouraged?
- When are teachers affirmed? How? By whom?
- How are school principals affirmed? When and by whom?
- What is the school's policy for teachers' professional renewal, and ongoing learning?
- Are communication sub-systems clear and regularly evaluated?
- And so on . . .

JEAN: Education is not a zero-sum game in which one party gains at the expense of another. We all stand to benefit from the success of each other. How to ensure that? We need to encourage teachers to care in an overt, skilled way, and we need to ensure that teachers are also cared for – we are all in relation, and our relationships need to be relationships of consideration for the other. We need to provide appropriate and adequate provision for teachers to discover and celebrate their own caring practices, in collaboration with peers, students, parents, and all partners in education. We need to shout constantly that we have actively to care, to commit ourselves to taking the extra step; and that takes energy, commitment and courage.

If this all sounds too much, we need constantly to ask ourselves: when children have nowhere else to turn, where do they go but to their teacher? Can we meet their needs? It is our responsibility as caring professionals to educate ourselves in the service of those children. For if we don't, who will?

BIBLIOGRAPHY

Antoniuk, J. (1997) 'Living Artistry in Teaching: One Teacher's Story'. Unpublished masters thesis, University of Alberta, Edmonton, Alberta.

Appleyard, B. (1992) *Understanding the Present: Science and the Soul of Modern Man*. New York, Anchor Books, Doubleday.

ASTI (Association of Secondary Teachers Ireland) (1993) *The Transition Year*. Dublin, Oval Publishing.

Atweh, B., Kemmis, S. and Weeks, P. (1998) *Action Research in Practice*. London and New York, Routledge.

Axline, V.M. (1990) *Dibs – In Search of Self*. London, Penguin Books.

Baldwin, J. and Wells, H. (1979) *Active Tutorial Work, Book 2, The Second Year*. London, Basil Blackwell.

Bassey, M. (1990) *On the Nature of Research in Education*. Nottingham, Faculty of Education, Nottingham Polytechnic.

Bazalgette, J. (1979) *Learning to Handle Oneself in a Hostile Environment*. London, Grubb Institute.

Bazalgette, J. (1983) *On the Psychology of Being a Student*. London, Grubb Institute.

Bazalgette, J. and Reed, B. (1971) *Becoming Adult*. London, Grubb Institute.

Beck, L. (1994) *Reclaiming Educational Administration as a Caring Profession*. New York, Teachers College Press.

Best, R. (1994a) 'Care, Control and Community', in P. Lang, R. Best and A. Lichtenberg (eds), *Caring for Children: International Perspectives in Pastoral Care and PSE*. London, Cassell.

Best, R. (1994b) 'Teachers' Supportive Roles in a Secondary School: A Case Study and Discussion', *Support for Learning*, 9 (4).

Best, R. (1995) 'The Caring Teacher in the Junior School', CEDARR Occasional Paper No. 1. London, Roehampton Institute.

Best, R. (ed.) (1996) *Education, Spirituality and the Whole Child*. London, Cassell.

Best, R. and Decker, S. (1985) 'Pastoral Care and Welfare: Some Underlying Issues', in P. Ribbins (ed.), *Schooling and Welfare*. Lewes, Falmer.

Best, R., Jarvis, C. and Ribbins, P. (1977) 'Pastoral Care: Concept and Process', *British Journal of Educational Studies*, XXV (2).

Best, R., Jarvis, C. and Ribbins, P. (eds) (1980) *Perspectives in Pastoral Care*. Oxford, Heinemann.

Best, R., Ribbins, P., Jarvis, C. and Oddy, D. (1983) *Education and Care*. London, Heinemann.

Blackburn, K. (1975) *The Tutor*. London, Heinemann.

Blackburn, K. (1983a) 'The Pastoral Head: A Developing Role', *Pastoral Care in Education*, 1 (1), 18–23.

Blackburn, K. (1983b) *Head of House, Head of Year*. Oxford, Basil Blackwell.

Bohm, D. (1980) *Wholeness and the Implicate Order*. New York, Routledge.

Bowden, P. (1997) *Caring: Gender-Sensitive Ethics*. London and New York, Routledge.

Brookfield, S. (1987) *Developing Critical Thinkers*. Buckingham, Open University Press.

Button, L. (1974) *Group Tutoring for the Form Tutor*. London, Hodder and Stoughton.

Calkin, L. McCormick (1991) *Living Between the Lines*. Portsmouth, NH, Heinemann.

Capra, F., Steindl-Rast, D. and Matus, T. (1992) *Belonging to the Universe*. London, Penguin.

Carr, W. and Kemmis, S. (1986) *Becoming Critical: Education, Knowledge and Action Research*. Lewes, Falmer.

Casti, J. (1994) *Complexification: Explaining a Paradoxical World Through the Science of Surprise*. London, Abacus.

Chomsky, N. (1995) *Manufacturing Consent*. London, Paladin.

Christiansen, H., Goulet, L., Krentz, C. and Maeers, M. (1997) 'Making the Connections', in H. Christiansen *et al.*, *Recreating Relationships*. Albany, State University of New York.

Clandinin, D.J. (with Connelly, F.M.) (1986) 'Rhythms in Teaching: The Narrative Study of Teachers' Personal Practical Knowledge of Classrooms', *Teaching and Teacher Education*, 2 (4), 377–87.

Clemett, A.J. and Pearce, J.S. (1986) *The Evaluation of Pastoral Care*. Oxford, Blackwell.

Coleman, J.C. and Hendry, L. (1991) *The Nature of Adolescence*, 2nd edn. London, Routledge.

Collins, Ú. (1980) *Pastoral Care: A Teachers' Handbook*, Dublin, School and College Services.

Collins, Ú.M. (1993) *Pastoral Care: A Teachers' Handbook*, 2nd edn. Dublin, Marino Institute of Education.

Collins, Ú. (1996) *Developing a School Plan*. Dublin, Marino Institute of Education.

Collins, Ú. (1998) 'Fiche Bliain ag Fás', in P. Lang, Y. Katz and I. Menezes, *Affective Education*. London, Cassell.

Daubner, E. (1982) 'Deified, Depraved, Denied or Deprived: Moral Nature and Counselling', *Counselling and Values*, 26, April.

Delong, J. and Wideman, R. (1998) *School Improvement through Research-Based Professionalism*. Ontario, Ontario Public School Teachers' Federation.

Department of Education (1993a) *Transition Year Programmes – Guidelines 1993/1994*. Dublin, the Stationery Office.

Department of Education (1993b) *Guidelines for Counteracting Bullying Behaviour in Primary and Post-Primary Schools*. Dublin, Stationery Office.

Dermody, B. (1986) 'Towards a Sex Education Programme'. Unpublished masters thesis, University of Galway, Galway.

DES (Department of Education and Science) (1989) *Report of Her Majesty's Inspectors on Pastoral Care in Secondary Schools: An Inspection of Some Aspects of Pastoral Care in 1987–8*. Stanmore, Department of Education and Science.

Dewey, J. (1963) *Experience and Education*. New York, Collier Books.

Dowling, E. and Osbourne, E. (1994) *The Family and the School*, 2nd edn. London, Routledge.

Drudy, S. and Lynch, K. (1993) *Schools and Society in Ireland*. Dublin, Gill and Macmillan.

Eisner, E. (1993), 'Forms of Understanding and the Future of Educational Research', *Educational Researcher*, 22 (7), 5–11.

Elliott, J. (1991) *Action Research for Educational Change*. Buckingham, Open University Press.

Erikson, E.H. (1968) *Identity, Youth and Crisis*. London, Faber and Faber.

European Commision (1995) *White Paper: Teaching and Learning – Towards the Learning Society*. Brussels, European Commission.

European Study Group (1997) *Report: Accomplishing Europe Through Education and Training*. Brussels, European Commission.

Freire, P. (1970) *Pedagogy of the Oppressed*. New York, Seabury Press.

Fukuyama, F. (1995) *Trust: The Social Virtues and the Creation of Prosperity*. London, Penguin.

Fullan, M. (1993) *Change Forces*. London, Falmer.

Fullan, M. and Hargreaves, A. (1991) *What's Worth Fighting for in Your School?* Ontario, Open University Press.

Gardner, H. (1983) *Frames of Mind: The Theory of Multiple Intelligences*. New York, Harper and Row.

George, V. and Wilding, H. (1976) *Ideology and Social Welfare*. London, Routledge.

Glasser, W. (1984) *Take Effective Control of Your Life*. New York, Harper and Row.

Glasser, W. (1986) *Control Theory*. New York, Harper and Row.

Goleman, D. (1996) *Emotional Intelligence*. London, Bloomsbury.

Goodlad, J.I., Soder, R. and Sirotnik, K.A. (eds) (1990) *The Moral Dimensions of Teaching*. San Francisco, Jossey-Bass.

Government of Ireland (1992) *Green Paper: Education for a Changing World*. Dublin, Stationery Office.

Government of Ireland (1995) *White Paper: Charting Our Educational Future*. Dublin, Stationery Office.

Halsall, N.D. and Hossack, L.A. (1996) *Act, Reflect, Revise: Revitalise*. Ontario, Ontario Public School Teachers' Federation.

Halsey, A.H. (1972) *Educational Priority*. London, HMSO.

Hamblin, D. (1978) *The Teacher and Pastoral Care*. Oxford, Blackwell.

Hamblin, D. (1989) *Staff Development for Pastoral Care*. Oxford, Blackwell.

Hamblin, D. (1993) 'Pastoral Care: Past, Present and Future', *Pastoral Care in Education*, 11 (4), 3–6.

Hamilton, M.L. (ed.) (1998) *Reconceptualizing Teaching Practice: Self-Study in Teacher Education*. London, Falmer.

Handy, C. (1991) *The Age of Unreason*, 2nd edn. London, Arrow Books.

Hannan, D.F. and Shorthall, S. (1991) *The Quality of their Education*. ESRI No. 153, Dublin.

Hargreaves, A., Baglin, E., Henderson, P., Leeson, P. and Tossell, T. (1988) *Personal and Social Education: Choices and Challenges*. Oxford, Basil Blackwell.

Hegarty, E. (1989) 'The Work of William Glasser: Its Promise for Irish Post-Primary Schools'. Unpublished masters thesis, St Patrick's College, Maynooth.

Henderson, H. (1978) *Creating Alternative Futures*. New York, Putnam.

211

Holt, J. (1969) *How Children Fail*. Harmondsworth, Penguin.

Holt, J. (1971) *The Underachieving School*. Harmondsworth, Penguin.

Hopkins, D. (1993) *A Teacher's Guide to Classroom Research*, 2nd edn. Buckingham, Open University Press.

Horgan, J. (1996) *The End of Science*. London, Little, Brown and Company.

Huber, J. (1992) 'Narrative Inquiry and Evaluation in a Primary School Classroom'. Unpublished masters thesis, University of Alberta, Edmonton, Alberta.

Humphreys, T. (1993) *Self-Esteem – The Key to Your Child's Education*. Cork, Tony Humphreys.

James, W. (1917) *The Will to Believe: Selected Papers on Philosophy*. New York, J.M. Dent and Sons.

Jerusalem Bible (1968) (ed. A. Jones). London: Eyre and Spottiswoode.

Johnson, D., Ransom, E., Packwood, T., Bowden, K. and Kogan, M. (1980) *Secondary Schools and the Welfare Network*. London, Allen and Unwin.

Lang, P. (1983) 'Pastoral Care: Some Reflections on Possible Influences', *Pastoral Care in Education*, 2 (2).

Lang, P., Katz, Y. and Menezes, I. (1998) *Affective Education*. London: Cassell.

Lang, P. and Marland, M. (eds) (1985) *New Directions in Pastoral Care*. Oxford, Blackwell.

Lawrence, D. (1987) *Enhancing Self-Esteem in the Classroom*. London, Paul Chapman Publishing.

Leonard, D. (1995) 'Aspects of Data Gathering'. Paper presented at Marino Institute of Education, Dublin, May.

Lomax, P. (1994) 'Action Research for Professional Practice: A Position Paper on Educational Action Research'. Paper presented at the Practitioner Research Workshop at the Annual Conference of the British Educational Research Association, Oxford.

Macdonald, B.J. (1995) *Theory as a Prayerful Act: The Collected Essays of James B. Macdonald*. New York, Peter Lang.

McGuiness, J. (1989), *A Whole School Approach to Pastoral Care*. London, Kogan Page.

McNiff, J. (1986) *Personal and Social Education: A Teachers' Handbook*. Cambridge, Hobsons (CRAC).

McNiff, J. (1988) *Action Research: Principles and Practice*. London and New York, Routledge.

McNiff, J. (1993) *Teaching as Learning: An Action Research Approach*. London and New York, Routledge.

McNiff, J. and Collins, Ú. (eds) (1994) *A New Approach to In-Career Development for Teachers in Ireland*. Bournemouth, Hyde Publications.

McNiff, J., Lomax, P. and Whitehead, J. (1996) *You and Your Action Research Project*. London and New York, Routledge.

McNiff, J., Whitehead, J. and Laidlaw, M. (1992) *Creating a Good Social Order Through Action Research*. Bournemouth, Hyde Publications.Magee, B. (1997) *Confessions of a Philosopher*. London, Weidenfeld and Nicolson.

Magee, B. (1997) *Confessions of a Philosopher*. London, Weidenfeld and Nicolson.

Marland, M. (1974) *Pastoral Care*. London, Heinemann.

Marland, M. (1980) 'The Pastoral Curriculum', in R. Best, C. Jarvis and P. Ribbins (eds) *Perspectives in Pastoral Care*. Oxford, Heinemann.

Marland, M. (1989) *The Tutor and the Tutor Group*. Harlow, Longman.

Marland, M. (1993) *The Craft of the Classroom*. Oxford, Heinemann Educational.

Marland, M. (1995) 'The Whole Curriculum', in R. Best *et al*. (eds), *Pastoral Care and Personal-Social Education*. London, Cassell.

Midgley, M. (1989) *Wisdom, Information and Wonder: What is Knowledge For?* London and New York, Routledge.

Milner, J. (1983) 'Pastoral Care: Myth or Reality?', *British Journal of Guidance and Counselling*, 11 (1), 35–45.

Monahan, L. (1995) 'Developing the Role of Pastoral Care Coordinator in Chanel College, with Particular Reference to the Teaching Staff', unpublished dissertation, St Patrick's College Maynooth and Marine Institute of Education, Dublin.

Monahan, L. (1996) *Making School a Better Place*. Dublin, Marino Institute of Education.

Monahan, L. (1997) *The Class Tutor*. Dublin, IAPCE.

Monahan, L. (1998) *The Year Head*. Dublin, IAPCE.

NCC (1990) *The Whole Curriculum. Curriculum Guidance 7*. York, National Curriculum Council.

NCC (1993) *Spirituality and Moral Development: A Discussion Paper*. York, National Curriculum Council.

National Education Convention Secretariat (1994) (ed. J. Coolahan), *The Report of the National Education Convention*. Dublin, Stationery Office.

Noddings, N. (1992) *The Challenge to Care in Schools*. New York, Teachers College Press.

Noddings, N. (1993) *Educating for Intelligent Belief or Unbelief*. New York, Teachers College Press.

Nuttall, L. (1988) 'Transmitted, Caught or Taught? – A Whole School Approach to Personal and Social Education', *Pastoral Care in Education*, 6 (1), 3–7.

O'Connor, J. and McDermott, I. (1997) *The Art of Systems Thinking*. London, Thorsons.

OECD (1989) *Schools and Quality: An International Report*. Paris, OECD.

OECD (1991) *Reviews of National Policies for Education, Ireland*. Paris, OECD.

OECD (1996a) *Lifelong Learning for all*. Paris, OECD.

OECD (1996b) 'Combating Failure at School'. Draft Report (unpublished).

O'Murchu, D. (1997a) *Quantum Theology*. New York, Crossroad Publishing Company.

O'Murchu, D. (1997b) *Reclaiming Spirituality: A New Spiritual Framework for Today's World*. Dublin, Gill and Macmillan Ltd.

O'Neill, C. (1992) *Dealing with Disaffection*. London, Longman.

Parsons, C., Hunter, D. and Warne, Y. (1989) 'Skills for Adolescence – An Analysis of Project Material, Training and Implementation'. Canterbury, Evaluation Unit, Christchurch College.

Popper, K. (1985) *Unended Quest*. La Salle, IL, Open Court.

Presentation Sisters (see Sisters of the Presentation of the Blessed Virgin Mary).

Prigogine, I. and Stengers, I. (1984) *Order out of Chaos*. New York, Bantam.

Pring, R. (1984) *Personal and Social Education in the Curriculum*. London, Hodder and Stoughton.

Pring, R. (1988) 'Personal and Social Education in the Primary School', in P. Lang (ed.), *Thinking About . . . Personal and Social Education in the Primary School*. Oxford, Blackwell.

Reid, K., Hopkins, D. and Holly, P.J. (1987) *Towards the Effective School*. London, Blackwell.

Ribbins, P. and Best, R. (1985) 'Pastoral Care: Theory, Practice and the Growth of

Research', in P. Lang and M. Marland (eds), *New Directions in Pastoral Care*. Oxford, Blackwell.

Riso, D. (1988) *Personality Types*. London, Aquarian Press.

Robson, C. (1993) *Real World Research: A Resource for Social Scientists and Practitioner-Researchers*. Oxford, Blackwell.

Rodger, A. (1996) 'Human Spirituality: Towards an Educational Rationale', in R. Best (ed.), *Education, Spirituality and the Whole Child*. London, Cassell.

Rogers, C. (1961) *On Becoming a Person*. London, Constable.

Ryan, L. (1993) 'Counselling the Adolescent in a Changing Ireland'. Dublin, Institute of Guidance Counsellors.

Schön, D. (1983) *The Reflective Practitioner*. New York, Basic Books.

Senge, P. (1990) *The Fifth Discipline*. New York, Doubleday.

Sewell, I. (1993) 'The Folkloral Voice'. Unpublished doctoral dissertation, University of Alberta, Edmonton, Alberta.

Sexton, J. (1991) 'The Varied Masks of Pastoral Care', *Pastoral Care in Education*, 9 (1), 9–12.

Sisters of the Presentation of the Blessed Virgin Mary (1986) *Constitutions and Directives*. Dublin.

Stenhouse, L. (1975) *Introduction to Curriculum Research and Development*. London, Heinemann Education.

Stenhouse, L. (1983) Site Lecture presented at Simon Fraser University, Vancouver 8/1980, quoted in M. Skilbeck, 'Lawrence Stenhouse: Research Methodology – "Research is Systematic Enquiry Made Public"', *British Educational Research Journal*, 9 (1), 11–20.

Stuart, M.F. (1990) 'Social Perceptions and Social Skills in the Classroom'. Unpublished PhD thesis, Queen's University, Belfast.

Sugrue, C. (1998) *Teaching, Curriculum and Educational Research: Proceedings of an International Invitational Symposium*. Dublin, St Patrick's College.

Van Manen, M. (1991) *The Tact of Teaching: The Meaning of Pedagogical Thoughtfulness*. Albany, NY, SUNY Press.

Wall, W.D. (1977) *Constructive Education for Adolescents*. London, UNESCO.

Watkins, C. (1985) 'Does Pastoral Care = PSE?', *Pastoral Care in Education*, 3 (3).

Watkins, C. (1990) *Whole School Personal-Social Education Policy and Practice*. Oxford, NAPCE Base.

Watkins, C. and Wagner, P. (1987) *School Discipline: A Whole-School Approach*. Oxford, Blackwell.

Wheatley, M.J. (1992) *Leadership and the New Science: Learning about Organization from an Orderly Universe*. San Francisco, CA, Berrett Koehler.

Whitehead, J. (1989) 'Creating a Living Educational Theory from Questions of the Kind, "How Do I Improve my Practice?"', *Cambridge Journal of Education*, 19 (1), 41–52.

Whitehead, J. (1993) *The Growth of Educational Knowledge: Creating Your Own Living Educational Theories*. Bournemouth, Hyde Publications.

Williamson, D. (1980) 'Pastoral Care or Pastoralization?', in R. Best, C. Jarvis and P. Ribbins (eds), *Perspectives on Pastoral Care*. London: Heinemann.

Winter, R. (1989) *Learning from Experience*. Lewes: Falmer.

Young, R. (1992) *Critical Theory and Classroom Talk*. Clevedon, Multilingual Matters.

Zuber-Skerritt, O. (1996) *New Directions in Action Research*. London, Falmer.

INDEX